Women and Men Speaking

Frameworks for Analysis

CHERIS KRAMARAE
Department of Speech Communication
University of Illinois at Urbana-Champaign

D0023818

Newbury House Publishers, Inc. / Rowley / Massachusetts / 01969
ROWLEY • LONDON • TOKYO

Library of Congress Cataloging in Publication Data

Kramarae, Cheris.
  Women and men speaking.

  Includes bibliographical references.
    1. Language and languages—Sex differences.
2. Sexism in language. I. Title.
P120.S48K7   401'.9   80-16802
ISBN 0-88377-179-9

Cover design by Jean Ploss

NEWBURY HOUSE PUBLISHERS, INC.

 Language Science
Language Teaching
Language Learning

ROWLEY, MASSACHUSETTS 01969
ROWLEY ● LONDON ● TOKYO

Printed in the U.S.A.

First printing: January 1981
5   4   3   2   1

Preface

In each of the past ten years we have seen an increased number of studies of sexism in language and other topics dealing with the relationship of gender and language use. The researchers often explicitly acknowledge an interest in current social tensions, and in the relation between research questions and social conditions. Yet seldom do they draw upon a general framework of social interaction to help articulate their understanding of why specific findings are present, why they are important, and how they may be related to other language and gender studies. In the following chapters I work with these questions to make some initial connections across studies, and explanations.

The following anecdote illustrates the importance of considering gender research within a discussion of the social organization of women and men. Several years ago, I bought a "women's" magazine in an English supermarket because one of the feature articles was a report on physiological changes experienced, according to the article, by women who work outside the home. According to the article, women with demanding, professional jobs were reporting symptoms of maleness—in particular a rearrangement of body hair with more on the chest and face and less on the top of the head, and an increasing huskiness of voice. The question in the article's title—"Ambition, stress, power, work—IS IT ALL TURNING WOMEN INTO MEN?"—was answered by subtitles stating that a Cambridge University professor had found such evidence. The professor, identified as a "top endocrinologist and Professor of Medicine," was quoted in the article as saying that the various problems of women who develop a compulsive work drive are the most difficult to treat. According to the report, the professor believes that women become overwhelmed when they try to take on too many responsibilities—hold down a tough job, keep house, raise a family. His final word is cautionary: "It is vital that women recognize their limits before it's too late" (*Women's Own*, 23 July 1977, pp. 14-16). Getting that tough "man's job" may also get you a tough, deeper "man's voice."

Actually, according to an investigative follow-up report by Lyn Owen titled "The Myth of the Hairy Lady," the professor had been studying primarily women with a lot of housework who become depressed and take on volunteer work in the evenings in order to vary their activities (*Manchester Guardian*, 23 July 1977, p. 11). He had not actually categorized people according to their jobs inside or outside the home. Other endocrinologists, physiologists, and psychiatrists who were interviewed for the newspaper account said they had not noticed any increase in the number of hairy, husky-voiced women among their patients. They pointed out that the professor had knowledge only of women who came to him for help with problems. His study had not included the millions of women who work outside the home and do not get too hairy or husky-voiced. The reporter for the *Manchester Guardian* suggests that the professor assumed that careers outside the home are not good for women (or for society) and used what he saw to advocate his position. Theories about what is true and good for women vary, depending on whether or not the economy needs women to work outside the home. This article, in a popular magazine edited by men, came at a time of relatively high unemployment in Great Britain.

Jessie Bernard (1973b), Stephanie Shields (1975), and Rhoda Kesler Unger (1979) have discussed the way that scientific statements about gender are made to fit the changing "needs" and myths of a society. It is customary for science to support the dominant values of society by justifying those values, including women's subordinate social roles. Scientific concerns, such as female and male brain structure and size, the range of intelligence variation between females and males and among members of the same gender, and maternal instinct, fade in and out of importance for the scientific community in accordance with the concerns and questions of the greater social community. Shields writes, "As the times change, so must the [scientific] myths change" (p. 740).

Many of the so-called scientific arguments about innate differences in the biological and social behavior of females and males of the human species and of other species are based on methods or descriptions that are called objective but that can bury evidence. Ruth Herschberger (1970), reviewing the studies and conclusions of biologists, writes about the difficulty (or unwillingness) of the masculine population to think of women as other than creatures responding to them or creatures who are deviations of them.

In a review of several recent books in sociobiology, Sarah L. Hoagland (1980) suggests that, in defensive reaction to feminist efforts to present rape as action that demonstrates and helps preserve the differential power of women and men, sociobiologists have begun to argue (from purportedly objective descriptions of animal behavior) that male domination—including rape—is necessary for the preservation of the species. Social scientific research is not impersonal, apolitical, and factual, but interpretative.

In this book I am interested not only in collecting research findings about sexism in language, about the use of language by women and men, and about evaluations of the use of language by men and women; I also want to consider ideas about language within several theoretical frameworks in which assumptions about the relations of women and men are made explicit. Probably few, if any, of the language usages discussed in the following chapters are particular to either females or males. However, the usages are performed or experienced or evaluated

To Brinlee and Jana

who are not silent.

Permissions

in different ways. Language is used in social contexts; used to construct and maintain social relationships between and among women and men. So our inquiries need to be extended, to include explicit disscussion of social structure and the social organization of gender. In this work, then, I start with abstracts of several theories about social structure and then link findings about speech and language structure to those theories. The frameworks offer varying explanations about the interactions of women and men in contemporary society; I believe they can be developed as conceptual tools, enabling us to work out our own individual and collective models for the study of language and gender. I include many references to the writings of others to indicate the range of discussions in related areas of research. The contents of many of the works referenced are annotated in the bibliographies in Barrie Thorne and Nancy Henley (1975), and Nancy Henley, Barrie Thorne, and Cheris Kramarae (in preparation).

Many of the authors I cite are women;[1] this fact, and even more important, the topic, may immediately make the discussions suspect in the minds of some. Catharine Stimpson (1979), the founding editor of *Signs: Journal of Women in Culture and Society*, has spoken of the particular responses that feminist scholarship receives from the academic community. Indifference is perhaps the most frequent response. But other responses include a fear of separatism ("But what about the men?") and the accusation that the women are being political, that their inquiries are not as value-free as men's writing. (The assumptions here seem to be that there are no political implications in most academic work, and that politics and truth are in necessarily separate realms.) Another response is the accusation of irrationality. Women are thought to be intuitive, not logical. The term "women's scholarship" itself is thought by some to be a paradox. The theoretical frameworks discussed in this volume can be used as methods for analyzing these and other derogatory responses to women's expressions; and, by referencing many women, I hope to call attention to the work of some of those people who are confronting and challenging these responses.

I have tried to acknowledge a variety of perceptions about the relationship of women and men, particularly the perceptions of those people who are questioning the symbols and values that are basic to traditional explanations of our world. Most attention is given to discussions that present women as full, active members of society—discussions not generally heard in classrooms, or found in textbooks, in popular literature, or in the media.

I began this book during a year in England, where I participated in several women's study groups and worked on several language research projects. I came to recognize then that a person's understanding of the social organization of gender is closely tied to that person's background—not only the immediate beliefs and actions of parents, siblings, friends, and teachers, but also the general cultural assumptions about what the important ideas are and who the acceptable authorities are. In the chapters that follow I often write about American and British culture as if they were one—and indeed women in these countries do share many concerns and ideas about the relationship between social structure and language structure and use. Yet I recognize that a person's understanding of social continuity and social change is situated in a specific time and place. The (perceived) histories of countries, the different family, educational, legal, and political institutions, and one's position in those institutions, make a difference in an individual's experiences and in her or his perceptions about the world. I feel most comfortable with the last two frameworks I discuss—theoretical approaches that deal explicitly with social change and with economic and class relationships and stratification as well as with gender stratification. However, I have found each of the four frameworks helpful for exploring issues in language and gender.

This book owes much to the network, now international, of people discussing language and gender. The sharing of references, papers, ideas, and suggestions is making this study process very much a cooperative, and collective, work. In the process of writing about language and gender I have corresponded with hundreds of women and men, and have talked with many faculty members and students at the University of Illinois at Urbana-Champaign and at other universities, with persons attending conferences, and with women in study groups in Urbana-Champaign and in London. I thank them and hope for continued discussions and correspondence. I list by name only a few people, who have been of special help in discussing the material in this volume: Louise Adler, Shirley Ardener, Margaret Deuchar, Carole Edelsky, Diana Gibney, Howard Giles, Nancy Henley, Mercilee Jenkins, Cora Kaplan, Tom Nixon, Trevor Pateman, Michelle Rosaldo, Phillip Smith, Muriel Schulz, and Paula Treichler. Dale Spender provided encouragement, friendship, and citations. Sally McConnell-Ginet read the entire manuscript and gave me many valuable suggestions. Dale Kramer typed drafts. Barrie Thorne frequently and continually has provided me with ideas, corrections, and support since the days in 1972 when we began corresponding about language and gender research. I am especially appreciative of the suggestions she made on early drafts of this work. The value in talking and corresponding with these people and others has in large part come from hearing about their ways of interpreting the world, ways that differ somewhat from each other's and from my ways. So although interaction with them has been very important to me, it should not be assumed that they are in full agreement with my treatment of the material in this volume.

One additional note about names involved in this study: In their article "Toward a Feminist Aesthetic" (1978) Julia Penelope Stanley and Susan J. Wolfe (Robbins) write: "The most obvious and striking evidence of women's concern for language and its role as a naming process is the frequency with which women are choosing new names for ourselves" (p. 60).[2] Their own names were in transition when they wrote; they now call themselves Julia Penelope (with a tie back to a courageous Great Aunt Penelope alive during the Civil War), and Susan J. Wolfe. At the time I married in Ohio, the state laws did not allow a married woman to legally retain her own name. So my name became, at the direction of the state, Cheris Rae Kramer. My middle name was the same as that chosen by my mother for herself when she left home for college. Now that state laws allow married women to name themselves independently of their husbands, and I am able to legally change my name according to my own wishes and directions, I have reordered the sounds to Cheris Kramarae.

I am sorry that I did not carry with me a tape recorder to collect the variety of responses as I talked with family, friends, and university and government officials about my name change. Family members and many friends offered encouragement and, at my request, advice on spelling. (I wanted the new spelling similar enough to the old so that I would not lose mail and so the two names would be next to each other in my bibliography). Several times when I introduced the subject of Women and Proper Names to a group of women, the spirited discussion about their own names continued for more than an hour. Some other people clearly think that self-naming is a joke. And some people, who hear nothing strange in giving all children the surname of only their father and giving wives the surname of their husbands, think that the disruption of a system of patronymic naming is quite wrong;[3] or senseless. Several people shrugged their shoulders and said, "Well, it's your name." And I replied, "Exactly."

NOTES

1. I have included first names of researchers and writers the first time they are mentioned in each chapter.

2. Women are now providing material for a new chapter in the history of women's name changing, a history documented in Una Stannard's book, *Mrs. Man* (1977).

3. The symbolic carrying of the continuity of the family is given to the male in several respects. He is more likely to be given a kin name for his first name. A girl is more likely to receive a fashionable or playful name (Alice S. Rossi, 1965).

Contents

Introduction

This world taught woman nothing skillful and then said her work was valueless. It permitted her no opinions and said she did not know how to think. It forbade her to speak in public, and said the sex had no orators.

Carrie Chapman Catt (1902)

Women's speech is devalued. Women's words are, in general, ignored by historians, linguists, anthropologists, compilers of important speeches, news reporters, and businessmen, among others. People who control public-speaking platforms and public airwaves have effectively restricted women's access to these resources. In more private settings also, women are more likely than men to be interrupted or ignored. In the chapters that follow, I consider, within several theoretical frameworks, many beliefs, speculations, hypotheses, and findings about women's speech, men's speech, and the language code they use.

As adult, native-English speakers, we have a ready stock of terms, concepts, and reference works with which to begin such a discussion. Our culture has a large lexicon of derogatory terms for women, most of which refer to sexual activity. Julia P. Stanley (1977b) has compiled a list of 220 terms referring to women as sexual creatures—terms that demean them and put them in opposition to men. We also have a number of terms with derogatory meanings that are used primarily to label women speakers: *shrews, bitches, cats, hens; shrill, sharp-tongued,* and *gossipy.* The speech of individual men may be called overbearing or illogical—but as a class, men are not thought to be poor speakers.

My examination of books that advise American women on how and where to talk or, in most cases, how to keep silent, indicates that these concerns have persisted over the past 150 years (Cheris Kramer, 1975a; Kramarae, 1978). Diane Bornstein (1978) found that courtesy books of the Middle Ages also gave very gender-specific advice on how to talk. The characteristics of speech discussed in these books are much the same as those thirty-six traits listed by young, white, midwestern American adults as distinguishing the speech of females from the speech of males (Kramer, 1977). For example, traits that both female and male high school and university students thought were characteristic of women but not of men included (in the students' terminology): *gentle, fast, friendly, emotional, polite speech, a lot of talk, gossipy, good grammar*, and *gibberish.* Traits thought characteristic of male speakers included: *dominating, forceful, blunt speech, deep demanding voice, sense of humor,* and *use of slang.* Women's speech is certainly not heard as all bad, and men's speech is not thought all good (Kramer, 1978; Kathryn Scott, 1980), but they are considered different kinds of speech, serving different functions.

Women who speak publicly and to audiences that include men experience particular difficulties. Women's presence at many public events—even when they do not speak—is not always fully acceptable. Yet—although there are few public discussions about whether "qualified" women should attend academic conferences—the evidence so far is that they do not talk proportionately as often nor for as long as men do at those conferences (Marjorie Swacker, 1976). Women may sit in the choir in front of the congregation, but they seldom address the congregation. They appear, although infrequently, on the floor of state legislative bodies, yet they talk even more infrequently on the floor. My historical survey of women's efforts to speak in public (Kramarae, 1978) reveals that their public presence has been tolerated at times when their speech was not.

Relatively few women (or men) desire to speak in public forums. However, since public speech by a few can have a powerful, widespread impact, we can usefully examine who has access to the public forums and who does not. Although women do not necessarily encounter hostility in all public speaking situations, women's public speech is especially restricted when women wish to address mixed-sex or male adult audiences, and when women attempt to speak on issues and in places considered important to men.[1] St. Paul's declaration that women should be silent in public places is not quoted when a woman addresses a large gathering of the women's service auxiliary church group in the church basement, on the topic of collecting money to aid hungry children. But St. Paul is often cited when a woman tries to talk from the pulpit.

Women's speech has been restricted in a variety of ways. In the nineteenth century women often had difficulty locating a lecture platform open to them. Today, women have more difficulty than men finding a radio or television employer who will give them on-air speaking jobs. Contemporary discussion about women as public speakers—for example, as politicians or as radio and television news reporters and announcers—is not an aberration of history, but part of a continuing discussion about whether or not women should have the same amount of freedom of speech that men do. The arguments used to deny or restrict women's access to public platforms and airwaves do not usually make overt reference to the importance of public speech in influencing the attitudes and behavior of listeners. Rather, the arguments make reference to Biblical imperatives, to tradition, to women's "natural" occupations, to the inferiority of women's voices for public speaking, and to women's physical weaknesses.

In this volume I explore reasons for the differing evaluation of women's and men's speaking—their speaking in private as well as in public situations. Women are encouraged to talk softly and adopt nonassertive posture and intonation patterns, and then they are criticized for not having authoritiative voices. They are kept out of "important" jobs and then they are criticized for talking "chitchat" about "trivial topics." The expectations concerning volume, eye contact, body language, and vocabulary differ for women and men. In the past men—who have the greater speaking rights—have been largely responsible for establishing the criteria by which women's and men's speech is judged.

At the present time these criteria are being called into question. Especially since the inception of the Women's Liberation movement, many researchers and writers have discussed language and gender differences. This literature has come from people working from many different perspectives and publishing in a variety of publications—in particular, linguistics, literature, speech communication, psychology, sociology, anthropology, philosophy, literary criticism, education, and feminist journals. Several book-length discussions of the relationship of language and gender are available.[2] The annotated bibliographies in Mary Ritchie Key (1975), Barrie Thorne and Nancy Henley (1975), and Nancy Henley, Barrie Thorne, and Cheris Kramarae (in preparation); the questions raised in Kramarae (1980); and the review essays by Barbara W. Eakins and R. Gene Eakins (1978), Francine Wattman Frank (1978) and Cheris Kramer, Barrie Thorne, and Nancy Henley (1978) can be used as guides to (selected) writings and issues in this field.

Interest has increased as many people have come to see that through studying language structure and language use we can study the beliefs about and the social enactment of relationships between women and men. Study of the language structure indicates the elements and images that are perceived as important by the people who do the encoding of symbols in our culture. Study of language use can give us information about social organization, such as the hierarchical organization of speakers, and about linguistic strategies used to maintain superiority and to establish group solidarity.[3]

Recognition of a diversity of perspectives is valuable—and vital if our descriptions are not to be distorted and impoverished. The researchers start from somewhat different assumptions about society, about what constitutes proof, and about how results are interpreted. The guidelines suggested for study, and the data and analysis supplied by the various types of research, have helped sensitize us not only to the complexities of "natural speech," but also to the variety of interpretive processes and the varying assumptions from which questions arise and studies grow.

Some researchers follow traditional academic methods, insisting, however, that women as well as men be observed so that generalized descriptions of language behavior apply accurately to the entire language community. Some work with popular statements about women's speech, questioning the accuracy of these stereotypes and considering the consequences of their acceptance. Others work on new questions about the type and import of the categories of our language code.

Responses to these studies have also varied. The same pieces of work are described, depending upon the perspective of the evaluator, as elegant, provocative, insightful, balanced, calm, graceful, reasoned, cogent, wise, brilliant, disciplined, and creative—or radical, misguided, polemic, illegitimate, shrill, wrongheaded, overgeneralized, biased, and insignificant. Language and gender research has attracted much interest and quite a lot of anger. Trying to understand and explain that anger has become one of the concerns of workers in this field.

Research to date has documented many gender-based differences, and—just as significantly—in many cases has failed to support hypothesized differences. For the most part these findings have been considered as discrete items. Yet theoretical analysis exists that is both relevant and useful as a quilting pattern to supply directions and organization for our research. In the following chapters I attempt to develop connections and to suggest future possibilities for research. I organize the material around four theoretical frameworks which are being developed by sociologists, linguists, psychologists, anthropologists, and other thinkers. These frameworks, formulated to explain the relationship of contemporary women and men in Western cultures or the relationship of language and ethnicity in Western cultures, can fruitfully be used as well to explain speech similarity and diversity between women and men. They can help us work toward a conceptualization of the social factors involved in women's and men's language use and attitudes.

The first theoretical approach is based on the research and editing work of Shirley Ardener (1975, 1978) and Edwin Ardener (1975), both anthropologists at Oxford University, England, and their colleagues. This "muted group" framework, which posits a male-dominated social hierarchy that determines the dominant communication system of our culture, serves as the organizing structure for Chapters I, II, and III.

The work of Jacques Lacan, a French psychoanalytic theorist, as discussed and modified by, in particular, Cora Kaplan, provides the framework that is used in Chapters IV and V. Kaplan teaches American and British literature at the University of Sussex, England.

The third theoretical framework, the base for discussions in Chapters VI and VII, comes from the work of Howard Giles and his social psychology colleagues, many of whom are or have been associated with the University of Bristol, England.

The last theoretical approach, labelled the "strategy model," is a composite of the work of several American and British anthropologists. Chapters VIII, IX, and X draw on that model to interpret language and gender research in terms of these researchers' assumptions about the division between private (female) and public (male) spheres of labor, and assumptions about the rationality of all speakers.

These four approaches were chosen because (1) I found them of value in framing discussions of language and gender; (2) they each deal with social relations; (3) the analyses they provide are different: what is treated as problematic and what is assumed differ in each case; and (4) the frameworks are based on theories of people from different academic and geographical backgrounds.[4] In general, I do not attempt to standardize the terminology across discussions of the four frameworks; rather I use that of the authors. I have tried to make the four main sections of the book relatively independent units, at the same time trying to avoid a great deal of repetititon of discussion and support material.

This organization of the material tends to stress the differences in the assumptions and arguments made by people working with the four frameworks. There are, however, important similarities. The first framework ("muted group") and the second (labelled "reconstructed psychoanalysis") are both concerned with general organization of culture and thought, and the relation of language structure to both women's and men's self-conceptions and to their articulation of their experience. These two frameworks emphasize speakers' attitudes toward their language and its role in organizing their perceptions and the expressions of perceptions. The focus in these theoretical models is on the abstract structures of beliefs and language rather than on the minutiae of social interaction. Both models deal with the concepts presented, and the restrictions imposed, by language, and with women's and men's differing relationships to language construction and use. The reconstructed psychoanalysis model is, in addition, concerned with a wide range of psychological issues.

The last two frameworks, "speech styles" and the "strategy model," stress the uses of language in social life—the how and why men and women speak the way they do. The focus is on the interweave of people's social roles and the particular situations, i.e., on the complex relationships among speakers.

Using this organization I attempt both to review much of the language and gender research and to indicate possible future directions for this work. New questions and problems are generated when different frameworks are used. Considerations of several frameworks can help us sort through our assumptions and make them more explicit.

The use I make of these frameworks for discussing language does not, of course, draw upon all of the aspects that their founders have articulated. I have pulled threads selectively, drawing forth lines of argument most applicable to my concerns. In particular, I have focused on language and gender research, an aspect of intergroup and interpersonal relations work that not all of these theorists discuss explicitly. Language, an organizer and product of social interaction, affects and is affected by the lives of its speakers. Use of these theoretical frameworks should help us work toward coherent statements about gender differences and similarities in language use, and sexism in language structure.

NOTES

1. In her essay, "The Progress of Fifty Years," published in 1894, Lucy Stone wrote about a nineteenth century public speaker (who spoke for abolition of slavery):

Abby Kelly once entered a church only to find herself the subject of the sermon, which was preached from the text: 'This Jezabel is come among us also.' They jeered at her as she went along the street. They threw stones at her. They pelted her with bad eggs as she stood on the platform. Some of the advocates of the very cause for which she endured all this were ready to drive her from the field. (Stone, 1894:59)

Lucy Stone thought that by the 1890s the situation was much improved: "The first [U.S.] woman minister, Antoinette Brown, had to meet ridicule and opposition that can hardly be conceived to-day. Now there are women ministers, east and west, all over the country" (p. 60). She was right in saying that men placed fewer restrictions on women's public speech in the 1890s than they had in the 1840s. But now, almost 100 years after she wrote of the new freedoms, women are still being put down when they try to speak up in public places—east and west, north and south.

2. Following the argument made by Suzanne Kessler and Wendy McKenna (1978) that "the element of social construction is primary to all aspects of being female or male" (p. 7), I use the term *gender* to refer to the cultural expression and expectations of masculine or feminine features and behavior. What is considered "essential" to being male or being female differs depending upon the time and the society. Erving Goffman (1977) discusses some institutional methods used to maintain gender—such as "appropriate" division of labor, and separate toilet facilities. He argues that biological sexual differences are greatly embellished by institutions that are designed in part to separate the activities and the rights of females and males. In using *gender* rather than *sex* I am not denying that most of the people called *male* share some biological traits not shared by most people called *female*, but I am stressing the many and pervasive social distinctions and definitions concerning social strata and power that are used to separate women and men. (For a related discussion of gender terminology and maintenance techniques see Barbara Westbrook Eakins and R. Gene Eakins [1978].)

3. The distinction between structure and use is widely used in language study. Language structure usually means *lexicon* and *grammar* while language usage usually refers to people's speech and writing in a particular context for particular purposes. (See Penelope Brown and Stephen Levinson [1978] for a discussion of this division and its limitations.) Although these definitions of the terms are assumed in the discussions that follow, I do not see *language structure* and *language use* as dichotomous terms. Language use and language structure are intimately connected (Kramer, Thorne, Henley, 1978) in many ways which many people continue to explore.

4. I might have used other approaches. For example, although many of the people contributing to these theoretical explanations of the relationship of women and men work from a Marxist orientation, this collection includes no explicitly Marxist-feminist position, which would include discussion of kinship and class relationship as the base of discussion of public (state) and private (family) relationships.

Women and Men Speaking

I

WOMEN AS A MUTED GROUP

Two women who began working together in 1966, the early days of the present women's movement, write, "We didn't have the words to describe what we believed in; Women's Liberation didn't exist. We called ourselves radical women, coming out of the experience of the civil rights and student movements. . . . At that time, *sexism* wasn't yet a word in the language, and we were trying to identify and figure out what to do with the problem that had no name, the so-called 'women's issue' " (Naomi Weisstein and Heather Booth, 1978:27).

The muted group theory provides the following explanation and expansion of their experience: The language of a particular culture does not serve all its speakers equally, for not all speakers contribute in an equal fashion to its formulation. Women (and members of other subordinate groups) are not as free or as able as men are to say what they wish, when and where they wish, because the words and the norms for their use have been formulated by the dominant group, men. So women cannot as easily or as directly articulate their experiences as men can. Women's perceptions differ from those of men because women's subordination means they experience life differently. However, the words and norms for speaking are not generated from or fitted to women's experiences. Women are thus "muted." Their talk is often not considered of much value by men—who are, or appear to be, deaf and blind to much of women's experiences. Words constantly ignored may eventually come to be unspoken and perhaps even unthought.

The muted group theory provides a way of conceptualizing and visualizing two types of structure: the underlying "template structures" of a group of people (the mesh of beliefs and categories that comprise their world view) and the "structure of realization" (the articulation of their world view). The underlying structures cannot be directly known; we can know them only by their reflections through language and other signs. Edwin Ardener (1975) states that groups that are on top of the social hierarchy determine to a great extent the dominant communication system of a society. Subordinate groups (such as children and women) are made "inarticulate" (pp. 21, 22).

A visual representation of the relationship women and men have to language (a modification of a diagram by E. Ardener [1975:26]) will make clearer how women, according to this theory, adapt their ideas and expressions in order to speak through the communicative modes of men.

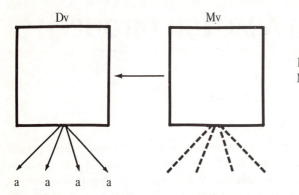

Dv=dominant world view
Mv=muted world view
a=articulation(s)

According to this theory, women are "inarticulate" because the language they use is derivative, having been developed largely out of male perception of reality. A system of division of labor between males and females means that the ingredients of everyday life will differ for women and men—and thus their perceptions will also differ. The public areas of life—and public discourse—in most societies appear to be controlled by males. The work, interests, and talk of women are not considered as important to men as men's own work, interests, and talk. Women do, of course, speak. However, in public discourse especially, "the appropriate language registers often seem to have been 'encoded' by males, [and thus] women may be at a disadvantage when wishing to express matters of peculiar concern to them." Unless their views are presented in a form acceptable to men, and to women brought up in the male idiom, they will not be given a proper hearing (S. Ardener, 1975:ix). The male system of perception, which is represented in the language used by both men and women, does not provide a good "fit" for the women's expression of their experiences. While individual men may have difficulty in expressing their model, there is presumed a close correspondence between the men's position in the society and the dominant model. Women are a "muted group" in that some of their perceptions cannot be stated, or at least not easily expressed, in the idiom of the dominant structure. To give a rather specialized example, but one that provides a clear instance of a misfit between the models of women and the idiom of the dominant structure: for nuns it becomes almost impossible to describe accurately one's "marriage" to Christ because the usual terms for marriage are inappropriate in the context (see Drid Williams, 1975 [in S. Ardener]).

Another example is offered by Hilary Callan (1978), who writes of the manner in which women are muted by a language structure that incorporates men's but not women's experience. She writes of language as a "conceptual toolbag" which contains terms such as dominance, hierarchy, status, control, and possession, which describe a traditional male authority pattern. The description of the organization of female groups in those terms often makes it easy to see female groups as incompetent, as poor imitations of the male groups. Callan writes of the problems nurses, for example, have in defining themselves. They have been defined by others as angels of mercy and as battle-axes, depending upon whether they are seen as accepting a supporting, nurturing role or whether they are seen as renouncing "femininity" (p. 211). The language imposes its structure on the way the nurses and the observers of nurses describe them, although that language code may not include terms that reflect interaction patterns of nurses or the important aspects of their own professional training or professional history.

The discussion of muted groups was initially inspired by a debate about the methods of social anthropologists (Edwin Ardener, 1973). The framework can be applied, Edwin Ardener argues, with equal validity to research about any groups in society, including all-male groups (e.g., blacks and whites; children and adults; working class and middle class), in which members of one group are in an asymmetrical power relationship with members of another contrasting group. The concept of mutedness is partly a means of conveying the manner in which boundaries of perception are defined by the experiences of the members of the groups, and the manner in which the dominant group engulfs the subordinate group and "blocks the power of actualization of the other" (E. Ardener, p. 25). Of course, not every member of a group will have the same perceptions as every other member; but common experiences will lead to some general, if sometimes not explicit, agreement as to what constitutes reality.[1]

Because the gender division is so basic to the organization of our society, because the assignment to a gender category is made at birth, usually for a lifetime, and because men are dominant in so many areas of public life, the discussion of the mutedness of women is of particular concern.

The basic assumptions of the muted group theory pertaining to the relationship of women and men appear to be:

1. Women perceive the world differently from men because of women's and men's different experiences and activities rooted in the division of labor.
2. Because of their political dominance, the men's system of perception is dominant, impeding the free expression of the women's alternative models of the world.
3. In order to participate in society women must transform their own models in terms of the received male system of expression.[2]

The proponents of the muted group theory hold that a language reflects a world view. They argue that over the years a dominant group may generate a communication system that supports its conception of the world and then call it *the* language of the society, while at the same time subjecting others to experiences that are not reflected in that language. Edwin Ardener writes: "The muted structures are 'there' but cannot be 'realized' in the language of the dominant structure" (p. 22).

Although the authors of the essays in *Perceiving Women* (S. Ardener, 1975) do not, except in very general terms, deal with the method by which the dominant/subordinate relationship between men and women was established and is perpetuated, I think their argument could reasonably be expanded along these lines: Society and its communication system are defined by men. The importance of the male/female division itself is likely a product of the male definition of the social structure. Some features of women's experience cannot be expressed or expressed easily within this social structure. The resulting relative "inarticulateness" of women presently aids in consigning them to positions of little freedom or power; women and their concerns continue to be of marginal importance in men's perception.

Below I list several hypotheses, concerning female and male expression, which I think are suggested by the muted theory.[3]

1. Females are more likely to have difficulty expressing themselves fluently within dominant (public) modes of expression.
2. Males have more difficulty than females in understanding what members of the other gender mean.
3. Females are likely to find ways to express themselves outside the dominant public modes of expression used by males in both their verbal conventions and their nonverbal behavior.
4. Females are more likely to state dissatisfaction with the dominant public modes of expression.
5. Women refusing to live by the ideas of social organizations held by the dominant group (example: women who are active in the modern Women's Liberation movement) will change dominant public modes of expression as they consciously and verbally reject those ideas.
6. Females are not as likely to coin the words that become widely recognized and used by both men and women.
7. Females' sense of humor—what relationships between persons, places, and things they consider incongruous—will differ from males' sense of humor.

The discussions below are designed to explore the evidence for the existence of different men's and women's world views.

Shirley Ardener and Edwin Ardener and the other authors of the essays in *Perceiving Women* (S. Ardener, 1975) (as well as others who have been involved in the women's anthropology group seminar at Oxford) are concerned with the value of this general theoretical approach for research in several cultures, including British. Their work provides valuable evidence for the usefulness of this approach as a tool for social anthropology work.[4] Here, my interests are more limited; I am primarily interested in what questions the theory raises and what explanations it may provide for the communication patterns among and between women and men in Great Briatin and the United States.

In this chapter I consider the first, second, third, fourth, and fifth hypotheses above; and in the following two chapters I include material relevant to the sixth and seventh hypotheses.

VERBAL SKILLS OF WOMEN AND MEN

That females will have more difficulty than males expressing themselves seems implicit in the muted group theory. Most of the information available on sex differences and verbal skills does not seem to support such an hypothesis. But experiences common to many women suggest an area of inarticulateness that has not yet received much research attention. Women are writing of their "silencing" because the tools of expression have been shaped by men. And men also often suffer, and cause others to suffer, from an inability or unwillingness to self-disclose, to discuss feelings, and to do interaction support work. References to these specific topics are found in a variety of sources, from academic journals to writings coming from men's consciousness-raising groups and from feminist periodicals.

Eleanor Emmons Maccoby and Carol Nagy Jacklin (1974) state that "female superiority on verbal tasks has been one of the more solidly established generalizations in the field of sex differences" (p. 75). Their generalizations are based almost entirely on data from studies of children and young adults. Girls are found to show more maturation in verbal abilities in the first years of life. Few differences have been found in the preschool to early adolescence years but at about age eleven females begin to outscore males at a wide variety of verbal skills—spelling, punctuation, vocabulary, fluency, comprehension of written tests including complex logical material, and various tests of verbal creativity (p. 84).

As always, the way the studies are set up makes a difference as to what results are found and how they are interpreted. The confidence with which generalizations can be made about the linguistic skills of very young children is in question, since studies of the past two decades in this area have been concerned with the linguistic skills of only a few, carefully selected groups (Maccoby and Jacklin, p. 77). Not much information on the linguistic skills of adults is available—at least not in academic linguistic studies.

Furthermore, the gender of the researcher appears to have had some bearing on study results regarding differences. At least in pre-1960s studies, research teams composed partly of males were more likely to find male superiority on various measures while teams of women were more likely to find female superiority. (Barrie Thorne and Nancy Henley, 1975: 286-287. See their annotated bibliography, and Henley, Thorne, and Kramarae, in preparation, for reports of studies of gender differences in some aspects of verbal ability.) So some caution is important in making generalizations. However, a comparison of study results now available reveals that when gender differences have been found among children and young adults, usually females have slightly higher test scores and are said to have "superior" overall linguistic abilities. Differences in phonology seem solidly established. Studies by Lewis Levine and Harry Crockett (1966), Roger Shuy, Walter Wolfram, and William Riley (1967), Wolfram (1969), William Labov (1972), Peter Trudgill (1975), Jenny Cheshire (1978), and Patricia Nichols (1978) show females are more likely to use "standard" or "higher prestige" pronunciations. (However, the particular conditions and work opportunities for the women and the men studied must be considered before such generalizations can be drawn for the people in any geographical area [Nichols, 1978]. Maryann Hartman [1976] has begun a study of the language use of Maine women and men over seventy years of age, a study that has found occupation an important factor.)

Multiple explanations have been offered: Girls' neurological systems are more mature at birth; they are more responsive to sounds and thus perhaps get a head start on language learning. Stuttering and reading disorders are more frequent among males; perhaps genetic factors enable girls to handle language more easily (Cinthia Lee Gannett Conrad, 1978). Girls are more social, and spend more time interacting with friends. (Maccoby and Jacklin [1974:349] call the latter statement "unfounded belief.") Roger Abrahams (1972) suggests that groups with relatively little power may learn to place a high value on verbal skills in order ro present themselves verbally in a way not to create offense. Perhaps women use what they perceive as "correct" speech in order to compensate for lack of status in other areas of their lives (Trudgill, 1975). Nancy Henley (1977) writes that underlings must be more circumspect, more correct, in following the rules of proper speaking than those people in dominant positions (pp. 84-86). Ronald K. S. Macaulay (1978) points out that test differences between males and females are usually slight; they have been, he writes, overemphasized and misinterpreted.

The muted group theory itself would not predict that adult females are more fluent. If females have to speak through a social system and a language structure which to a large extent overlook females or consider their interests subordinate to the interests of males, we could expect that females would be less fluent, perhaps particularly after puberty and through the teens when gender differences, social expectations for boys and girls, and relationships between boys and girls are given so much attention by the teens themselves (often with the encouragement of the media, teachers, and parents). Yet, as indicated, evidence of female linguistic superiority is strongest in studies concerning males and females eleven years and older. Perhaps females are *not* particularly handicapped by the dominant communication system. Perhaps females are forced to monitor their speech in a way boys are not, that is, to develop superior verbal facility and a consciousness that recognizes multiple perceptions and interpretations of the world. Perhaps care by, primarily, female teachers in the lower grades (as well as care by mothers at home) gives girls a chance to develop language skills within a structure that is supportive of girls' linguistic expression. Teachers are more likely to underestimate the abilities of boys in the early teens, especially boys from working-class homes, and to reprimand them more (Sara Delamont, 1976:57). The school systems in the United States and Great Britain may *expect* girls to develop better reading and writing skills (Dale Spender, 1979), to be correct in their writing and speaking; and that expectation might enable girls to have a positive approach to some aspects of language learning.

Studies of the brain organization for speech and writing skills indicate women, in general, might have a biological predisposition toward linguistic processing which uses both hemispheres of the brain—the left hemisphere with its linear, sequential, analytical, and externally focused mode of processing and the right with its holistic, gestaltist, imagistic, and inner-focused mode. Men's language processing appears more lateralized in the left hemisphere (Conrad, 1978; but for a countering argument see Anthony W. H. Buffery and Jeffrey A. Gray, 1972). Relatively slightly different predispositions at birth, perhaps strengthened by cultural experiences, might explain some of the perceived differences between females' writing and speech styles and males' styles.[5]

Although females, at least young females, appear to have an edge in many types of language skills, perhaps researchers have not looked at other salient characteristics of speech behavior. For example, we know little about the importance male and female school children place on their language. Perhaps males do not care as much about developing linguistic skills, at least within the school system. Perhaps what are considered important skills by the academic researchers are not considered to be important by the boys. Perhaps girls, who are evidently somewhat more sensitive to negative comments (Maccoby and Jacklin, 1974:158), are more concerned about performing in the "right" way ordained by the teachers. Perhaps we are too ready to equate "superior control of language" to the "appropriate language behavior of the classroom." Young black males put great value on verbal skills developed outside the school—skills that are not likely to be highly evaluated by teachers. Researchers have paid little attention, however, to the verbal skills of black or white *girls* outside the school.[6]

As this discussion indicates, the muted group theory, as I have outlined it, offers little help in explaining the sex differences that have been found in "verbal ability" in the types of empirical studies completed in recent years. On the other hand, the empirical studies have worked with the language common to both genders; they do not consider the possibility implicit in the muted group theory that experiences peculiar to the subordinate group have not yet been encoded in a language. I have attended seminars (in Great Britain and in the United States) that had as the explicit topic for discussion the limitations of language for women. The women attending discussed shared experiences for which there are no labels, and lists were drawn up of the things, relationships, and experiences for which there are no labels. For example, one woman talked about a common occurrence in her life which needed a label. She and her husband, both working full-time outside the home, usually arrive home at about the same time. She would like him to share the dinner-making responsibilities but the job always falls upon her. Occasionally he says, "I would be glad to make dinner. But you do it so much better than I. " She was pleased to receive this compliment but as she found herself in the kitchen each time she realized that he was using a verbal strategy for which she had no word and thus had more difficulty identifying and bringing to his awareness. She told the people at the seminar, "I had to tell you the whole story to explain to you how he was using flattery to keep me in my female place." She said she needed a word to define the strategy, or a word to define the person who uses the strategy, a word which would be commonly understood by both women and men.

Then, when he tried that strategy she could explain her feelings by turning to him and saying, "You are _____ ," or "What you are doing is called _____ ."

Spender (1977), who organized one of the seminars, set out to collect perceived gaps in the language, experiences of women that need a name: A term for normal sexual power in women (a counterpart for *potent*); a term for *a woman* that connotes an individual, an autonomous human being rather than a qualifying term which calls attention to the woman/man division (Simone de Beauvoir [1964] writes that "woman represents only the negative . . . it is vexing to hear a man say: 'You think thus and so because you are a woman.'. . . It would be out of the question to reply: 'And you think the contrary because you are a man'; for it is understood that the fact of being a man is no peculiarity" [p. xv]); a word equivalent to *effeminate* for a woman with "manly" qualities; a word for a man who takes a woman's *No* to mean *Yes* and appears to think this is clever; a word for a woman who is not flattered by male propositions (the last example mentioned is by Julia Stanley, 1974); and a positive word to take the place of the phrase "not sexist." As I indicate in later sections, many women are now working to name themselves and their activities; and they are very conscious that this action is not traditionally women's action. Many of them speak of having been "silenced" by men who have been the definers of the worlds of both men and women. Their discussions indicate how language, the symbolic system, is closely tied to a patriarchal social structure.

MISUNDERSTANDINGS BETWEEN WOMEN AND MEN

Another hypothesis which I draw from the muted group theory states that males will have more difficulty than females in understanding what members of the other gender mean. Many men have discussed in print the difficulty of understanding women; some men have set forth what they think is different and/or wrong with women. Ortega y Gasset says, "The core of the feminine mind, no matter how intelligent the woman may be, is occupied by an irrational power"; although he is not a native-English-speaking commentator, his words are similar to those used by English-speaking males who talk and write about the mystery and irrationality of women (quoted by Julius Fast, 1971:49). "Women are intuitive rather than analytical," writes the author of a 1936 book on the art of conversation (Milton Wright, 1936:100). He explains that if we hear a woman who is logical "it will be found that she has a man's mind" (p. 99). (There's logic for you.) He cites as corroboration the words of Andre Maurois:

> Women's thoughts obey the same laws as do the molecules of gases. They go with much rapidity in an initial direction, until a shock sends them into another, then a second shock into a third direction. It is useless to choose a theme with women. (Wright, p. 99)

Other men do not try to explain women's minds and conversations, or they try and then decide that explanation is impossible. For example, one linguist, discussing the possible reasons that women use more standard or "correct" pronunciations, gave several possibilities but concluded by saying perhaps the explanation is that women are one of the mysteries of the universe. Shulamith Firestone (1970) calls that type of "explanation" part of an "exaggeration process" that labels woman as a particular creature that cannot be understood or treated by the laws that govern *man*kind (p. 100).

Many cartoons in popular magazines portray men as showing incredulity at the inexplicable things women are saying (Cheris Kramer, 1974a; 1974b). The representation of women's reasoning and talk as peculiar, stupid, irrational, irritating, charming, or a delightful mystery is an important element of folklinguistics.

Several explanations for men's stated difficulties in understanding women seem to be offered by the muted group theory. The explanations are not necessarily either/or, but can be complementary possibilities. First, men have helped set up and maintain the social opposition *male* and *female* partly by professing not to understand what females (as a class) say, by asserting that women as a group are outside comprehension. Gender differentiation and a sense of distance between men and women are reinforced by this behavior. While women have also been involved in maintaining the dichotomy, men are perhaps more interested than women in stressing sex differences and ridiculing women's behavior since such conduct acts to support male domination. If women were thought to be as rational and as clear-speaking as men, the present social/legal treatment of women would be harder for men to rationalize.

Second, men, in determining the "acceptable" values and assumptions (which include the inferior status of women), subject women to experiences that men are not subjected to; but men's language structure does not include the ready means for women to express the thoughts and behavior that result from their subjugation. While women have had to learn the language structure of the dominant group, men have seldom had to discern or have wanted to discern the women's model of the world. Women, even though barred from many of the work, pub/bar, and sports experiences of men, still receive much information about the male model of the world through the institutions that men have set up. Textbooks and encyclopedias are organized and written to describe, primarily, male activities. Men's activities are highlighted in the newspapers except in the relatively small section of "women's news." Prime time evening programming relies heavily on war and crime, primarily male activities (although they have important consequences for women). In television drama men outnumber women 3 to 1; 56 percent of the prime time characters are "involved in violence," with white and minority women characters more likely to be victims of the violence than white or nonwhite men characters (George Gerbner and Nancy Signorielli, 1979:5, 25-26). Weekend television programming gives us the filming and description of many basketball and football games. Women spend much of their time hearing, seeing, and reading about the men's models of the world. On the other hand, experiences thought to "belong" to women, such as sewing, child car, and running a household, are given much less attention in information- and attitude-sharing exchanges when both genders are present. Thus, we could expect that men will not be as likely to understand women as women are to understand men.

Do men really have major difficulties in understanding women? Do they have more difficulty in accurately understanding women than women have in understanding men ("accurately" meaning close correspondence to what is intended by the speaker)? Women's voices have not been heard publicly as often as men's, on this topic as on so many others. Perhaps women have as much to say about the difficulty of understanding men as men have had to say about the difficulty of understanding women. And, as I have suggested, men may see advantages in saying they do not understand women when they talk. Below, I briefly look at evidence from one area of study: What spouses say about their partners. In a subsequent chapter I summarize some of the agreements and disagreements women and men have over what is humorous, i.e., what relationships are incongruous or ludicrous, or amusing. If women and men, at least to some extent, have different world views, we would expect that they will at times be amused by different things.

Talking about One's Spouse

One method of testing the hypothesis that men do not understand what women say as easily as women understand what men say consists of listening to what males and females say about the ease/difficulty of understanding what is said by members of the other group. I have already reported a few statements by males on what is different/wrong about women's speech that makes it difficult to understand. Here I look at some comments, made by wives as well as by husbands to professional interviewers, about the speech of their spouses. Although the women and men interviewed were not asked to make checks on rating scales, what is said is still, of course, somewhat structured by the interests of the interviewers. Reporting on the methodological problems of the interview as a research instrument, George W. Brown and Michael Rutter (1966) write of the advantages of structured detailed questioning, since respondents' general comments about activities, they find, are often misleading to the interviewer. Brown and Rutter believe that asking general questions prompts answers reflecting attitudes rather than actual behavior. Their assumption that for each question there is "a true answer" is one commonly made in the past by researchers of family life, who were not much interested in whether or not the wife and husband might have differing perceptions of the "truths" of their interaction. Although wives and husbands in many interviewing sessions must have discussed their perception of the mental world of their partners, few of the resulting study reports contain such references.

One of the exceptions is Mirra Komarovsky's *Blue-Collar Marriage* (1967), a report based on interviews with fifty-eight working-class couples. Her chapters on "Barriers to Marital Communication" and "Confidants Outside of Marriage" contain many hints of what those fifty-eight women and fifty-eight men think causes misunderstandings. Komarovsky gives excerpts from some of the interviews, which in part attest "boredom of the wives, the contempt and exasperation of the husbands" (p. 149). Many of the men talk not so much about not understanding their wives as not wanting to listen to them. "Women talk about the silliest details that don't matter and they don't want to talk about interesting things. This isn't just my wife. It is almost any woman" (p. 150). This theme was repeated by many men. Komarovsky writes:

> Similar dissatisfactions were expressed by a wife who was trying to explain why talking with girl friends frequently proved more satisfying than conversations with her husband. When she once told her husband about a young woman in the community who had an illegitimate baby, he ended the discussion with: "It happens all the time." But with her girl friends she can talk over such matters in detail. (Does the girl really want to give up her baby? Should she? Would she marry the father of her baby if he asked her to? And so on.) (p. 150)

A twenty-one year-old wife is quoted as saying: "Men are different; they don't feel the same as us—that's one reason men are friends with men and women have women friends" (p. 151).

The women were more likely to endorse the therapeutic value of talk. It is important to note, however, that the interviews were conducted by women. Given what the wives and husbands said about the talk of women and men, surely the sex of the interviewers was a factor in what the wives and husbands decided to talk about. (At least six hours were spent with each family, including two interviews, each two hours, with the wife, and one two-hour interview with the husband.) Quite possibly the women were more likely to be willing in this situation to talk about talk. However, Komarovsky considers the women's repeated complaints that the men will not talk things out an important aspect of the study. She believes the husbands' relative silence comes from a "trained incapacity to share" (p. 156)—at least with their wives. Possibly men have less to talk about because of the closeness of fit between their experience and the conventional modes of expression.

Lillian Breslow Rubin (1976), who also bases her statements on interviews with working-class families, says that "I just don't know what she wants" is the "plaintive and uncomprehending cry" of most of the men she interviewed. Rubin says that often the wife does not know either; she only knows that her dreams for marriage are not realized. However, part of the problem lies in conflicting world views:

> The problem lies in the fact that they do not have a language with which to communicate, with which to understand each other. They are products of a process that trains them to relate to only one side of themselves—she, to the passive, tender, intuitive, verbal, emotional side; he, to the active, tough, logical, nonverbal, unemotional one. From infancy, each has been programmed to be split off from the other side; by adulthood, it is distant from consciousness, indeed. (p. 116)

A *real* man is strong and silent and does not talk about his troubles, feelings, and pain. He is surprised when his wife asks him to talk about feelings, and he replies, "What is there to tell?" (p. 177). This indicates that *men* are the muted ones on some subjects. However, the men's reticence leaves the women thinking they are the ones with the faulty perceptions. Some of the women told Rubin that their feelings are so seldom validated that they are left thinking that perhaps they are crazy. Rubin thinks that this outcome of the interaction between couples is "the most common interactional pattern in American marriage," although particularly critical in the working class where traditional norms set up more distinct activity boundaries for women and men (p. 119). Both of these studies were completed with the cooperation of working-class women and men, who experience more gender segregation than middle-class women and men. Relatively few of the women interviewed were employed outside the home, a much lower percentage than in the overall population.

Komarovsky and others, observing what they perceive as husbands' reticence, have offered other explanations of this asymmetry in sharing talk and experiences. The reason most commonly given is that wives are excluded from their husbands' world of work—perhaps men do not talk much because they do not think their wives will understand the job experiences. Yet as Komarovsky points out, men and women could "have their separate tasks and still share common interests in the psychological problems of child rearing, in their personalities, in social life and aspirations for the future" (p. 155). Women are still saying that they are more willing to talk with their husbands than their husbands are willing to talk with them, even now when more than half of the married women in Great Britain and the United States hold wage- and salary-paying jobs. (And not all men have paying jobs. The rate of employment for adult males is now under 80 percent.) Women appear to be the ones still working hard to get and keep conversations going.

The muted group theory could explain the male/female asymmetry in willingness to talk to the partner in terms of the dominant model of the world. Men have structured a value system and a language that reflects that value system. Women have had to work through the system organized by men. So they are more likely to have an understanding of the men's world view than the men are likely to have an understanding or appreciation of the women's world view. (Within the strategy theory discussed in Chapters VIII, IX, and X this inexpressiveness is explained as a technique used by males to withhold information about their physical and psychological limitations.)

WOMEN'S VERBAL CONVENTIONS

The muted group theory suggests that females are likely to find ways to express themselves outside the systems used by males. Here, I look at just a few forms of expression by women that have recently received attention as significant forms of expression: diaries and letters; conversations among women; essays written collectively by members of small groups with interaction norms that are viewed as based on women's experiences; and art work utilizing materials of the home.

For example, while women's correspondence and diaries have occasionally been used in scholarly historical analyses, they have certainly more often been destroyed or packed away in the attic. First, they have been ignored or destroyed because letters and diaries, particularly those of women, are seldom considered to be literary genres. Second (and these reasons are closely related), they have been ignored or destroyed because women's correspondence and diaries are seldom thought to deal directly with what have been considered weighty matters. When the content of women's private letters and diaries have been remarked upon, it is usually in the context of revealing something about the lives of important men, rather than, for example, in way of learning more about the nature of long-term, intimate female friendship. (Carroll Smith-Rosenberg [1975] shows how such manuscripts can be profitably used for the latter study.) Even though relatively little interest has been shown in such material as *writing*, much of it does exist in various archives. Women who have searched for collections have been surprised to discover a vast literature (Mary Jane Moffat and Charlotte Painter, 1975). Might these unpublished (for the most part) diaries and letters represent efforts by women, at least middle-class women, to find modes of expression that more adequately allow them to express their interests and experiences than, say, novel writing or essay writing? Of course women write diaries for various reasons. Some women, like some men, write diaries or journal entries to keep a record of ideas for possible later use in writing poetry, fiction, or nonfiction—the recognized public genres. Mary (Mrs. Humphrey) Ward in her introduction to Charlotte Brontë's *Villette* writes that women are "the equals" of men novel writers in part because "the arts of society and of letter-writing pass naturally into the art of the novel." But, although we have little information on how many women and men keep diaries, the information we do have indicates that men are more likely than women to keep such records *in addition to* expressing themselves as public writers and speakers, and that there is a difference in the audience and purpose of women's and men's writing.

Some women who have studied the amount of diary writing and the content of the entries have suggested that diary writing fits the experience of the women. In the introduction to *Three Women Diarists*, Margaret Willy (1964) writes, ". . . there is something in the activity which strongly appeals to female instinct and inclination" (p. 7). Mary Jane Moffat (1975) suggests a match of experience and form:

> The form has been an important outlet for women, partly because it is an analogue to their lives: emotional, fragmentary, interrupted, modest, not to be taken seriously, private, restricted, daily, trivial, formless, concerned with self, as endless as their tasks. (p. 5)

The closer look being given these days to women's letter and diary writing may reveal that women use private diary and letter writing partly because they are not as likely to have success at finding encouragement and time to write (and a publisher to print) other types of writing even if women did write for a public audience. Although they are still using the language of the dominant group, women, through letter and diary writing, may also have more flexibility in the manner in which they articulate their experiences and ideas. Letters to other women, and diaries to themselves, will not have to measure up to, or be evaluated against, the models males have produced for "creative" writing. Anthony Burgess says he seldom finds the following characteristics in the contemporary "woman writer": "humor, poetry, the power of the exact image, the ability to be both hard and compassionate, a sense of place, all the risks of impersonation, and finally, a historical eye" (quoted in Rosalind Miles, 1974:41). The muted group theory would suggest that the "man writer," using literary genres and language developed primarily by males for males, finds his own literary forms more acceptable than the forms produced by women who do not have that same relationship to their language.

While diary and letter writing may not be considered "real" creative writing by the governors of literary criticism, women have won recognition for five types of writing considered at least marketable if not "high" art—children's stories, detective fiction, science fiction, historical romances (Karen Trenfield, 1978; Miles, 1974) and, in the nineteenth century, the very popular novels by American women about women for women (Nina Baym, 1978).[7] Because writing to the public is tied to finding a publisher willing to print and distribute the work, and because women's writing and discussion of women's experience has not been considered as publishable, or as valuable, as that of men, we will have a hard time determining the most instrumental reasons that women's writing has often taken different forms from that of men. If men were cut off from public forums, would they continue to write the same amount and in the same form or would they turn more to letter writing and diaries? Is it the male-designed language that women find restricting, or is it the male-controlled publishing concerns? Or both? Feminist critiques of publishing concerns are difficult to find. However, it evidently has been the belief of many women that only by controlling the presses—usually through collective effort—will women be able to start writing for themselves and be read by others. This belief has resulted in the establishment in the 1970s of many feminist presses throughout the western world. (This new use of talent and ink is described in issues of *Media Report to Women* and in a book on women's publishing by Polly Joan and Andrea Chesman [1978].)

Nancy Faires Conklin (1974) has suggested that the many women (in the United States in particular) who in the late 1960s and 1970s joined together in consciousness-raising (CR) groups were employing a forum, a type of interaction, that is specific to women. The early CR groups discussed various types of group behavior and consciously chose a type of interaction that seemed comfortable and effective for them. The talk in CR groups, which explored and altered the significance of established values, took place in a distinctive social setting. It was unlike a bull session, cocktail party, or business, bowling, or therapy session. CR groups existed to explore the dimensions of society's expectations and their ramifications for women. Descriptions of some of the early CR discussions were published in early issues of *Ms.* and other feminist periodicals, and were used as guidelines for many other groups.

The CR groups set out to make explicit some of the interaction norms that were already in operation in many women's groups, and to state what was good about those norms. Perhaps women have never believed that their group interactions were cackling hen parties. However, they have realized that the discussions in bridge club meetings are not about the same things said in the same way in men's groups, professional or recreational. Most published academic small group research is about groups of males—and is study conducted by groups of males. We have to go to diaries, letters, fiction, underground publications, and our own experiences to find out what women have been saying about women's groups. Mercilee Jenkins and I (1978) did that in part—by searching through many underground publications and our own experiences. Through our textbook education in small group research we had learned that maximum productivity, "objective" facts, competition, leadership development, and conflict were the major concerns of, if not the participants, at least the male researchers studying small groups. In our own study we found women conscious of relating to each other, and also of the possibilities and realities of interaction in their own groups.

For example, several women have discussed the way narrative is often handled in women's groups. A kernel story, a reference to the action, subject or dialogue from a longer story, told by a group member, becomes part of the repertoire of the group, referenced, retold by members, and used to support other stories with similar themes. Narrative is not so much sequential episodes told by various members as it is a group activity. New stories are often linked to the old by transitions that indicate the connections to the rest of the discussions. Many sentences are left unfinished by the speakers—to be finished silently or out loud by others (Susan Kalčik, 1975). These patterns of speaking seem to be more characteristic of women's groups than men's groups. At least women perceive members of men's groups as being more competitive with each other for individual attention than are members of women's groups.

In some cases the new types of verbal interactions have resulted in new types of writing activity. Women in Great Britain have not partipated in CR groups in such large numbers. British women in the movement have shown more interest in political theory than have American women; the British group meetings are more likely to deal with "women's issues" in terms of the way the issues may affect and are affected by the ideology and the workings of political parties and political theory, rather than how they may affect individual women. Many British women, with similar interests but from diverse jobs and locations have held many conferences and study group sessions. From some of these meetings and similar ones in the United States has come collective writing, a method of writing that runs counter to the unwritten rules that say writing is very much an individual act. In general, in our society, rugged individualism is exalted. Often this means that jealousy, selfishness, and exclusiveness are encouraged and rewarded in writing and speaking activities (Arlie Russell Hochschild, 1975). The new writing collectives are experimenting with an alternative approach that rejects the notion that ideas are owned and expressed by individuals. That is, they are using unconventional forms and forums of expression, unconventional in the sense that they do not pay tribute to the form and forums set by men. Members exchange rough drafts and suggestions, sometimes writing the papers during group sessions. The papers are considered either as the product of the group rather than of individuals or as essays that explicitly acknowledge the aid of others. The approach combines writing and speaking interaction.[8]

This is not to say that collective writing has never been used before. Many political speeches are written through collective effort—although the efforts of their writers are not usually acknowledged. Business firms and government offices often send forth papers without authors' names or with many names—but this is often done so no one person has to take responsibility. (One of President Jimmy Carter's early innovations was to direct that all new government regulations be written in nonlegal language, and be signed by their authors.) Sometimes groups of people protesting proposals or decisions or actions of other groups may work together to write a statement that all involved in the writing sign to show their solidarity. However, many women are writing together because, by working collectively, and supportively, they can have an impact on other groups in society that individually they do not. Individualism, competitiveness, and ruggedness are concepts that are being critically inspected and often rejected. The style and production of the writing are part of the message, and new types of creativity may be developed this way. Often this type of interaction includes a great deal of talk about language, especially if the groups include people from various social classes, and various educational backgrounds; language is then not a given but something to be constantly negotiated, and the underlying values discussed. Under such group questioning some language concepts are identified as "malestream".

Looking for the modes of expressions used primarily by women is not always easy; if the expressions are used primarily by women, quite likely we will not see them immediately as communicative expressions. Judy Chicago, a professional artist, points out that the work of women artists "has been taken out of the historical context and put into a mainstream [art] context it doesn't belong in; then it is ridiculed, or incorrectly evaluated" (quoted in C. Kurt Dewhurst, Betty MacDowell, and Marsha MacDowell, 1977). Furthermore, if art is defined by men, expressions in forms other than the "legitimate" forms might not be recognized as important expressions. Women either accept the terms set forth by men or do something other than art.

Dewhurst et al. write that the same social and historical factors that have limited the number of women who have become professional artists have also had an impact on women folk artists. They write that the exhibits of women's art and handicraft at the 1876 Centennial Exhibition and the 1893 World's Colombian Exposition did not include quilts—an American art form which flourished at the time and belonged almost exclusively to women.

Other handiwork done primarily by women and seldom recognized as art includes bed rugs, samplers, embroidered pictures and paintings, and crewel-worked bed hangings. Women working in the home have worked with the materials of the home. Only rarely have these items been considered art, and only rarely have these art forms been studied in terms of the limitations within which they were produced. Dewhurst et al. suggest that the study of this work can provide rewarding glimpses into the creative lives of women in the seventeenth, eighteenth, and nineteenth centuries.

The words of some of the British women who have organized a postal club to send each other small art works through the mail suggest that they feel their ideas or models of the world are not easily expressed through traditional modes. The women through their works of art and through their letters state that they once had a difficult time viewing their work as valid expressions of their experience. The works include a pink and blue knitted panel, hanging from the needles, reading "Heart not Art, Homemade I'm Afraid"; Friendship Samplers sent to each other with stitched messages such as "Wife is a Four Letter Word"; knitted zippered sandwiches. One woman said that before she began to participate in the postal art event she "made things, hid them, destroyed them and grew increasingly frustrated with the whole process." She now sees herself "as part of a large group of women working in different media, using different skills" (Rozsika Parker, 1977:7).

Of course, many thousands of males have felt isolated in their work and have felt that their art expressions have been scorned or ignored. However, because of their "muted" status, women experience special difficulties. Using materials and images from their everyday lives, they are consciously trying to develop a visual language that corresponds to their own experience. Yet, domestic crafts have always been considered an art form secondary to the male-dominated portrayals of historical or mythological subjects. Prestige is conferred on man's achievements in this area as in others. When women have used traditional skills, such as crocheting, for furnishing the home (rather than for money), its creativity has been discounted (Parker, 1977).

Similarly, while men often assume that women are in general naturally better than men at maintaining affiliative relationships—women are expected to write letters to aunts and uncles and smooth over rough spots in conversations—men call such activity "small talk." What could be, and probably is by many women, considered to be one of the most vital activities in the daily maintenance of life is often ridiculed by men as chit-chat. Deborah Jones in her paper "Gossip: Notes on Women's Oral Culture" (1980) points out that the topics, forms, and functions of "gossip" and "chit-chat" are very seldom discussed in terms of the experiences and values of women. The ways women orient much of their speech to serve the needs of others is often seen by men as natural to women but also as a weakness. This orientation has seldom been mentioned in small group research—and when it is mentioned it is labelled socio-emotional activity and usually placed in opposition to leadership activity. Men have indicated that they hear differences between the communication styles of women and men. But men evidently do not perceive the content and style associated with women's speech as essential to communication experiences. The linguist Otto Jespersen (1922) called it the "small change" of talk.

WOMEN'S NONVERBAL BEHAVIOR

Another mode of expression to study while considering the muted group theory is nonverbal behavior. Possibly, women restricted by a language structure determined primarily by males rely on nonverbal expression to a greater extent or in a different way. Phyllis Chesler (1972) writes that she thinks women comment on other women's feelings "by reflecting them in a very sensitive matching process."

Their facial expressions, pauses, and signs are more integral to their discussion than are men's (p. 268). Nancy Henley writes in *Body Politics: Power, Sex, and Nonverbal Communication* (1977), "Women's facial expressivity (with their emotional expressivity) has been allowed a wider range than men's, encompassing within the sex stereotype not only pleasant expressions, but negative ones like crying" (p. 174). She argues that this greater variability in facial expression is used to ridicule them as emotionally unstable. Her book is a serious study of what academicians have often passed over as trivial; she is concerned with the ways in which nonverbal behaviors of women and men express subordination and dominance between women and men, blacks and whites. Her review and discussion of nonverbal behavior of women and men might also be helpful in developing and evaluating the muted group theory. To illustrate the way that the subordinates learn to sensitively "read" the emotions of others, she refers to study results that show that women in general, and black men, usually perform somewhat better at identifying emotions portrayed nonverbally. Maccoby and Jacklin (1974:214, 349) discuss the complexities of "empathy" research; they indicate caution should be exercised in concluding that females are more attuned to others. However, the material presented by Henley, and by Judith Hall (1977), suggests that women may learn to rely more on nonverbal cues in interactions because customary terms of talk do not serve the language needs of women as well as they do the needs of men.

Nonverbal communication is of course part of the total communication system; we probably learn nonverbal codes in much the same way we learn verbal codes. Surely Henley's material on the way nonverbal expression can be used to establish and maintain power differentials indicates that both sexes understand basically the same communication system. But they may not have equal access to all parts of the system. The muted group theory suggests that we need to look at the possibly different ways women and men use verbal and nonverbal methods of communication. Perhaps women have a greater sensitivity to nonverbal cues because they are handicapped by a verbal code that is inadequate for women yet not significantly open to change from women. Perhaps the greater nonverbal expressivity expected of women, although often ridiculed, allows them more flexibility in expressing themselves nonverbally than verbally.

The examples above, coupled with indications (Rae Carlson, 1972) that women psychologists prefer to do research that is based on naturalistic observation and participation, while men psychologists prefer research based on "objective" quantitative analysis, illustrate the value of considering what methods women and men are using to express themselves. Here as always the exceptions are important; Erving Goffman is one man who has received wide recognition for his qualitative studies. However, as Jessie Bernard (1973a) points out, in general the qualitative approach (which is said of course to give "soft" data) is not as well respected these days as the quantitative, "hard" analysis; Bernard writes of the "machismo" element that is prevalent in academic research. Through the muted group theory, these different "surface expressions" can be considered as reflections (although likely imperfect) of different underlying world views.

Women and men are not equally able to say what they want, when and where and how they want.

WOMEN'S EXPRESSIONS OF DISSATISFACTION

I have suggested that, if females are muted by the communication system of men, we would expect to hear women allude to hardships that that system imposes on them. In the following section, and in Chapters II and VII, I give many illustrations of what women have said about the communication system of men. In this section, voices of several women writers are given a hearing as they discuss the difficulties they experience as women trying to speak about their experiences, through or around the *literary* language and form accepted by men.

Women writing poetry are much more likely than men writing poetry to discuss their difficulties in handling the language and poem structure. As part of her review of what women poets have said about being women poets, Jane Donovan (1976) looked at poetry anthologies, and found women represented only in small numbers. And the information on those poets indicates that the few recognized women poets wrote a relatively small body of work.

Adrienne Rich (1975) in her poetry and essays writes frequently of her difficulties, as a woman:

> In the late fifties I was able to write, for the first time, directly about experiencing myself as a woman. The poem was jotted down in fragments, during children's naps, brief hours in a library, or at 3 a.m. after rising with a wakeful child. I despaired of doing any continuous work at this time. Yet I began to feel that my fragments and scraps had a common consciousness and a common theme, one which I would have been very unwilling to put on paper at an earlier time because I had been taught that poetry should be "universal," which meant, of course, nonfemale. Until then, I had tried very much *not* to identify myself as a female poet. (p. 97)

She also describes how she initially learned about the craft of poetry from male poets before eventually trying her own form. Anne Sexton also thought of appropriate poetry form learned from men as constraining. Form was, Sexton once thought, the providing of cages for the wild animals of the imagination. Eventually she relied less on the tightly structured forms (Sexton, quoted in Patricia Marx, 1966).

The muted group theory can be used to explain the unease women feel with the methods and tools of writing accepted as conventional and useful by males. Males impose restrictions on the publication of women's public speaking and writing, and males in general determine the words and the forms that are to be used. Women have to write with what is for them an impoverished language. The two restrictions are, of course, related—the constant attempts made to silence women mean that women, to be heard by men, try to present themselves in speech forms recognizable and respected by men.[9] The muted group theory would indicate that often what women want to say and can say best cannot be said easily because the language template is not of their making; it does not allow them to reveal some of their perceptions and experiences. Yet if women try to change their lexicon, grammar, and style, men will not listen or will likely reject what they hear. Men can, perhaps, take their language for granted in a way that women evidently cannot. Annette Kolodny (1975b) writes that "the struggle to create a form, a means of articulation, is a struggle shared by every artist, male or female, in every medium. But it is a struggle, apparently, with qualitatively different components for a woman" (p. 85). She adds that we do not even know much about the variety of women's experience, let alone the ways in which women have experimented with stylistic devices, genre forms, and image making (p. 86).

In the 1950s and continuing through the 1970s a change occurred in the way women approached their poetry writing, as they frequently and explicitly called attention to the differences in men's and women's experiences and perspectives. For example, Erica Jong (1973) writes of the difficulty and necessity that women in particular have in seeing themselves as individuals and in trusting their own voice. She writes of her own experiences at finding her voice and making poetry of it:

> I stopped writing about ruins and nightingales. I was able to make poetry out of the everyday activities of my life: peeling onions, a trip to the gynecologist, a student demonstration, my own midnight terrors and dreams—all the things I would have previously dismissed as trivial.
>
> Because of my own history, I think women poets have to insist on their right to write like women. . . . As long as femininity is associated with ruffles and flourishes and a lack of directness and honesty, women artists will feel a deep sense of ambivalence about their own femaleness. In a culture where *woman* is a synonym for *second-rate,* there's no mystery about why women want to "write like men." (p. 118)

These women work as writers, naturally highly conscious of the role of words in their lives, and their feelings may not be representative of the feelings of most or even many women. However, because they are probably more sensitive than most to the relationship among ideas, feelings, and conventional writing norms, what they are saying should receive attention.

Obviously neither the cognitive nor the communicative problems they refer to are as yet precisely defined. And we would not, in keeping with the insights of the muted group theory, expect them to be. The dominant structure does not provide clear, neat labels for the ideas the women are discussing.

Actually, these women are not less explicit in their discussion than are the many critics (mostly male—literary critics are usually male) who indicate that writing is divided into two major groups, feminine and masculine. Mary Ellmann (1968) writes about a dichotomy she has witnessed in literary criticism: "Women [are thought unable to] comprehend male books, men cannot tolerate female books. The working rules are simple, basic: there must always be two literatures like two public toilets, one for Men and one for Women" (pp. 32-33). The critics seldom provide specific examples to illustrate what is "feminine" writing and what is "masculine" writing.

Recently, Mary Hiatt (1977) with the aid of a computer examined four long passages from each of one hundred books (equally divided between fiction and nonfiction and between those written by women and those written by men) picked from library shelves. She found that the results of her study do not tally with the stereotype of women's writing as being repetitious and circumlocutory.

(For example, she found that women write fewer long sentences than men and more short sentences [although the average sentence lengths of women and men were similar].) She concludes from her study that women use fewer exclamation points, use more parentheses, offer more reasons and justifications for their arguments, use approximately the same number of parallel constructions, and use fewer similes. In the 200,000 words of prose she found several adverbs used only by men and several used only by women. (She compares the fiction and nonfiction separately; my description is generalized from her more specific comparisons. Sally McConnell-Ginet [1979] has written a careful description and evaluation of Hiatt's computer study.)

Actually, the similarities appear much greater than do the differences in women's and men's fiction and nonfiction writing. However, Hiatt's tabulated results do not indicate whether or not writing is any more difficult for women than it is for men; whether or not more women than men find the conventional forms of fiction and nonfiction less "fitted" to what they want to say; or whether or not the published books on the library shelves are representative of the efforts of women who write and of men who write.

From her study of various literature courses and publications, Tillie Olsen (1979) estimates that there are many more men writers than women writers, that in critical studies one page in thirty is devoted to discussion of women writers, and that the ratio of published books is one book by a woman to every four or five by men. Olsen writes that any ratio other than one-to-one calls for an explanation. Certainly, that explanation will have to be complex and to include discussion of how much encouragement—and what resources such as uninterrupted time—women interested in writing receive during the writing process as well as during a search for a publisher. In addition, we might well listen carefully to what women, "successful" and "unsuccessful" writers, are saying about the difficulties that come from writing about women's experiences in what many call a male language.

WOMEN CHANGING THE COMMUNICATION SYSTEM

The muted group theory suggests that women who explicitly express their discontent with many of the values and actions of the dominant group will do so by revising, getting around, and resisting the conventional communication system. Certainly many women are discussing communication systems and possible alternatives to what is now considered conventional talk and writing. These discussions *can* be read and heard, for example, at times when feminists talk together and in the feminist press. (As early as 1973 approximately 150 feminist publications and periodicals were listed in *The New Woman's Survival Catalog* [eds. Kirsten Grimstad and Susan Rennie]. Most such periodicals do not have a sure financial base, but although each month some periodicals discontinue, others begin.)

Women have suggested or employed alterations in the lexicon, argumentative proof, topics considered appropriate for conversation and debate, and channels of communication used. Some women consider the construction of a new language the most important activity of the current Women's Liberation movement. For example, Nelle Morton (1972), a theologian, writes that "the new language of the lips of those experiencing liberation" (p. 181) is more indicative of the changes that will come through the movement than are the political actions. She titles her essay "The Rising Woman Consciousness in a Male Language Structure." Another feminist, Judith McDaniel (1978), writes, "If feminism is the final cause—and I believe it is—then [attention to] language is the first necessity" (p. 17).

Increasingly, women in the movement have become dissatisfied with having to write and speak through what they call a male language structure. Stanley's (1975b) way of putting it is that most of the semantic space of the English language is occupied by male definitions. Men have been the custodians of the lexicon, as studies of etymologies reveal (see Chapter II). Sheila Rowbotham (1973), a British Marxist feminist, writes, "As soon as we learn words we find ourselves outside them." The language that males have developed to reflect and maintain the framework of their world model is, says Rowbotham, "carefully guarded by the superior people because it is one of the means through which they conserve their supremacy" (p. 32). Ann Bodine (1975) points out that males through an Act of Parliament in the nineteenth century determined that "he" would also stand for "she" (p. 136).

Women who wish to articulate the manner in which their values differ from the values received from men have difficulty in doing this within a language structure that is a part of the received values. Betty Friedan (1963), trying to express her dissatisfaction and yearning, wrote of "the problem that has no name" (p. 17). Rowbotham argues, "It is not just a question of being outside existing language. We can never hope to enter and change it from inside. We can't just occupy existing words" (1973:33).

She wrote that in 1973. In the late 1960s, in the initial days of the contemporary Women's Liberation movement, women did attempt to use the language of the males around them even though they were trying to express ideas counter to many ideas held by those males. Some of the rhetoric they employed and some of the problems they experienced with that rhetoric were recorded in the feminist press. (The examples I include here come from the United States. The greater influence of the labor and socialist movements in Great Britain may have produced a different early liberation talk there, although it too would likely have been based on male rhetoric.)

In the late 1960s, some of the women in the New Left, dissatisfied with their (subordinate) roles in that movement, began meeting apart from the men, forming the first of what are now called consciousness-raising or rap groups. Of course, not all women who were active in the early Women's Liberation movement were first active in the New Left movement, just as not all women in the movement now have exactly the same goals. Some groups within the movement are primarily interested in working through established channels to obtain equal legal rights, while other groups are more interested in what they see as a larger struggle against capitalism and against patriarchy. The influence of the New Left language was pervasive in the Women's Liberation movement prior to the 1970s. The language used by the movement, at least in the manifestoes of those first early groups, was very similar to that employed in the New Left literature. (See, e.g., "S.D.S. National Resolution on Women," in *Masculine/Feminine: Readings in Sexual Mythology and the Liberation of Women,* eds. Betty Roszak and Theodore Roszak, 1969:254-259). Discussing the S.D.S. National Resolution on Women, Roszak and Roszak write: "The language of the resolution is an unfortunate example of the pompous jargon employed in S.D.S. literature since it has taken a strong Marxist-Leninist line. Even the defensive feminists here seemed trapped by their self-imposed terminology" (p. 254). Paradoxically, while identifying the male as the agent of their oppression, the women used a rhetoric that many women now believe reflects the male-oriented world model, which they now seek to challenge.

In an article written relatively early in the movement, Margaret B. McDowell (1971) observed: "In spite of their anti-war stance, Movement women depend heavily on a militarist vocabulary (*struggle, tyranny, power, enemy, hostility, solidarity, front, power, organize, unite, resist, mobilize, regroup, destroy, attack, liberate*)" (pp. 190-191). She notes also the "obscenities shouted with a vehemence rivalling that of the Weathermen" (p. 191), the seriousness "bordering on paranoia, of much of the radical Liberationist rhetoric" (p. 192), and the "mocking, raucous, taunting humor" (p. 192) of the early movement.

Robin Morgan (1978) writes that in the Leftist consciousness of the late 1960s, "being tough, butch, 'heavy,' and 'a street fighter' were now prerequisites for being a radical, male or female" (p. 115). She "dutifully" inserted words such as "imperialism, running-dog-of-a-capitalist-swine, and other phrases which would have given George Eliot the vapours" into her essays for a radical newspaper written and published collectively by women (p. 119).

While other women involved in the women's movement in the late 1960s think that these descriptions are exaggerated, the descriptions do point to a problem experienced by some movement women. A "tough" language when used by males commanded attention. Women who were accustomed to supportive, democratic modes of interacting in rap groups and other more informal groups had not developed a corresponding style for public speaking.

Sometimes the public styles interfered with the small group interaction. The writing of the women trying to assess the failures and successes of the women's movement in the early 1970s testifies to the discontent that was soon felt with the use of the masculine rhetoric. Two women who toured the country trying to determine the status of the movement wrote:

> In every group or grouping we've been in, those women who by some chance have acquired the typical "male" traits of aggressiveness, forcefulness, articulateness, loud voices, and especially public self-confidence, have become the leaders. This reinforces the female tradition of expecting leadership to always have these qualities. Those who are more typically "feminine" (i.e. passive, not self-confident, inarticulate, "illogical," soft spoken) didn't see themselves as leaders any more than they did in the male-oriented student movement. (Caltha Mellor and Judy Miller, 1970:79)

The concern was that, by using the words and delivery constructed and valued by males, women would fail to provide the base for a new social system based not on competition and division but on connections between people.

The masculine rhetoric was not working for two reasons. First, women, even when using the language structure set up by men, are still outsiders to the male power structure. Nancy Henley (1977), writing on the politics of touch, points out that when women initiate touching it is often seen as a sexual advance; when men initiate touching (the more frequent happening) it generally functions as a gesture of dominance. Hearing a similar *verbal* phenomenon, a feminist sociologist writes:

> It may be argued that women too use what I have called "male" language [dominance] and customs. True, but when they do, the behavior immediately loses its political significance. Dominance gestures don't work when women use them. They are transformed into sexual signals or indications of lesbianism; or they may provoke male violence. Towards women male culture is utterly exclusive. Furthermore, women never carry the thing off properly. They underdo or overemphasize everything to such an extent their behavior almost seems a caricature: the traditional fate of oppressed who try to "pass for" oppressors. (Ann Battle-Sister, 1971:419)

So the first reason women's use of male rhetoric was found ineffectual was that it was not heard as containing the same power and significance it conveyed when males used it.

The second reason comes out of the first. The "male" language did not establish the base the women wanted. Two participant-critics in the early feminist movement wrote about the danger of applying the competitive (masculine) linguistic norms: "We must avoid the inclination to rank women according to men's standards: articulateness, intellectual cleverness, verbal aggressiveness. Being straight-shooting, fast talking, clever performers is not what we're after; we don't need debating points" (Anne Rogers and Aleen Holly, 1971:55).

Evaluating in the late 1970s an article—on teaching women survival tactics—which she wrote in the early 1970s, Robin Morgan (1978) talks about the incongruity of the form and content. The article had

> ... Leftist style mixed uneasily with Feminist content, the whole thing whipped to a froth of urgency to avoid curdling at the boil. There is an aura of Playing War in this article, which at the time did seem preferable to Playing House, but which now strikes me as equally infantile and even more unsatisfying. (p. 131)

Rae Carlson (1972) saw the ultimate futility of using masculine language to protest the masculine-hierarchical-competitive social structure. In referring to the verbal devices used by early feminists, she wrote:

> "Sigmund Freud was a male chauvinist!" "Anatomy is not destiny!" "Anything you can do, I can do better!" These slogans, possibly quite valid statements, miss a fundamental point: Since the protest is couched in the language of the "oppressor," it is unlikely to transcend the basic assumption embedded in that language. (pp. 17-18)

The awareness of the difficulties of talking new ideas through the old leftist language structure for public speaking did not come immediately after the break of the women from the New Left movement. In fact, problems with the rhetoric perhaps slowed down the movement. A member of one group formed by women who had been active in the New Left recalls:

> We had heard about women's groups being formed in other parts of the country, but our experience in the [New Left] movement had burned us so badly that anything that hinted

of organizing, meetings, or objectivity was synonymous with manipulation, rhetoric, and ego-trips, so for a long time we didn't seriously consider meeting in any kind of formal way. (Pat Hansen, quoted by Judith Hole and Ellen Levine, 1971:121)

When the CR groups, thousands of them, organized, there was explicit recognition of the need for alternative modes of self-expression (Anita Lynn Micossi, 1970). The women tried in their discussions to be as supportive as possible.[10] Additionally, women encouraged each other to speak about subjects that had formerly been taboo to them and about subjects that are not considered important by many males.

The table of contents in a 1971 Women's Liberation movement anthology indicates some of the topics that women were discussing: prostitution, the sexual double standard, lesbianism, depression of middle-aged women, the socialization of women, the image of women in textbooks, and the dimensions of femininity. Even rape, the threat of which constrains so much female activity, had previously seldom been discussed by women's groups. These topics had not been treated as legitimate discussion topics in our encyclopedias, textbooks, or in popular "women's" journals.

For many years women have been stating that men's language does not fit the expressive needs of women. Virginia Woolf wrote in 1929 that the established grammar and literary forms make writing more difficult for a woman. She states that examples from men's writing do not help a woman in her writing, for immediately in reading men's writing, the woman finds that there is "no common sentence ready for her use." Woolf argues that the sentences in male writing are unsuited for the woman who writes (reprinted 1972:76). Her statements are provocative, if ambiguous. What is it about those sentences that women find unsuitable for their own? Morton (1972) wrote that women in the women's movement are no longer speaking "a male speech," that they are working toward "a new language of the *full human experience*" (pp. 189, 190). "Women's writing," "a feminine text," and "male writing" are the topic of Hélène Cixous' article "The Laugh of the Medusa" (1976). She states that writing has been run by males; she encourages the woman writer to "write her self, because this is the invention of a *new insurgent* writing" (p. 880). Others have written of the need for linguistic reclamation, of "shaping a new tool for new uses" (e.g., June Arnold, quoted in *Media Report to Women,* 1 April 1976, p. 10). Adrienne Rich (1978) writes of the many forms of silence that have muted women's voices: "namelessness, denial, secrets, taboo subjects, erasure, false-naming, non-naming, encoding, omission, veiling, fragmentation and lying" (p. 18). She, like many others, believes that an examination of women and language will also bring an examination of the connections between not only the polarization of female and male, but also the polarization of black and white women and of heterosexual and homosexual women. If women are not allowed a voice and our own words, we are not permitted examination of the interconnections between oppression of black and white women.[11]

These statements, and there are many other, similar, statements, are clear indications of dissatisfaction with the conventional communicational system. They are declarations that what we sometimes call "our" language leaves unencoded much of women's experiences, and that many women see poverty in what is so often called the wealth of words and language. A closer look at the work of some contemporary writers gives further, more specific, signs of the limitations and possibilities of language code and structure, as perceived by them.

First, as the Rich quotation above indicates, some women are calling attention to the man-made polarities in the language. Naming is a power used to tame and domesticate women and nature; naming separates men from nature and women, separates the social and public from the domestic and natural. Several authors (Annette Kolodny, 1975a; Mary Daly, 1978; Susan Griffin, 1978) have recently looked at this polarization and have written about the reining in, domestication, and frequent maiming of the environment and of women. Griffin, for example, writes:

> And it is written that in the inferior world of brutes and vegetables man was created to act as the viceroy of the great God of heaven and earth, and that he should then name the brutes and the vegetables. For there is power in words, it is said, and it is put forward that by knowing the names of natural things, man can command them, that he who calls the creatures by their true names has power over them.
>
> (Thus it is decided that earth shall be called land; trees, timber; animals to be called hunted, to be called domesticated; her body to be named hair, to be named skin, to be called breast, vulva, clitoris, to be named womb.) (p. 20)

Also tomato, chick, peach, sow, bitch, cow, mare, bunny, shrew, beaver, dog, bat, pussycat.... Recognizing and responding to the male/female polarity and the muting of women as subjects in the language, the French writer Monique Wittig (1975) splits the first person pronouns, possessive adjectives, and reflexive pronouns. She uses I [J/e], m/y, and m/e to remind the reader that the writer is in a male-controlled language, not one of woman's making.

Second, what Griffin calls the "paternal voice" is analyzed and rejected by some writers. The Griffin quotation above is a parody not only of sacred writing but also of male scholarly, objective, nonemotional, authoritative writing and speaking. In Griffin's writing, patriarchal thought is represented by the passive voice; this construction implies a universal consensus—that is, fact—not personal opinion. (Stanley [1975a] also discusses some of the effects of this construction.) This so-called objective voice introduces assertions without their agents: It is discovered/ advised/ stated/ agreed/ determined/ written/ said/ cautioned/ put forward/ observed. To reveal that disembodied voice Griffin sets up a dialogue with what she calls her voice joined by the voices of other women, to produce an embodied, impassioned voice (p. xvi). For example:

> And it is written in the law that "Women should be subject to their men."
>
> *And we learn*
>
> And it is advised that women not be allowed to teach nor should they baptize. That "even the Virgin Mary" was not allowed to baptize.
>
> *that our speech is unholy*
>
> And it is stated that nature should be approached only through reason....
>
> (1978:19-20)

Her book catalogues what she feels are the patriarchal attitudes toward women and nature, and offers style alternatives.[12] Her dialogue is about what she feels has caused women's mutedness and about what forms women's own speech can take: *"And they say that muteness is natural in us"* (p. 26). *"We open our mouths. We try to speak. We try to remember"* (p. 44). If women's experiences are not recorded in civilized literature, how can women know about women's experiences? Below, Griffin writes about tracing the cause of a woman's death to an abortion (and about tracing women's lives in general).

> It is said from the body of the dead woman no proof of innocence or guilt can be issued. *We go back. We ask what happened then. We find no mention. No reference. No books. Books out of print. Lost, destroyed. Pages torn away. Days missing. We find documents.* She finds letters. Diaries. Stories are repeated. *We discover* she was operated on four times before she died, *we discover* a hairpin was removed from her bladder, *we read* they took salts of lead, copper, zinc and mercury, *we read* they let themselves fall down staircases. . . . *We can tell you something of what they went through, we say.* (1978:215)

Women in the movement now consciously use the *personal* as proof, in an attempt to correct a situation in which women and their experiences have been slighted. (Karlyn Kohrs Campbell [1973] writes that this emphasis on "effective proofs and personal testimony" contributes to making the rhetoric of women's liberation a separate genre [p. 83] .)

In writing of the way man regards and makes use of woman and nature and of the resulting muteness of women, Griffin does not follow standard English usage or traditional sequencing of time or arguments. A third way the writing of feminist innovators differs from traditional styles is in their use of a holistic, open form, which rejects linear time sequence and a static cause and effect. Some twentieth-century male authors have also used this "women's style" but, as Susan J. Wolfe (Robbins) (1978) points out, they do so for the purpose of stylistic experimentation, not to challenge "knowledge" nor to express the essence of their existence and their perception. Wolfe notes that most of the innovations are coming from the pens of lesbian/feminists who have made perhaps the most complete break with male perspective. A prefatory statement in Jill Johnston's (1973) *Lesbian Nation* provides a short example of the merging of time, and the breaking of rules about structural logic. Johnston writes of the book's style as an "interlocking web" of personal experience and history:

> All repetitions of thoughts ideas material projections plans reflections reveries fantasies in the same or varied phrases in different contexts constitute my way of working circles within circles, like the quadriga, the four horsed chariot, constantly returning to its point of origin. Every departure from a point of origin carries with it a renewed approach to it. Each return to the point of origin completes the cycle of one existence and begins another. The style and the subject are the same: the return to the harmony of statehood and biology through the remembered majesties of women. (Introductory Remarks)

Another way some women are taking liberties with language is by coining words. A short passage in Daly's (1978) *Gyn/Ecology*, a book about wrenching back word power, gives some idea of the seriousness of her word playing. She creates a new set of terms to draw attention to the inadequacy of existing ways of expression:

> The rulers of patriarchy—males with power—wage an unceasing war against life itself. Since female energy is essentially biophilic [life-loving], the female spirit/body is the primary target in this perpetual war of aggression against life. Gyn/Ecology is the re-claiming of life-loving female energy. This claiming of gynergy requires knowing/naming the fact that the State of Patriarchy is the State of War, in which periods of recuperation from and

preparation for battle are euphemistically called "peace." Furies/Amazons must know the nature and conditions of this State in order to dis-cover and create radical female friendship. (p. 355)

Some words coined or used in a new way by Mary Daly include *Crone-ology* (women's history), *male-functions, man-ipulated, gynergy, stag-nation, biophilic*. She includes 160 entries in her "Index of New Words" (pp. 469-471). (In Chapter II, I look more closely at the ingredients of our language, and the ways it is altered or not by its speakers.)

These words give an indication that, in addition to creating new words, some writers are engaged in what Muriel Schulz (1978) calls the task of dredging, bringing to the surface the accretions of generations of speakers in order to use language afresh. Daly writes:

Since the language and style of patriarchal writing simply cannot contain or carry the energy of women's exorcism and ecstasy, in this book I invent, dis-cover, re-member. At times I make up words. ... Often I unmask deceptive words by dividing them and employing alternative meanings for prefixes (for example, *re-cover* actually says "cover again"). I also unmask their hidden reversals, often by using less known or "obsolete" meanings (for example, *glamour* as used to name a witch's power). ... When I play with words, I do this attentively, deeply, paying attention to etymology, to varied dimensions of meaning, to deep Background meanings and subliminal associations. (1978:24)

So, for example, she looks at the etymology of *hag*, finds that it comes from an Old English word meaning harpy, or witch, and formerly meant "an evil or frightening spirit," and she asks evil and frightening to whom? She traces the history of words for labelling women such as spinsters, lesbians, harpies, crones, furies, to record the relationship of language and myth, and to redefine the terms. At the beginning of her book she lists the "fair game" of the Playboys' Playground (p. 7); at the end, the game/the named are no longer silent. Daly writes of the "Paradise" that is outside and beyond the patriarchal Playboys' Playground:

We hear the call of our wild. We play games to end their games. Those who have been called bitches bark; pussies purr; cows moo; old bats squeal; squirrels chatter; nags whinny; chicks chirp; cats growl; old crows screech. Foxy ladies chase clucking biddies around in circles. (1978:423)

Another new way of dealing with the old language is illustrated by Daly's use of exploded and fused terms. Daly makes new connections through her frequent uses of slashes—writing, for example, that "Radical feminist consciousness spirals in all directions, dis-covering the past, creating/dis-closing the present/future" (p. 1).

Taken out of context these bits of prose/poetry passages can only give hints of the new language and new styles some women have been using and discussing. The examples do, however, suggest the dissatisfaction with and the challenges to conventional discourse—through the women's discussions of passive voice and dichotomies in the language, through the breaking of the rules of a linear, logical style, and through the creating and redefining of words.[13]

Finally, women are writing and speaking in a greater variety of forms and channels. As I have indicated, feminists have shown a great deal of interest in collective writing. In the past, women have, as Karlyn Kohrs Campbell (1973) points out, seldom talked to each other through public forms (p. 79); as reported in the publication *Media Report to Women*, groups of women especially in the large cities are critiquing radio and television programs, writing and publishing their recommendations for changes, and some women are producing programs especially for women on, for example, social and political issues. The underground communication network, through which are heard thousands of women who would otherwise never have a local, let alone a national, audience, grew rapidly during the early days of the movement. Conscious that men's control over language has extended to control of the publication of words, several groups of women in the United States and Great Britain have organized their own presses and distribution networks.

SUMMARY

In all, the evidence is that many women who are questioning the perceived dominant male world view see changes in language and in interaction patterns as central to their concerns. Talk about change in relationships among people has entailed talk about the resources of our language and about changed communicative behavior.

The muted group theory offers us a framework for looking at the ways a language, and the accepted methods of using language, present images of what women are "supposed" to be, of what is "natural" and "unnatural." The theory posits that the values and assumptions encoded in our language are primarily those of males; thus the theory offers an explanation for some of men's protestations that they cannot understand women or what they say. In addition, the difficulties many women experience in detailing their concerns and values can be explained by use of this theory.

This discussion has looked primarily at what women have said about their difficulties with the English language and the recognized and respected modes of interaction supported by our schools, businesses, and other social institutions. I have written about a few of the efforts by women to call attention to alternative or additional lexicon items and interaction models that support and reflect other than the accepted interpretations of what interaction is desirable. The muted group theory provides a structure for looking at these efforts. It does not provide as much support for an analysis of the ways the English language and conventional communication systems handicap men in their interaction with others. What about men's muteness, their difficulties in talking with others in the domestic sphere, and in discussing their and others' feelings? Men are writing increasingly about their inexpressiveness and the problems they encounter when they try to find modes of speaking that can serve them in both their private life with family and friends, and their public life in which they are often encouraged by others to be competitive and relatively unconcerned with people's feelings.

Some of the women in the early slavery abolition movement in the United States were encouraged to use in their writing the rhetorical principles set up entirely by male British and American orators, and to sit silent on the platform while male ministers and relatives read the women's public address. Today we still get our public statements primarily from males. Women, however, are primarily responsible for the maintenance of friendship networks. Many long distance male friendships are kept warm largely through the work of women married to the men, women who send the letters, gifts, and birthday greetings (as well as clean the houses, and make the meals and beds for visitors). *Men* in these cases seem to be handicapped with inadequate language resources or with underdeveloped communication competencies.

Boys are more likely to meet aggression with aggression; girls more likely to meet aggression with a variety of verbal responses. Even when they are working with a language that encodes the values and interests primarily of males, females have been encouraged from the beginning to use verbal rather than physical resources and to learn more verbal strategies for dealing with people. They are encouraged to use speech rather than swings and blows. When boys play with trucks and planes they imitate the sound of the machine, not the drivers or pilots. Meanwhile the girls who are playing house with other children or are playing with dolls are taking the roles of the family members within the home and are practicing various domestic interactions. Ideally, it seems to me, girls need more encouragement to use their physical strength. Likewise, boys need more encouragement to use verbal resources in personal relationships.

We need to look not only at the way women's and men's world views are reflected or not in the language, but also at the amount and types of speech practice of females and males. And then we need to determine if "chit-chat" and "small talk" are the terms that most adequately define what it is that women have learned. What happens if women define the nature of their interactions? In the following chapters, I discuss more specifically the words and concepts of the English language as well as some recent alterations by women.

NOTES

1. A French anthropologist, Nicole-Claude Mathieu (1973 [trans. by D.M. Leonard Barker, 1978]), has taken issue with some aspects of E. Ardener's analysis and with some of his assumptions about the relationship of women and men anthropologists. Her critique of the E. Ardener essay "Belief and the Problem of Women" and his reply (in S. Ardener, ed., 1975) to her critique will be valuable for anyone wishing to explore further the participation of women and of men in determining the focus and boundaries of the discipline of social anthropology.

2. Debate continues over the constraints a particular language places on its speakers' perception of the world. I use "constraints" rather than "determination" since most people writing today about the Humbolt-Whorf-Lee-Sapir hypothesis (which states that language determines the way we think) argue that although the concept/articulation capabilities of any particular language do influence what speakers of a language are able to "see" and to think about, people are able to perceive things outside their particular language.

3. Edwin Ardener and Shirley Ardener (conversation, 1977) warn that the underlying structures of women's and men's models of the world cannot be easily detected and that if they are elicited the difference between women's and men's models may be found to be quite small—although perhaps very important in male/female interaction. Further, they warn that talking about the theory by way of listing and testing several hypotheses brings an element of reduction into discussion of the theory. While, as they point out, the women/men relationship appears to be an extremely clear example of a relationship between dominant and subordinate groups, the muted group theory is designed to look at the relationship between all asymmetrical groups.

4. The study of women by social anthropologists has continued with the publication of *Defining Females: The Nature of Women in Society,* edited by Shirley Ardener (1978). Some of the papers in that collection also make use of the theory that posits that there are dominant modes of expressions in any society (generated by dominant groups) which cause the "muting" of the subordinate groups. In that work, S. Ardener writes, "The 'mutedness' of one group may be regarded as the inverse of the 'deafness' of the dominant group, as the 'invisibility' of the former's achievements is an expression of the 'blindness' of the latter. Words which continually fall upon deaf ears may, of course, in the end become unspoken, or even unthought" (p. 20).

5. I am, however, very reluctant to suggest biological imperatives as answers to our questions about female/male differences in behavior. The possibilities, limitations, and dangers of a biosocial perspective (which at present is built on little solid data from either primates or humans) have been recently evaluated by many (including eight writers in *Signs: Journal of Women in Culture and Society,* 1979, 4 (4), 695-717). Rather than focusing on "innate differences" we might do well to listen to many women talk about their perceptions of the degree, costs, and types of asymmetry in our human relationships. Those perspectives have been largely missing in previous research on and discussions of women's and men's nature and behavior—research and discussions that too often in the past have been basically arguments for the status quo of the social structure.

6. Marjorie Harness Goodwin (1978), however, has spent hundreds of hours listening to, recording, and analyzing the conversations of black working class children, seven through thirteen years old, playing in their neighborhood streets in Philadelphia. She describes the boys' speech as much more directive than that of the girls, who use fewer "bald" commands.

7. Women *have* been involved in literary innovation, of course. Elizabeth Hardwick (1975) has spoken of the influence on other writers of, for example, Emily Dickinson, Jane Austen, Virginia Woolf, and Colette. However, these women, like others, have received attention *as* women writers. Carol Ohmann (1971) writes that critics are much more likely to analyze the poetry and other writing of women in terms of what is known about their lives as women, while the poetry of men is thought to exist more independently. Mary Ellmann (1968) writes, "Books by women are treated as though they themselves were women, and criticism embarks, at its happiest, upon an intellectual measuring of busts and hips" (p. 29). See also Margaret Uroff's (1979) analysis of the criticism of Ted Hughes's and Sylvia Plath's writings. They often wrote on similar topics when they lived together. Critics often discuss Plath's writing, but not Hughes's, in terms of the author's personal life.

8. This is certainly not to say that all others recognize the product of this interaction as a valuable alternative. University tenure review committees are usually more interested in competitive rather than noncompetitive behavior. When more than one author is listed on a publication, records are kept in some universities on who is the first (i.e., the controlling) author. Evidence of a hierarchy is demanded. (However, more frequently now than five years ago, I see footnotes that state the authors tossed coins to determine name order on a publication, and footnotes that give acknowledgements to others who had some part in the study.)

In many respects writing collectively is not easy. There are few conventions to provide guides. Several women in writing collectives in England discussed at a 1977 feminist conference in Bristol the methods, benefits, and difficulties of collective writing. I heard several references to collective writing as "not high art," which indicates that some of the participants still evaluate collective writing in terms of more established literary forms and are still influenced by beliefs that the personal voice is more honorific than collective forms. Those statements also indicate that these women do think collective writing produces something that differs from traditional forms. Working from the muted group theory, my question is, do we find women using modes of expression that are not used frequently by males? Women writing collectively *are* questioning the value of conventional forms of writing.

9. Not that this technique works frequently or well. The praise which was applied to the work of George Eliot, Ellis Bell, and Currer Bell was modified or withdrawn when those

works were revealed as coming from the pens of Mary Ann Evans, Emily Brontë, and Charlotte Brontë. One male reviewer of the first edition of Emily Brontë's *Wuthering Heights Heights* likened the author to a "rough sailor [with] a powerful imagination" while a reviewer writing after the author's sex was known likened her to a "bird fluttering its wings against the bars of its cage, finally sinking exhausted" (Carol Ohmann, 1971:908, 909).

10. Yet, this explicit attempt to make the groups "structureless" resulted in other difficulties. Jo Freeman (1975) writes of the "tyranny of structurelessness." She believes that some militancy and some form of leadership may be needed to confront those in power in order to bring about political and social changes. If we pay more attention to the social organization of girls' and women's groups we might be better prepared to discuss present and possible harmonious, effective structures for various activities.

11. Women share oppression, but the oppression is differentiated along race and class lines. The authors in *Capitalist Patriarchy and the Case for Socialist Feminism* (edited by Zillah R. Eisenstein, 1979) discuss the relationships between gender and class, and gender and race. Eisenstein suggests that the important question to ask is not how women of varying class and race are oppressed, but how the process of power functions.

12. We can find another dialogue with contrasts between the formal voice and the voice of actual experience in Dorothy Parker's short story "The Waltz." In this work Parker gives us both the proper, humble, accommodating, sweet, stereotypical feminine speech as the woman speaks to her male dancing partner, and her internal monologue in which she rages against the situation (Paula Treichler, 1977).

13. Women in several cultures are discussing the forms and functions of a language that would better serve women. For example, Simone de Beauvoir discussing the ways a language can be altered and enriched by women says,

Language . . . is inherited from a masculine society, and it contains many male prejudices. We must rid language of all that. Still, a language is not something created artificially; the proletariat can't use a different language from the bourgeoisie, even if they use it differently. . . . Women simply have to steal the instrument; they don't have to break it, or try, a priori, to make of it something totally different. Steal it and use it for their own good. (In Alice Jardine, 1979:229-230)

II

FROM ANDROCENTRISM
TO ZYGOSTYLE

If, as suggested by the muted group theory, the code we call English is more closely aligned with the world view of the dominant group, we would expect to find that men are the primary developers of our language. Two issues are involved here and should be considered separately. First, is there evidence that women have generally been excluded from language construction, particularly from contributing to the vocabulary and the writing and speaking genres used by both women and men? And second, is there evidence that women (other than those writers and poets quoted in Chapter I) feel constrained in perception and/or expression by the present language?

WOMEN'S EXCLUSION FROM LANGUAGE CONSTRUCTION

First, the evidence that women are excluded from the making of words that become accepted by many people, both women and men, although extensive, is largely "negative evidence"—that is, women are not credited with making words. Women are seldom identified as participants in the construction of what is repeatedly referred to by lexicographers as our marvelous, living, English language—a language that is said to reflect its speakers' interests and to change as speakers change interests and ideas, invent things and concepts, and explore their surroundings.

Of course, most men will live a lifetime without coining a word recognized by anyone outside their family and friendship circles. However, they are not excluded from the process on account of their gender, or, according to etymologists, on account of their race or formal education.

Mario Pei (1967), author of more than two dozen books on language structure and language usage, writes in *The Story of the English Language* that it is chance that makes language. The English language, he writes, is the result of a long series of accidents. But he makes an observation that indicates that at least one constant has been operating: men have made the language. "Many men, famous and obscure, have had a part in fashioning what goes into the tongue we speak and write. Few if any of them had any clear idea of what they were doing as they did it" (p. 4).

Perhaps he meant to include women under the label *men*. (A possibility, although investigators are finding that generic usage of *man* and *men* is relatively rare; see Norma Shepelak, 1977; Donald G. MacKay and David Fulkerson, 1979; and Wendy Martyna, 1980.) However, his story of the English language is a story of the linguistic activities of males. If his history and other histories of the English language are accurate, the contributions of women in constructing our language could be erased and no one would notice. (I am considering women's *active* role in language construction. Clearly, men have used [perhaps created] and maintained women's "otherness" in building language; words designating women have, at least for the past few hundred years, constituted a noticeable segment of the vocabulary. See Julia P. Stanley, 1977b.)

The people responsible for the introduction of new words into the English language vary depending upon the decade and the humans and activities esteemed or feared. J.L. Dillard (1975) writes of the impact on the language of those involved in maritime trade and frontier travel and trading. He also notes (1976) the influence of the stagecoach riders, paying and nonpaying passengers on railway trains, cowboys, pioneers, gamblers, drinkers, smokers, trappers, loggers, miners, advertising men, farmers, scientists. (These are, of course, activities or occupations that are considered male activities, although most would not have to be gender specific.) He notes the influence of the French, Dutch, British, and other nationalities and the contribution, virtually ignored by other United States language historians, of blacks. Dillard's work on American talk is an important addition to our understanding of the American language, since he documents in particular the contribution black males have made to the language. He does mention the activity of Sojourner Truth, a black pre-Civil War feminist/orator, "an inspired public speaker," who was one historical figure involved in a language shift from a variety of Dutch to nonstandard English (1976:30). However, Dillard's "the Black" appears to be gender specific. His examples usually refer to activities identified with males (e.g., street corner verbal games, and pimping). In general his historical account is about men with no discussion of the reasons why—no matter the decade, the race, or ethnic group—women rarely participate, or are not recorded as participating, in the development of the English language.

The best-known American etymologist, H.L. Mencken, is also parsimonious with references to women as word creators. Each edition of H.L. Mencken's *The American Language: An Inquiry into the Development of English in the United States* is considered classic. The first edition is dated 1919; the sixth printing of the fourth edition was published in 1977. (References here are to the fourth edition.) As the editor of the fourth edition, Raven McDavid, Jr., writes: "A list of those whose concern with linguistics was stimulated by correspondence about 'The American Language,' or whose research was furthered directly by Mencken himself, would include most of those who have made the study of American English a respectable discipline in its own right" (p. vi). Mencken's account of the history of the American language is almost entirely about *men* and language, whether moneylenders, theologians, medicine quacks, politicians, sailors, trappers, mountain men, ministers, or nomads. The few mentions of women as actively involved in public use of language are seen as digressions. In a chapter on "English Difficulties with American" he mentions in one section three English women authors who use Americanisms in their work. (Two of them he says use these forms incorrectly.) I was surprised at Mencken's reference to women authors, three in a row even. Mencken also was aware of this phenomenon and identified his next author as "a he-novelist" (p. 303), and his historical account returns to "normal." Mencken's book and—with very few exceptions—other histories of American or English language(s) are books about the linguistic activities of men written for men. For example, Mencken, writing of the value of the word "rubberneck," says that whoever invented it "would be worthy not only of a Harvard LL.D. but also of the thanks of both Rotary and Congress, half a bushel of medals and thirty days as the husband of Miss America" (pp. 706-707). The assumptions are that the inventor is male, and that the reader is a heterosexual male who will appreciate Mencken's idea of a perfect reward. Brian Foster (1976) also writes about English as a male invention and project as he writes in *The Changing English Language*: "In the mind of many a young Briton and his girl, American speech is the hall-mark of the tough guy and the he-man" (p. 14). Although Foster's book is almost entirely about male involvement in language change there is no explicit discussion of the exclusion of women.

Some of the histories do mention women as persons to be named or as persons who utilize the words made for them by others. Mencken, for example, writes:

During the mid-Nineteenth Century it was usual for American wives to borrow the honorifics of their husbands. (p. 331)

... the English newspapers frequently refer to *lady secretaries, lady doctors, lady inspectors* and *lady champions.* (p. 351)

But the women at work in the shipyards and other war plants were seldom if ever called *ladies*, and the Pennsylvania Railroad, when it put female trainmen to work in 1943, marked their caps simply *trainman.* (p. 351)

For many years there has been a quiet effort to find a substitute for *mother-in-law*, which has been cursed with unpleasant connotations by the cheaper humor of the press and stage, and also, perhaps, by personal experience. Gene Howe, editor of the Amarillo (Tex.) *News-Globe* ... began a movement for rehabilitating the lady in 1930, or there about, but did not invent a softer name. (p. 354)

Many disarming names for a house of prostitution are in common use. ... There are even more for prostitute. (p. 365)

[In a study with college student participants] the word most abhorred by the men was *puke* and by the women *bitch.* (p. 365)

... *she* is a derogatory prefix in many parts of the country. ... (p. 365)

Maurer says that prostitutes are so stupid and so little group-conscious that they have never developed "the technical vocabulary which characterizes all other criminal groups." (p. 727) (Mencken adds that "Nevertheless" there are a number of trade terms used widely by them.)

[Females who] devote themselves to entertaining soldiers and sailors on leave ... were usually called *V-girls.* (p. 727)

[The women of burlesque] were called *hill horses* or *beef trusts,* the last a reference to Billy Watson's famous "Beef Trust" company, the billing of which announced that it offered "two tons of women." (p. 736)

Mencken's editions of *The American Language* are massive, and in his treatises on the inventions and definitions of words he often discusses groups of men who have been labelled by others, not by themselves. For example, he writes that blacks (male and female) often "inherited" English and Welsh surnames. Men (and women) of all ethnic groups in the United States have experienced being labelled by others. The word *skibby,* once "used on the Pacific coast to designate Japanese, is extremely offensive to them, for it was applied originally to a loose woman" (p. 373). Other terms of abuse include *grease ball, dago* and *wop, wetbacks, spick,* and *kike.* Blacks have been given the greatest number of derogatory names—*boy* or *girl, buck, coon, darky, nigger,* and *pickaninny* are just a few.

However, women are seldom presented in Mencken's history as anything *but* recipients of labels or as genteel searchers for "euphemisms" (for references to parts of the body or to items of clothing). Mencken mentions that most words used for labelling women, no matter what their original meaning, acquire derogatory connotations (p. 357), but he does not explore the reasons or the implications of this for women. (Muriel Schulz [1975] does what Mencken did not.[1]) And in Mencken's work, and in other such discussions, when women are mentioned it is often their sexuality that is discussed. (Prostitution is one occupation of women that does receive attention.) Mencken does quote Earl Wilson, described as a saloon editor and expert on Broadway lexicography, on the terms that "chorus girls" use to refer to men who make advances and to refer to pads which alter their body shape (p. 736). He writes of words such as *falsies* and *sex appeal* (body pads), *body* (man), *square* or *creep* (undesirable person), and *fractured* (drunk). Several of these have been widely used since they were reported in the 1940s. In Mencken's book Earl Wilson is reported as having asked Toots Shor, described as "a [male] Broadway savant" (p. 736), for precise definitions of several of the words. That is, even though the words were evidently created by women the words were defined and reported by males. Few other women word-creators are mentioned. In his chapter on slang, Mencken notes only in passing that "even nuns in cloisters have developed their own slang (amusing, but of course genteel)" (pp. 702-703).

If one assumes that any group of people engaged in common activities and in frequent contact develops some specialized terms, it is likely that groups of women have coined words and have altered meanings for other words in common usage. So many occupations are gender segregated that many groups of women probably use terminology that would not be immediately understood, or used, by other women or men. However, women's groups in general have been very little studied (see discussion in Lee Jenkins and Cheris Kramer, 1978), and the activities of women's groups are seldom considered newsworthy. So there is relatively little publicity or concern about what women talk about and what they say. They are not as likely to be involved in the activities or careers considered adventuresome, or worth much attention. From my discussions with other women I know that mothers are often the coiners and preservers (through usage) of many words particular to individual families. However, women are not as likely as men to be in positions to publicize their talk. They are perhaps less likely to be in occupations where new words are explicitly needed. (Women even in their homes use cleaning and cooking devices which have been named and marketed by men. As several students in my classes have noted, the expression "a household word" means that almost everyone knows the term.) For these reasons at least, women are not as likely to be represented in language-change histories.

However, some women *have* played an active, if largely unrecognized, role in language development. Rosa Shand Turner (1977) writes of the influence of a number of women translaters, poets, and novelists. She adds:

> My point . . . is that women have never been so unusual in nonsexual roles as the English language would have us believe. This female invisibility, which is built into the way our language has been used, dictates that every woman who plays an independent role be seen each time as a new exception. . . . Our language has given us no new words with which to include her naturally. When each individual woman must refight the same battle—that she is always the exception—males can utilize as a powerful tool in their retention of power the language's insistence that she is by her very nature an exception. (p. 249)

Women are encouraged to use established, "reputable" language, not words that are considered pungent and picturesque. The etiquette books have for more than a hundred years advised women to avoid slang expressions. Just as Peter Trudgill (1975) has written of the high value that middle-class men place on the pronunciations used by working-class men—pronunciation considered more rough, more masculine—others have written about the interest men have in creating and using slang terms because slang is "tough." Writing that much of American slang expresses amorality, cynicism, and toughness, Flexner in the preface to Harold Wentworth's and Stuart Berg Flexner's (1975) *Dictionary of American Slang* states that men use slang "just because it is not standard or polite" (p. xii). He writes that while working on the dictionary he was constantly aware that most American slang "is created and used by males" (p. xii) and refers to male endeavors. He adds that since men "tend to avoid words that sound feminine or weak" there are differences in the standard vocabularies of men and women. (As examples of "feminine" words he gives *silver, crystal, china,* and *linens,* and as "masculine" equivalents the words *knives, forks,* and *spoons, glasses, dishes,* and *tablecloth and napkins* [p. xii]. Here again the "masculine" seems to be more closely associated with sterotypical working-class vocabulary.) Many of the slang words that men create and use concern sex, women, work, money, drink, politics, and sports.

A few men have written of the ways males can and do exclude women through careful choice of words. For example, Bob Lamm (1977), relating his experiences teaching a politics-of-sports course at a university, mentions what he thinks is the primarily desired effect of much sports terminology—male bonding and thus the exclusion of females:

> The trivia of sports, like the pseudo-complexity of academic language, makes the out-group, the oppressed group, feel awed and powerless. And that's just how men want

women to feel about sports and about life. Sports trivia is only one of a million subtle and blatant ways in which men bond together to oppress women. (p. 55)

Some members of women's groups must surely use original terminology to set themselves apart as a group and exclude others. (I think few, if any, of the linguistic activities discussed in this book are unique to males or to females, only performed or experienced to different degrees.) Again, certainly not all males are equally involved in the evolution of new slang or other words or in the determination of what becomes a part of the English lexicon for a period of decades. But, if the material in the histories of American language is believed, it is primarily men's and not women's interests, activities, and perceptions that are recorded. The language is primarily determined by men and, according to many people, helps support the power of men to dominate women.

I went to Raymond Williams's (1976) *Keywords*, the history of 155 words that Williams calls significant in formulating the way we see and discuss many of our "central experiences" (p. 13). The first twelve words, which will suggest the types of "keywords" included, are: aesthetic, alienation, art, behaviour, bourgeois, bureaucracy, capitalism, career, charity, city, civilization, class.[2] According to the information on the publisher's book-jacket, Williams "describes the complex interaction between the changed meanings of words, how these changes affect people's concepts and how people's concepts are once again changed by the changes." In giving an historical account of the changing meanings of the words, Williams mentions thousands of people who were influential in forming, influencing, modifying, or redefining the meanings. I searched for a long time before finding a mention of a woman (Jane Austen—"Improve") involved in this process.

Like any other writer, Raymond Williams approaches his topic with questions and positions derived from his own experience. Perhaps he overlooked or underestimated women's influence in this words-in-progress study. And likely his list of keywords differs from the lists others of us would draw up. However, women's near-absence from what Williams presents as a continual process of language development is not noted by him, or in any of the reviews of the book that I read. Women are, currently at least, actively involved in some phases of language change, as I have illustrated in other chapters. However, if the histories of our language are to be believed, women's role in the past in coining words and in determining meanings that are considered to be shared meanings has been slight. And this has seldom been considered even a curious fact.

WOMEN'S CONSTRAINT IN LANGUAGE EXPRESSION

The second question: Is there evidence that women feel constrained in their perceptions and/or in their expression by the present English language? Perhaps while the determination of our vocabulary is largely the activity of males, these words are for the most part peripheral to the needs of women. Or perhaps words coined by men but also widely used by women eventually acquire some of their meanings from their use by women. At first exploration this does not appear to be the case.

Women and men do share many experiences. Yet much of our folklore, and many of the essays in the popular and scholarly journals and books are full of information that suggests that women and men have many different experiences. Or at least women and men are *thought* to possess many gender-linked interests and behavioral characteristics that lead them to different experiences. Women, for example, are thought to be more talkative, more religious, and more sensitive to others than are men. Men are thought to be more knowledgeable about business, more objective, independent, aggressive, active, adventurous, and more likely to think men are superior to women. By itself alone, the constant reaffirmation that we are one gender or the other means that we have somewhat different experiences. Erving Goffman (1977) discusses cultural customs that he thinks serve not so much to acknowledge the (relatively slight) biological differences but actually *to produce* a sense of them: e.g., traditional courtship patterns, courtesy systems (protecting females from spiders, rains, cold, and other dangers), separate toilet facilities, and job placement (women in housekeeping and mothering jobs). These customs call for the frequent expressions of genderism and make gender *appear* "natural" and highly significant; they are not expressions of natural differences, but they do mean that women's experiences differ somewhat from men's.

Can a language structure (the language and its specified rules for use), which appears to be built primarily by males, be used with equal facility by both women and men? (I do not use the phrase "equal effectiveness" since for the moment I want to discuss the speaker's reactions and not the listener's evaluation.)

In searching for answers to this question I have paid particular attention to the statements women are making about their secondary relationship to, and their place in, the English language, and to responses made by people who do not think the language serves males and females differentially. In this next section I summarize some of this material.

The ideas and myths contained in the language are not, many argue, of women's making; yet the language we have learned as *the* language with its inherent concepts about women makes reanalysis of the nature of women and the nature of her rights difficult. Of course, not all women feel a reanalysis is necessary. And certainly the language is not the only barrier in reclassifying things. Other, related, problems exist. For example, men have collected the data upon which we base our ideas. There are more answers to men's questions than to women's questions. Dorothy Smith (1974;1978) has discussed the "bifurcation of consciousness" experienced by women academicians who are, on the one hand, engaged in research (usually through procedures and methods determined primarily by men), and on the other occupied with the many practical activities of keeping houses clean and children clean, fed, and loved. Additionally, women frequently have not been allowed or encouraged to come together to discuss notions of reality that may differ from those accepted by men. (Participants at women's conferences often express relief and delight at receiving confirmation from others about "radical concepts of reality." Many of the speakers and participants at the Feminist Scholarship 1978 Conference at the University of

Illinois, Urbana-Champaign, used personal experience as part of their proof—and often made reference to the freedom they felt at being able to make use of such naturalistic observations while in an academic conference, a setting where usually only "objective" research is respected and rewarded.)

However, these problems are seen by many people as based in the way the world has been named. This idea is familiar to those who have discussed the relationship between a ruling class that creates prevailing beliefs, and subordinate groups that internalize these beliefs, thereby coming to doubt or deny their own experience. The working-through and then the changing of some of the categories of the language is a part of any effort to change relationships between social groups and social institutions. Robin Morgan, an activist in the New Left movement before a "feminist consciousness trickled into [her] life," writes that for years she implored the men of the New Left movement to let women take an active part. But, she writes,

> Then, at a certain point, I began to stop addressing such men as "brothers" and began (O language, thou precise Richter scale of attitudinal earthquakes!) to use the word "we" when speaking of women. And there was no turning back. (1978:5)

Only as we perceive ourselves as prevented from defining ourselves and the world, and only as we perceive the possibility of changing the situation, will we work to reshape relationships between women and men. Only then will we come to see ourselves as possible creators of reality, rather than as recipients of a given, unchangeable position in reality. Only then will we claim the right to say our own word, to name the world.

The importance of naming as a way by which "men achieve significance as men" has been discussed at length by the Brazilian educator Paulo Freire, whose work has had a major impact in education theorizing in South and North America. He writes:

> Dialogue is the encounter between men, mediated by the world, in order to name the world. Hence, dialogue cannot occur between those who want to name the world and those who do not wish this naming—between those who deny other men the right to speak their word and those whose right to speak has been denied them. Those who have been denied their primordial right to speak their word must first reclaim this right and prevent the continuation of this dehumanizing aggression. (1970:76-77)

Freire is working from a Marxist perspective and a belief that the suffering of people of the Third World can be ended only if they are provided the tools and opportunity to engage in a dialogue with others—from a belief that social vision and policies to benefit all must come from all.

Feminists working from a Marxist or socialist perspective urge a study, in particular, of the problems faced by women in different social and racial groups; while Freire does not consider the ways capitalism and sexism may lead to and reinforce each other, his writings might well become a source of theoretical leads for people who *are* interested in class oppressions, male privilege, and the naming of the world.

Already we have available an important base of operations from which to inspect the English language anew. We have assertions by many women about what they hear and cannot hear in the language, documentation of the pervasiveness of sexism in the language, and historical studies of women's relative exclusion from language composition—that is, of the androcentrism revealed from a study of our language.

At times my statements and the quoted statements of others may seem to some people to be over-generalizations. However, from the perspective of the people quoted below, the statements may be, I think, considered as *challenges* to over-generalizations, calling for the investigations of assumptions about the linguistic behavior and rights of males and females. Insights, critiques, questions, definitions, and analyses can come in many forms and from many perspectives. If a coherent analysis representing the perspectives of many people, women as well as men, is desired, we will need to listen to and consider many descriptions of reality. The critics below are stating their distrust of some mainstream academic work and of some currently widely accepted "factual" information. They are asking that we re-examine our assumptions about language. Support of such a basic reorientation as they are asking may lead to many new investigations of women's and men's relationship to their language.

In recent years many people have made statements about English as a symbol system much more representative of men's vision of the world than of women's. Jessica Murray writes:

> I will argue that the male bias of language . . . is an indication of a male outlook that pervades human culture; that the grammar is only a reflection of a phenomenon which goes so deep as to be concerned with our very definitions of Humanity; that the language we use, like everything else that reflects our culture, is based on the archetypal assumption that *human* means *male*. (1973:46)

Jeanette Silveira (1978) writes that women have felt "a strong sense of individuality and existential aloneness whereas men that I knew felt themselves to be part of a social organism or herd" (p. 15). Our language, she writes, has contributed to this by presenting men as the whole, and women as worthy of little attention.

In an article entitled "What's in a Label: The Politics of Naming," Julia P. Stanley (1974) writes that, "Through naming, men have cast the nets of their own perceptual matrices over events, so that our every movement, action, or desire is defined in their terms." Men have defined women, and almost always in relationship to themselves. Radical feminist writer Mary Daly (1973) has considered the "net of meaning" controlled in the past by men as a power as real and as important as political power. She writes, "In a sexist world, symbol systems and conceptual apparatuses have been male creations [which] do not reflect the experiences of women, but rather function to falsify our own self-image and experiences" (p. 7). Dale Spender (1977) thinks the division of power so basic and pervasive that she writes of the world as composed of two groups of people, The Namers and The Named.

Many others in the contemporary feminist movement have written of the politics and power of language in dividing the sexes and in perpetuating their asymmetrical relationship. Some of their comments are included or summarized in Wendy Martyna's (1980) essay entitled "Beyond the He/Man Approach" and in

Judith Hole's and Ellen Levine's (1971) book on the contemporary feminist movement. The people quoted speak of the political, social, and intellectual power that comes from defining one's own symbolic reality.

These statements give evidence of a perception of language very different from that of many male authors and speakers. These women quoted, and other women and men, are discussing the way they see the English lexicon as a structure organized to glorify maleness and ignore, trivialize, or derogate femaleness.

In the language of the courts and legislatures women have been labelled as mother and wife, infantile and incompetent, seductive and immoral, and as nonpersons (Haig Bosmajian, 1977). In the language of the courts as elsewhere, men and women are presented not only as opposites but also as in opposition.

Naming customs of courtship and wedding and family life give us word pairs such as man and wife, playboy and old maid, mothering and fathering, and Mr. and Mrs. (Alleen Pace Nilsen, 1977). Clearly these pairings do not have components with similar or parallel meanings.

Textbooks, the presentations made by some of the educated elders to the learning youngsters of the ideas, histories, and facts the elders hold most worthy of transmitting, are—as many have documented—repositories of male-oriented stories (see, e.g., Nilsen, 1977; Joseph W. Schneider and Sally L. Hacker, 1973; James E. Stahlecker, 1978). Textbooks present a world in which most people are male: fathers are fathers of males (four or five times as often as fathers of females in one study of textbooks), sons outnumber daughters two to one, firstborn children are male, and aunts and nieces are almost nonexistent. The fathers, sons, uncles, and nephews are presented as the people who carry on the business of the world. Even in home economics texts women are often presented as peripheral (Alma Graham, 1975).

Similarly, the language of religious and secular literature, and of the literature of literary criticism, reveals "the sexist omissions and commissions of the English language [which are] the cultural legacy of writers and poets" (H. Lee Gershuny, 1977:107). For example, in biblical literature Adam receives the God-given right to classify, by naming, at least in the English translations (see Gershuny, and Phyllis Trible, 1978, for discussions of distortions of the English translations, distortions that give Adam, God, and Jesus more male characteristics than they have in the Hebrew texts). Gershuny writes that the language and traditions of the Bible are "continued and developed in secular literature, so that the idea of poetic creation as both masculine and divine has been a consistent part of our literary heritage" (p. 111).

Dictionaries also document and perpetuate cultural sexism. Working only with standard dictionaries, a group of women have composed a booklet of, to them, obscene or offensive words that men, primarily, use to address or refer to women, primarily—words that reveal a great deal of hostility toward women. This *Feminist English Dictionary: An Intelligent Woman's Guide to Dirty Words* (1973) records some of the misogyny of our culture. One of the editors said, " . . . as we consulted dictionaries and thesauruses, we found that words describing women ultimately led to ·the description 'prostitute'." (The same phenomenon is discussed in Julia P. Stanley's paper "Paradigmatic Woman: The Prostitute" [1977b] , in which she analyzes 220 terms used almost exclusively by men to label women; there are relatively few terms for promiscuous males.) The editors of the dictionary looked at the word *whore* in one widely used dictionary and found "a woman who engages in promiscuous sexual intercourse . . ."; but when they looked at the word *rapist* they found "a person who rapes." *Grandmotherly* is defined in terms such as "kindly, indulgent; fussy, interfering"; while *grandfatherly* often gets a more respectful description such as "benignant; old and venerable" along with a quotation such as "an eminently human person of grandfatherly years—Lewis Nichols" (interview; quoted by Laura Green, 1973:3).

A valuable analysis of our naming customs has been written by Casey Miller and Kate Swift (1976), who as free-lance writers and editors constantly experience the difficulties of finding expressions of assumptions shared by both women and men. Their discussions of their difficulties led them to review the process of labelling and to review various proposed guidelines for actively changing the language. Their book, *Words and Women: New Language in New Times,* was reviewed in *Time* (9 August 1976). The reviewer, Paul Gray, writes that the problem of sexism in language "is more than a joke and less than a national crisis." The magazine editors illustrate the review with a cartoon of a woman in a pulpit saying, "She leadeth me in the path of righteousness for Her name's sake" (p.72). Possibly the editors of *Time* perceive the cartoon of a woman speaking feminist ideas from the pulpit as funny in good part because women do not "naturally" belong in the pulpit saying anything. *I* found the caption a witty, concise composite of a number of feminist claims and demands. I thought, for example, of discussions of the female imagery for God. Phyllis Trible (1978), a Hebrew language scholar, writes of the imagery (conceiving, pregnancy, delivering, mothering) which was "lost" when the Old Testament was translated into English. For me the cartoon is both a challenge to the male language of faith and a prophecy of change for women as speakers and namers.

The documentation of the sexism of the language has extended to study of nonverbal gestures. For example, Nancy Henley (1977) interprets nonverbal gender differences as power differences which support a social hierarchy. She writes, "Slang and obscenity are generally taboo to women, and their nonverbal counterparts, such as obscene gestures and what we can call gestural slang, are likewise prerogatives of male culture" (p. 147).

While discussion of the evidence of English as a structure that perpetuates the male representation of reality is currently receiving much attention (in large part ridicule) in academic and popular journals and books, the basic issues have been voiced by women for many years. For example, Elsie Clews Parsons (1913a) introduced in her book on the status of women in the early 1900s many language and gender questions, and observations; questions that have not been cited by linguists in the sixty years following the publication of her work, and that are just now being rediscovered. She wrote of the slang phrases that are introduced and used almost exclusively by males, of the way that some words have different meanings depending upon the sex of the speaker, and of the shortage of specialized words to describe activities considered to be in the female domain.

Another example: In 1914 Beatrice Forbes-Robertson Hale—seeking, she writes, to explain the views she thought were "held by a majority of feminists"—states that through the years of women's enforced silence "Man the Romancer" had spoken for women, clothing them with his words. She writes of the vaudeville houses as institutions supported by men who there laughed at the "broad" joke, along with the "great mother-in-law joke, the famous divorce joke, and the delicious humour of the hen-pecked husband" (p. 115). The laughter from primarily one group but not from the other points to the different perceptions and definitions held by women and men. Hale writes that men's use of *Woman* holds no recognition of women, young and old, rich and poor, gifted or dull—no individuals—but is, rather, a label with very restricted meaning. Men's labels determine most of the concepts with which both women and men must deal. (Hale held out great hope for the end of male domination as a result of co-education, the opportunities for women in a democracy, and the efforts of feminists.)

In a 1942 report written at the request of the editor-in-chief of the *Encyclopaedia Britannica,* a feminist historian noted the many examples of the male bias that dominated the tone and content of the work. The category system of the encyclopaedia details the important elements of the world view of males, particularly scholarly males, but ignores many elements of the female world view. For example, "Weapons, Primitive"

> . . . are reviewed as features of the male's fighting function or inclination. But primitive weapons for social construction are not even hinted at. Surely they were even more important. We suggest introducing an article on constructive implements (not calling them weapons). (Mary Ritter Beard; quoted in Ann J. Lane, 1977:223-224)

Beard adds that such an article would include recognition of women's creativity in cooking, spinning, weaving, and the like. From a reading of the "Song" review in the encyclopaedia, one would suppose that no woman sang in Europe. The contributions of nuns, as composers and singers, are ignored (Lane, p. 220). What is labelled and defined in this encyclopaedic work, which seemingly details the knowledge of the age, represents the perceptions of men, not women. (The many recommendations made by Mary Ritter Beard and the staff working with her evidently have still not been heeded by the editors of the encyclopaedia.)

Additional evidence that men have organized and continue to organize most of the English language and the rules for its use comes from several historical linguistic studies. Stanley and Susan W. Robbins (1978a) review information available about changes in pronominal forms in Middle English, concluding that men have coined labels that have identified "maleness and humanity as mutually coextensive concepts, and other labels which isolate femaleness as a socially and biologically inferior trait." The grammars of the seventeenth, eighteenth, nineteenth, and twentieth centuries give "evidence that indicates that most of the names in English are used for exclusive masculine reference." Although in the mid-nineteenth century some grammarians did include *she* and *they* along with *he* as general pronouns when a sex distinction was not required or desired, by the mid-twentieth century American grammarians were declaring the necessity of using the masculine pronoun for indefinite sex referents (Stanley, 1978). (Grammarians have been particularly adamant about counting out women and girls. Ann Bodine [1975] has described the continuing efforts of grammarians to stop the popular use of the singular *they* and *their*; everyone should think twice about the origins of their grammar rules. Stanley notes that it is not the grammar school "Miss Fidditch" who has written the rules, but male grammarians.) Continuing their investigation into the "maleness" of the English language, Stanley and Robbins (1978b) review the types of predicates that are sex-marked "male" in English, the many missing female equivalents, and the cultural values expressed by the sex-marked terms. For example, castrating and emasculating a male (either literally or figuratively) denote unmanning him, making him a eunuch. We have no corresponding terms that denote unwomaning or the resulting state. Stanley and Robbins review some of the many English predicates that describe the male role in sexual intercourse—and the relatively few corresponding female terms. They conclude that, not surprisingly, the lexicon reflects the interests and preoccupations of the creators of English.[3]

In sum, many people are saying that the English language portrays and perpetuates the male experiences of the world; the language ignores or denies the reality of many experiences women have.

To ignore these statements and the evidence these people are accumulating is to acknowledge only the old standards about who can submit what type of evidence into discussions.

The implications of these statements and evidence are both basic and vast. As Gershuny (1978) points out, linguistic sexism is grounded in a belief in male supremacy and dominance. And such a belief affects what people think, say, and do about, for example, the education and the salaries of women and men, about abortion. It affects attitudes toward all the environment, including the land. (Annette Kolodny [1975a] has written in her book *The Lay of the Land* about men's naming of the land as woman, e.g., warm and with breasts, and of man's ambivalence toward the land, at times raping and dominating, and at times establishing an intimacy with her beauty.) The stories of the past, the realities of the present, and the visions of the future are all portrayed through and mediated by the language.

These critics do not see the English language in the way many historians have, as a marvelous, vital reflection of our most exciting and praiseworthy interests and activities. They do not agree with Mario Pei (1967) that "The English we speak is not the fruit of a deliberate human design [but] the sum total of a long series of historical accidents, behind which the only design that is perceptible is God's" (pp. 3-4). The language and most histories of the language only implicitly present English as put together by men and do not deal with the implications of the exclusion of women and minority groups from this construction. Pei writes that the task of the linguist is "to describe what has happened and is happening to a language rather than to philosophize upon it"—as if what he calls "a fascinating tale" can be presented as an "objective" account (p. 4).

As the writers mentioned above and others have spoken and written about inadequacies and indecencies of the language and have made specific recommendations for changes, other writers and speakers have protested; the resulting controversy indicates the political importance of the issues.

While the discussions about the deficiencies of the English language have been published primarily in feminist books and journals, the responses to the arguments and to suggestions for change have appeared in many popular publications with wide circulation. Most of the responses have focused on feminists' suggestions for elimination of the "generic" *he* and *man.* The types of responses that have been most frequently published are summarized by Martyna (1980) and by Maija S. Blaubergs (1978a, 1978b, 1980), and are reviewed in Chapter VII.

I make some mention of the controversy here because the basic question seems the same as that raised by the muted group theory: Is there evidence that the English language constrains women in their perceptions and in their expressions?

While many of the people quoted in this and the preceding chapter have shown concern with what they see as very large, basic issues concerning language—i.e., who invents it, and whether or not it represents the interests of both females and males—most of the discussions in the popular media have focused on the "generic" pronouns and on the type (and number) of representations of females and males in school texts.[4] Some critics have argued that we do not have enough evidence of sexism in textbooks, for example, to ask or require that publishers change their editing ways and teachers revise their grammar rules.

Two of those critics, Albert Kingston and Terry Lovelace (1978), review studies of what they call "alleged sexism" in texts and children's books and conclude that the studies on sexism have been conducted, in the main, in what they call an unscientific manner. They write:

> Terminology including *sexist, sexism, bias, stereotyped,* and *degrading* must be defined in a measurable, reliable, valid and unemotional fashion. (p. 157)

They quote a 1972 *Nation's Schools* survey based on a sampling of school administrators, which found that "Sexism in textbooks may be a hot topic with ladies who like Ms. in front of their names, but not with school administrators" (quoted by Kingston and Lovelace, who acknowledge that the gender of the administrators surveyed might be a contributing factor in the finding that 84 percent did not believe sex bias exists in curriculum materials [p. 157].) They argue that "students' preference for stereotyped versus non-stereotyped selections and the impact of those same selections on the formation of self-concepts and sex role development, must be studied scientifically, without bias on the part of the investigators" (p. 158). (They do not indicate whose definitions of *scientifically* and *bias* should be used. Many women would argue that the commonly used meanings of *bias* and *science* have been determined by men and do not tally exactly with the ideas of many women about what best constitutes proof [see, for example, Jessie Bernard, 1973a, 1973b, and Rae Carlson, 1972]).

Women have recognized that it is not enough just to say that when they look at the books, they see and read very narrow, unrealistic portrayals of women or often find themselves excluded. They realize that their objections are not considered by many as reason enough for changing the portrayals or the terminology, in the descriptions of activities or in the book illustrations. The observations of the women who say that many texts either exclude women or present very narrow, unrealistic portrayals of women are considered "emotional" responses by some who do not have similar experiences when viewing the books. Kingston and Lovelace do not directly challenge the findings of many women and men that, for example, male characters talk more frequently than females, males are portrayed in more numerous, more highly paid and more prestigious occupations, males are much more likely to be portrayed in leadership activities and in rescue activities, the illustrations in elementary school textbooks show a heavy preponderance of males to females, textbooks and standardized texts show a much higher frequency of male nouns and pronouns. Kingston and Lovelace do argue, however, that the operational definitions of terms were not made clear in most of the studies that, for example, found females represented as more *docile* and *dependent* than males. They ask for a "bona fide debate concerning the degree to which [policies and guidelines recommended by feminists and adopted by several publishers] actually may hinder learning by presenting an unreal, artificial life to school children" (p. 155). And they are critical of the studies that show that males appear much more frequently than females because the reporters of those studies, Kingston and Lovelace say, fail to explore the impact, if any, of the unequal representation of sexes upon the readers of the textbooks, males and females.

Of course, many of the studies they mention were published in newspapers, underground publications, and popular journals where one is more likely to find summaries of studies than the "operational definitions." However, Kingston and Lovelace are right in asking that we learn more about the methodology and the criteria employed in the studies. Their statements about the "unreal, artificial life" are more confusing. Do they believe that the present portrayal of women and men in the textbooks is realistic? And do they believe that schools should be about the business of maintaining the present stereotypes concerning women and men? The following passage indicates that they assume that in the past writers have been free spirits, uninfluenced by societal norms or by contemporary education ideology:

> Should materials that are used in instruction be neutral and/or controversial? Should a writer try to portray life realistically or should he portray an ideal if unreal world? In literature, the "ideal" often makes for saccharine reading. Similarly, literature that is over-edited or developed by a committee rarely stands the test of time. A genuine problem in producing literature is one of freedom for the writer to create independent works. (p. 136)

Here, however, I want to deal with their third area of criticism: that studies completed thus far have failed to explore the impact of the sexism in the books upon the readers.

Theoretical discussions of the ways in which sex differentiation in society is both reflected in and maintained by the language patterns are available in Elizabeth Lane Beardsley (1976, 1977), Patrick Grim (1977), Janice Moulton (1977), Carolyn Korsmeyer (1977), Virginia Valian (1977), Barbara Bate (1975), Maija S. Blaubergs (1975), and Jeanette Silveira (1978, 1980).

The work of researchers who have built upon such discussions is reviewed by Norma J. Shepelak (1977). College students asked to choose pictures to match titles such as "social man" and "urban man" were more likely to choose pictures of men alone (Schneider and Hacker, 1973). A similar study with grade school children resulted in similar findings (Linda Harrison and Richard N. Passero, 1975). Junior high students drew more male-only figures when illustrating historical accounts using the masculine "generic" than they did when responding to accounts using non-gender or feminine and masculine (i.e., *he or she*) gender cues (Linda Harrison, 1975).

Job descriptions that included a "generic" *he* or *man* were perceived by elementary, high school, and college students as classified for men only (Norma Shepelak, D. Ogden, and D. Tobin-Bennett, 1976). Sandra L. Bem and Daryl J. Bem (1973) experimenting with job advertisements found that gender cues could influence the job preferences of high school students. Spencer K. Thompson (1975) found that 78 percent of the three-year-olds in his study preferred same-sex labelled pictures as opposed to opposite-sex labelled pictures. Studies by Raymond Montemayor (1974) and by Leslie Zebrowitz McArthur and Susan V. Eisen (1976) found that children's performance in a game and on an assigned task was influenced by the gender label. Summarizing her review of studies that deal with the impact of the "generic" pronouns on the perceptions and actions of the students tested, Shepelak (1977:14) writes:

> The literature has shown that (1) gender cues serve as semantic markers which identify the sex of the person referenced in the linguistic structure and (2) those semantic markers function pragmatically by determining sex role classifications, possibilities, and preferences.

Donald G. MacKay has conducted a series of studies on the comprehension of the "generic" *he*. In a 1979 study he found that students reading textbook paragraphs containing the "generic" *he* made forty percent more pronoun comprehension errors (reading *he* to mean only males) than students reading paragraphs which are identical except that the *he* was replaced with *E, e,* or *tey*. On the basis of his research MacKay argues that prescriptive grammarians who advocate use of *he* to refer to both men and women have lacked "the proper data, techniques and theories with which to make sound prescriptions."

Wendy Martyna (1978a, 1978b) has also conducted a series of studies designed to determine people's use and understanding of "generic" terms, studies that indicate the connection of language structure and use. In one study she asked students to complete sentence fragments and found that women used alternatives to the " generic" *he* significantly more than men did when completing sentence fragments such as "When a person loses money. . . . " Women were less likely than men to use *he* in completing such fragments and more likely to use *they* and *he or she.* Only a few of the women were feminists. (And the students were unaware that their pronoun usage was being studied; they had been told that the researcher was interested in comparing written and spoken responses to various types of sentence fragments.) They evidently were not consciously making an effort to avoid "generic" terms. Evidently many just did not consider *he* as inclusive a word as the men did. Another Martyna study concerned the imagery the college students reported in response to the sentence fragments. For fragments with a male-related subject (such as "Before a judge can give a final ruling . . .") both women and men reported having male imagery. For fragments with a female-related subject (such as "After a nurse has completed training . . .") both reported receiving female imagery. For "neutral" subject fragments (such as "When a person . . .") sixty percent of the men reported specific images (almost all male-related images). However, only ten percent of the women reported receiving images (of specific males). That is, in her study many of the women who did use *he* in completing a sentence fragment did so without receiving a particular image. Her study offers specific support for the muted group theory. The women's production and interpretation of masculine "generics" are not linked in the same way the men's production and interpretation are. In another study children and adults were asked to read sentences containing "generics" (e.g., "A working person pays his own way") and then choose from a picture chart to indicate "Who the sentence is talking about." The researchers, Johanna DeStefano, Mary W. Kuhner, and Harold B. Pepinsky (1978), found that males tended to choose male referents, and females tended to choose gender-indefinite or inclusive referents. The "generic" terms appear to work differently for men and women.

SUMMARY

The muted group framework encourages an exploration of the possibility that the English language does not serve women in the same way that, or as well as, it serves men. My search for women's involvement in the development of the lexicon and grammar rules indicates that the contemporary historians of our language have not perceived women as actively involved in the continuing construction of our language and, further, for the most part the historians have not noticed the women's absence as anything remarkable or worth commenting on.

As reviewed above, many women have expressed dissatisfaction with their place in the language and with the perspectives and categories given them by the language. They have written and spoken of the handicaps imposed upon them as they try to express their dissatisfaction with the language through that language.

As I outline here and in other chapters, many women are presently involved in language controversy and change. Their activities are receiving a lot of attention, partly, I argue, because women's attempts to name themselves and to alter the language in other ways is in itself a revolutionary activity. The new terminology some women are suggesting and are using comes from a reassessment of their experiences as women. The new words and/or new uses for words provide not merely additions to the language but major alterations of the perspectives contained in the language.

Walter J. Ong (1977) has written of another time when women's entry into what had been men's activity alone brought about a change. He writes that Latin was a language learned by males from other males: "Not only were all of the teachers of Learned Latin males for well over a millennium, but all its learners were males as well, with exceptions so few as to be negligible" (pp. 25-26). This language was used for abstract, academic, philosophical, scientific, forensic, legal, administrative, and liturgical matters (p. 25) and "operated at a kind of formalized distance from the human lifeworld" (p. 35). As women came into academia in the nineteenth century the teaching and the use of Latin declined. He writes, "Many of the structures built into Learned Latin in academia derived historically from the way academia had been shaped around the needs of the male psyche. These structures set up to accommodate the male psyche were not congenial to women" (correspondence 1979). As women moved into the academic world Latin moved out.[5]

However, the influence of the Latin did not disappear. Ong writes that his "sex-linked, public, male language" encoded a very particular perspective into our lives, an influence which continues. Ong believes that

> An affinity seems to exist between early modern science, in its need to hold at arm's length the human lifeworld with its passionate, rhetorical, practical concerns, and Learned Latin as a tongue which had been isolated from infant development and thus from the physiological and psychosomatic roots of consciousness and which had been given instead an artificial base in writing. (p. 35)

> Modern science and much of modern technology ... developed out of an intellectual world which shaped its concepts and vocabulary and its cognitive style on Learned Latin, that is, out of the intellectual world of the medieval universities in the West and their continuators. (p. 35)

Ong, in writing of the manner in which Learned Latin contributed to the evolution of what we think of as intellectual thought and discussion, provides us with an illustration of the importance of the language structure in signifying relationships and in guiding and legitimating beliefs and actions. His discussion, along with the others cited in this chapter, also suggests the value of the muted group theory as a framework for investigating the restrictions of a male-oriented language upon those whose perspectives of the world is somewhat different.

However, that framework separates women's world views and their social roles, placing much more emphasis on the former than on the latter. The muted group theory neglects the complexities of gender, class, and race dominance. The theory does not provide us with clear possible explanations of *how* a dominant male language is established and maintained—although use of the theory for studying language gives us important indications of the importance of language in the maintenance of asymmetrical social relations. The theory is probably not, in isolation, a completely satisfying framework for many of us. However, the questions that the framework suggests offer some tantalizing possibilities for people interested in gender and language.

NOTES

1. Schulz describes the recurring debasement of terms used to designate women. Neutral terms used to name women gradually acquire negative implications and often finally carry obscene or debased connotations. (*Nymph, broad,* and *floozie* are a few examples of the words she traces through the years of their use. All once had either neutral or positive connotations.) The derogation of terms denoting men is much less frequent.

2. While Williams's list includes such words as *family, personality,* and *sensibility,* Barrie Thorne (correspondence) notes that most of the "key words" are *public* terms.

3. A university student reported to me a conversation with her health class instructor. The student asked for the specific terms for vaginal secretions during sexual arousal. The only answer the instructor had was "sweat."

4. Betty Lou Dubois and Isabel Crouch (1978) point out that "the great 'he/she' battle has become a shibboleth threatening to overshadow other issues" (p. 8). (They argue that in some instances *he* and *man* do serve as inclusive terms.) Sexism in language includes *all* the androcentric language uses and attitudes that are being detailed by feminists.

Robin Lakoff (1973, 1975) believes that a focus on the "generic" *he* and *man* is misplaced, that attempts to change pronoun usage are perhaps futile. However, the increased attention that "generics" have received during the past few years has already caused some changes. Politicians and teachers are now less likely to use the "generic" *he* when they are talking about activities involving both women and men—at least in the presence of women.

5. Ong does not propose a simple cause-effect relationship here. He writes:

> Other causes were also of course at work in the coming of women into academia and in the demise of the centuries-old Latin-based instruction (whereby all school subjects were taught *in* Latin), but most other causes were intertwined with the special agonistic needs of the male psyche. (correspondence, 1979)

III

JOKING MATTERS

If females perceive relationships between persons, places, and things in a somewhat different way than do males, as the muted group theory posits, I would expect to find gender differences in what is considered humorous. Certainly women and men share some joking interests. However, in our culture it has been unnecessary for males to consider closely females' world views as alternatives, although females have had to work with the social symbols of the dominant group. Concomitantly, it is more likely that females would recognize the joking interests of males than vice versa.

One consequence of this situation is that women are often put in the situation of having to choose between laughing at jokes that they do not think are funny (e.g., jokes in which women are presented as innately insane or stupid) or risking becoming an outsider in many female/male social groups. Laughter and despair are not always opposed impulses.

The question here: Are the models of the world that are used as the base for appraisal of joking the same for both women and men; or, as suggested by the muted group theory, do women understand the model used by men but do not find it an adequate description of reality?

Most analyses of humor have considered the content of jokes, the form of jokes, and the type and amount of response to jokes. Seldom do we hear discussion of the interactional nature of humor, discussion of conversational humor, discussion of the uses that are made of humor, and discussion of the privileged joking disrespect that dominant groups in Western countries take toward subordinate groups.

We do know that humor is largely culture-specific. We do know that much joking is based on ingroup/outgroup relationships: for example, Polish jokes, Jewish jokes, lady drivers jokes. (Those phrases mean that the jokes are *on* not *by* those groups).

However, not many Americans find it acceptable to tell a joke carrying negative presuppositions about the characteristics of a subordinate social group to members of that group. For example, no longer is it considered clever to tell racist jokes to blacks. In one recent study at a large southwestern university in America, researchers found that students were not keen to tell derogatory jokes about blacks to anyone. Yet the same students, male and female, showed a much greater willingness to tell sexist jokes about women to women (Nancy Wrather and Mary Sanches, 1978).

In terms of the muted group theory we might hypothesize that, since women's models of the world incorporate men's and are partly shaped by men, women are sensitive to the words and interests, including the jokes, of the dominant social group. The people who are in power have "legitimate" views of the world, including knowledge of what is incongruous or ridiculous. Women have not been as free to ignore the men's debates, the discussions, or the ridicule as men have been free to ignore those of women. Yet men have thought it strange when women do not always laugh as heartily at men's jokes as men do. Members of all subordinate social groups are muted to some degree. However, women as a class appear to be muted in a way other social groups that include men are not.

Men often complain that women do not understand men's jokes. Often they phrase it differently: Women have no sense of humor. This male assumption—that if women do not think men's jokes are funny, then women have no sense of humor—can be explained by the muted group theory. Men overlook the concerns of women because they are somewhat different from men's. The following [male voice] line from a feminist satire illustrates the asymmetrical relationship of the males' and females' models of the world: "We believe in the good old [pre-women's liberation] days, when men were men, and women were confused, and we all knew where we were" (Eileen Fairweather and Melissa Murray; quoted in *Spare Rib,* June 1977:26).

Below I look at some of the statements and explanations that have been made about gender differences in humor. I deal with this material at some length because male beliefs about gender differences in humor, or at least their *statements* about women's lack of a sense of humor, appear to be one of the firmest, more constant of the "accusations" made by men about women's speech behavior. Moreover, finding male/female differences in humor would indicate differences in world models of women and men.

WOMEN'S SENSE OF HUMOR

"Women often do and say funny, outrageous, and silly things, but they are very seldom intentionally and successfully witty; they are humorous but not humorists." This could be one possible conclusion of a study of the humor of and about women, especially one based on collections of after-dinner jokes and other handbooks of humor. Women as members of a gender category are the subject, or target, of many jokes, but women themselves do not have a ready sense of humor, according to these sources.

The editors of most joke books address their remarks to men. One editor (Evan Esar, 1949), who lists the authors of the jokes he publishes, distinguishes his compilation from others by explicitly stating that *his* collection includes many examples of the humor of "funny females." Some of these examples are even puns—not withstanding Oliver Wendell Holmes's declaration that there is no such thing as a female punster (cited in Maturin M. Ballou, 1971:311).

Most joke books do include many jokes *about* women as a peculiar class of people. Elizabeth Janeway (1975) counted 105 witticisms about women and only six about the funny qualities of men in one recently published book of humorous quotations (p. 151). Helen Rowland, one of the few female humorists whose quotations are included in many of the collections (although she is called a "lightweight" by one editor [Esar, p. 11]), writes that woman is "the peg on which the wit hangs his jest, the preacher his text, the cynic his grouch, and the sinner his justification" (in Herbert V. Prochnow and Herbert V. Prochnow, Jr., 1962).

Suggesting that women have no sense of humor or an inferior sense of humor is a serious charge in our society. Sinclair Lewis (quoted in Jacob Braude, 1958:11) wrote that accusing someone of a lack of a sense of humor is an insult "which no human will endure." (I wonder whom he is including in the *human* category or what he means by "endure," but I appreciate his sense of the importance of such an accusation.) As early as 1937 Louise Omwake pointed out that *women* think they have a sense of humor. She asked approximately six hundred students, female and male, from five colleges and one high school to give self-ratings (as compared to what they thought was the average of their classes) on "possession of a sense of humor." Only 1.4 percent of the students rated themselves below average, while 25 percent rated themselves as high in possession of sense of humor. (Omwake does not, unfortunately, give the percentages for each sex nor the number of males or females participating in the study. However, since 98 percent of the total rated themselves as average or above, and since the study was done at three coed universities and two women's colleges as well as at a high school, I assume that women are well represented in the totals.)

What evidence have men presented to support their claims that women have little or no sense of humor? What types of sex differences in humor have been claimed or reported? What *is* sense of humor? The difficulties in trying to answer these questions come from: 1) the confusion resulting from the lumping of many activities and responses under the one label of "humor"; 2) the scarcity of research or serious comment on humor; 3) the still greater scarcity of work that considers the humor of both males and females; 4) the customary focus on measuring people's ratings of ready-made jests rather than studying both an individual's appreciation of the humor of others and the individual's spontaneous production of humor; and 5) the paucity of studies completed in natural settings for males and females.

The general term "humor" is used to discuss many types of verbal and visual activities. Terms often used interchangeably with "humor" or "humorous" include: funny, witty, comical, satire, sarcasm, quick repartee, irony, waggish, droll, roguery, and amusing. While a number of theorists (e.g., Morton Gurewitch, 1975; Alvin B. Kernan, 1965) as well as many lexicographers have taken care to make distinctions among the various terms, many studies or discussions seem to be based on the assumption that any statement, joke, or cartoon that evokes laughter from many or most who come into contact with it can be used as stimulus for a study on "humor." This lack of discrimination, particularly as it involves sarcasm, satire, irony, wit, and humor, is not a new phenomenon. H. W. Fowler in the 1926 *A Dictionary of Modern English Usage* (excerpt included in John J. Enck, Elizabeth T. Forter, and Alvin Whitley, 1960) wrote of the "constant confusion" in the use of those words. What is of concern here is that what one researcher or theorist labels "humor" might involve sharp, unkind verbal attacks on others while what another labels "humor" might involve impersonal statements. Consider the words that can be used to describe aggressive teasing behavior: kid, poke fun, wisecrack, play a joke, satirize, caricature, make fun of, parody, ridicule, laugh at, twit, gibe, heckle, taunt, and mock (Jacob Levine, 1969:12). We will have a difficult time determining if males and females differ in their sense of humor until we take a closer look at how humor is defined by various authors. (Sometimes labels differ depending upon whether the activity examined is displayed by males or by females. Several writers have suggested that what is called wit in men is called cattiness in women [Anne Beatts, 1975:184; Mary Cantwell and Amy Gross, 1975:210]. Using different labels for the same activity may be one way the dominant group maintains the opposition between men and women.) Most reports of laboratory studies on humor give little information about the rationale used for the selection of the "humorous" material involved in the study, but since most cartoons and jokes in print are drawn and written by men, most of the material used in these studies has likely been composed for primarily male consumption (Antony H. Chapman and Nicholas J. Gadfield, 1976).

One reason there has been little concern with making firm boundaries between the various terms is that until recently psychologists and sociologists have not treated humor as a particularly worthy topic of investigation. While emotional states such as anger and fear have received much "academic" attention, such topics as love, friendly fun, play, and laughter have been neglected. Even now in the study of humor, hostile jokes receive more attention than other types of humor.

While humor of any sort has seldom been considered a topic worthy of more than passing attention, possible gender differences in humor have been looked at even less frequently. (The work of Freud, of course, offers an enduring exception.) Harry Levin (1972), who writes that "one of the sexes has been charged by the other with a lack of humor," suggests that the allegation "goes back to the days when it would have been considered unladylike to appreciate Rabelais" (p. 4). Alice Sheppard (1976) writes of a factor that she feels contributes to the long-standing accusation:

> It may not be unrepresentative that in one recent collection of thirteen research studies, nine humor studies were based solely on male subjects, one used only females, and two included both sexes. [She is referring to the collection edited by Levine, 1969.] This is consistent with the tendency of classical humor theorists to ignore the question of women's sense of humor or to doubt its existence at all.

Most studies of humor that have been concerned with possible sex differences have used questionnaires to measure the preferences for given jests. Yet Walter E.

O'Connell (1969) (working with groups of male patients, with "reasonably good contact with reality"—at a VA hospital) found no significant correlation between a man's appreciation of jests and his ability to produce them, as evaluated by others in his group. A number of investigators have, through the use of questionnaires on humor and the use of personality tests, studied relationships between appreciation of specific thematic content of humorous stimulus and personality traits such as aggressiveness, dominance, and introversion-extroversion (e.g., Levine, 1969:15). Again, the subject matter of the humorous stimulus may not be as salient here as the form; that is, whether or not the stimulus is in the form of a joke, a cartoon, and whether or not it is presented as an attack, say upon a specific person or group of people or as a jest about oneself. And, as Levine (1969) points out, critical judgments about humorous stimuli, as recorded on rating scales or through explanations of the funniness of the stimuli, are not identical with humor responses.

Furthermore, we have available very few studies of laughter and joking in natural settings, especially very few studies of girls' and women's humor. However, the studies whose reports are available are intriguing. Women staff members at a mental hospital who did make jokes and witty remarks in informal situations "hardly ever used their wit" at the formal staff meetings. While men made 99 out of the 103 witticisms observed at the meetings, the women provided much of the laughter response for the male witticisms (Rose Laub Coser, 1960).[1]

On the basis of her fieldwork in a rural parish in England, Ann Whitehead (1976) writes that "the content of cross-gender joking [in the pub] argues a consciousness of gender difference between the participants and a consciousness of sexuality" (p. 181). She found that the type of joking exchanges differs depending upon gender, sexual "availability," and age.

Although several researchers have observed and recorded the playground and street-corner joking and verbal play of boys, particularly black boys, they have seldom acknowledged the playground and indoor joking of groups of girls. Peter Woods (1976), in a study of laughter in a British school, writes that girls are more likely to "make capital out of their evening social engagements" (p. 179); he does not elaborate on that. Basing his reporting on his observations of children in two naturalistic settings, a nursery school and a summer day camp, Paul E. McGhee (1976) writes that at the nursery school level, no gender differences were found in amounts of laughter, in attempts to initiate humor, or in the hostility of the children's humor.

> The findings for the Day Camp subjects, on the other hand, show that by the middle childhood years (6-11) boys rated higher on all aspects of humor responsiveness studied. Boys showed more frequent laughter than girls, tried more often to make others laugh by clowning around or acting silly and by saying "funny" things, and showed more hostility in their laughter and humor. (p. 180)

With the increased interest in behavioral gender differences, actual and imagined, and the changing focus of gender difference studies, researchers are now changing their ways of looking for possible gender differences in humor. In the future, women will likely be involved to a greater degree in such studies, both as project originators and as the observed. The findings of a few recent studies indicate that some of the popular generalizations made about women and humor will need reconsideration, and they remind us that it would be useful if researchers involved in the study of female/male interactions consider those interactions as the surface reflections of differing world views.

No sex differences were found in the study of "mirth response" of grade school children in a study involving cartoons of different degrees of comprehension difficulty (Edward Zigler, Jacob Levine, and Laurence Gould, 1969). Adult females and males tend to rate comedy routines done by members of their own sex higher than those done by the opposite sex (Sheppard, 1976). Sven Svebak (1975) in studies conducted in Norway found that males include a "sarcastic" social style as a positive part of their social self-image, while females include a "funny" social style as positive.

People have offered a variety of theoretical positions to explain women's and men's seemingly somewhat different ideas about what is humorous. The theoretical work has been done almost entirely by men (see, e.g., the bibliography by Jeffrey H. Goldstein, 1976). Until very recently most of the essays on humor have been psychoanalytical in approach, based on Sigmund Freud's writings (Goldstein, 1976:104). Freud thought that women's incapacity to tolerate or enjoy undisguised sexuality or obscenity is the basis of men's sexual jokes. Men find their libidinal impulse inhibited by women; the sexual joke makes possible the expression of an instinct (whether lustful or hostile) in the face of this obstacle.

Assuming biological differences, Gilbert Highet (1962) writes that women are, innately, too kind to produce or enjoy satire (p. 235). Martin Grotjahn (1957) writes that it is women's "strangely realistic orientation" that makes the difference between the genders' outlooks on life (p. 58). Although he holds that women have as much "natural intelligence, hostility, and tendency to enjoy wit" as males (p. 52), he writes that females prefer the sentimental to the funny (p. 97).

Several researchers who hold that women and men differ in their perception of what is funny believe that the differences in perception are a result of cultural training. Writing about the self-rated "funny" social style of females and the "sarcastic" social style of males, Svebak (1975) states that "social learning seems to be a far more active contributor to the development of these sex differences than are biological factors" (p. 81). In a reflective analysis of her own childhood, Beatts (1975) writes that by definition all boys in her high school had a sense of humor while girls were thought to have a sense of humor if they laughed when they were the object of the joke. The socially accepted girls did not have an active sense of humor, that is, they did not crack jokes. She writes that the belief that women have no sense of humor has important consequences: "For many men, it is a rule to live by" (p. 182). Men fear women who try to be funny, she believes. Because, Beatts writes, "humor is aggression," because women are not rewarded socially for being funny (but rather for being nice to men), and because many women have had to live a life dealing with what she terms trivialities, there is likely to be a difference in women's and men's senses of humor: women's humor is subtler than men's—it is rooted in everyday events (p. 184). Beatts believes that girls learn, along with other rules pertaining to dating, how to laugh at the jokes of males but to stifle any clever remarks of their own. The rules are not presented to girls explicitly as a list of rules for proper female behavior, rather the rules governing female polite expression of the funny gradually become accepted and for the most part are unquestioned. (Explicit help was given to "ladies" in *The Behavior Book of 1853* by Eliza Leslie: "[In general] when you see a person slip down on the ice, do not laugh at them. . . . It is more feminine on witnessing such a sight, to utter an involuntary scream" (a selection in Helen Hoke, 1957:108).

Another reason given for assumed differences in male and female comic sensibility is that women, if they want to be taken seriously, have to be on the defensive, have to prove they are intelligent—and their defensive behavior makes them appear more humorless (Erica Jong, 1975:24). The more powerful can be more relaxed. (See Nancy Henley [1977] for discussion of this idea.)

Several writers have written of humor as a product that results from and maintains group solidarity. One theorist states:

> Laughter (as the overt expression of humor) produces, simultaneously, a strong fellow feeling among participants and joint aggressiveness against outsiders. Heartily laughing together at the same thing forms an immediate bond, much as enthusiasm for the same ideal does. Finding the same thing funny is not only a prerequisite to a real friendship, but very often the first step to its formation. Laughter forms a bond and simultaneously draws a line. If you cannot laugh with the others, you feel an outsider. (K. Lorenz; quoted in Jacob Levine, 1969:12)

A number of males have argued that males are more prone to joking than are females because males have a greater innate "need" to bond (e.g., Lionel Tiger, 1970). Gary Alan Fine (1976), whose study concerns obscene joking across cultures, offers an amendment to this approach. He writes that joking helps maintain male groups by providing cohesion for group members. And since men belong to and control more groups than do women, they are more likely to joke. The circularity in this argument is disturbing; but more disturbing is his conclusion to the article. He writes that "obscene joking serves to socialize members into the norms of the group, and once they have been socialized, to maintain these norms." Through joking, he writes, boys learn "the appropriate attitudes" toward sexuality. This is accomplished "without the negative side-effects of a direct hostile confrontation" (p. 139). His statements might be considered as an example of a male model of the world that fails to take into account the experiences and perceptions of women.

Julia P. Stanley and Susan W. Robbins (1976) suggested that lesbians had not developed an in-group vocabulary or humor because they did not have an awareness of themselves as a community with shared values and experiences. Possibly their argument could be extended. *Women,* who are a muted group, have not developed as much a sense of group humor as men since the language and the models of joking available to them do not reflect their world models.

I mention these approaches because they illustrate in their diversity that there has not been one common interpretation for perceived gender differences in humor production and appreciation. As the relationship between men and women changes and as our perceptions of the relationship change, our theories of humor have changed and will change. What the muted group theory has to offer at the present is an approach that has been developed in part by women and that, in offering a perspective that explicitly includes recognition of the male/female social opposition, challenges many of the assumptions that have dominated women's lives.

As stated more fully in the first chapter, women can be perceived as a "muted group," a subordinate group which, although it has generated its own models of the world, must recognize and deal with the world view (and the resulting conventions) of the dominant group. Women may laugh heartily at the jokes of men, not primarily because they think the jokes funny but because they must openly subscribe to the values of the dominant group in order to effectively cope with males. That is, both female perception of what is funny and the modes of expression for female perception may be inadequately recognized in the dominant model.

HUMOR AND GENDER, A STUDY

One useful way to interpret the results of studies mentioned above is through discussion of the "imperfect fit" between the women's models of the world and the values and codes of behavior of the dominant group, and by discussion of men's readiness to maintain distinct male and female categories. I think that the theory will best be tested by naturalistic studies of humor—studies that do not assume that female sense of humor must be seen as similar to or deviating from male humor but that begin with researchers' willingness to try to take the perspective of the individuals and groups involved and to examine the relationship of the humor of males and of females to their experiences and to the culture's male/female dichotomy.

Although what I offer below is not a report of a naturalistic study, it is an initial test of the relationship of gender to not only the enjoyment but also the production of one form of humor. I designed the study to test the hypothesis that women would show more appreciation of cartoon captions produced by women than they would of those produced by men, and men will show more appreciation of cartoon captions produced by men; and that women would rate the captions written by men as funnier than men would rate the captions written by women. I include information on it here because the study results and the flaws I now see in the methodology I used illustrate both the value of using the muted group theory as well as some of the difficulties that arise from employing traditional empirical study methods to test for muted world models.

The study was conducted with the cooperation of 205 students (111 women and 94 men) at two midwestern universities. For the first stage of the study twenty-five men and twenty-five women were asked to write individual captions for six cartoons. The cartoons, drawn by colleague and artist Stafford Thomas, pictured the following: 1) female nurse speaking to a male bed patient; 2) two males, each carrying a briefcase; one male is talking to the other, who is gripping the first by the arm; 3) woman seated in a livingroom talking to another seated woman while a group of men, walking down the sidewalk, can be seen through a picture window; 4) a man standing in a livingroom holding a drink talking to a woman, seated, also holding a drink; 5) woman driver talking to a woman police officer; 6) man talking to a man while they walk by a group of women who are holding placards (lettering is indecipherable) while marching in a circle outside a building.

For each cartoon the twenty-five captions written by female students were typed, and the cartoons and corresponding captions were given to a group of fifteen women who were asked to individually rate the captions on a five-point scale with polar ends of Not Funny and Very Funny. The students were told nothing about the gender of the caption writers. Similarly, the captions written by the male students were evaluated by a group of fifteen male students.

The mean rating was determined for each of the captions written and rated by males, and for each of the captions written and rated by females. The mean ratings given by women for female-written captions for the six cartoons and the mean ratings given by men for male-written captions were compared—the differences were not significant. (That is, women and men did not differ in their overall ratings of the funniness of captions written by members of their same sex.)

The five highest rated male-written captions for each cartoon and the five highest rated female-written captions for each cartoon were chosen for inclusion in the final questionnaire. The chosen male and female-written captions were typed in alternative order and put on five-point scales with polar ends of Not Funny and Very Funny. Approximately half of the questionnaires were administered by a woman and half by a man. One group (thirty men and forty-six women) was given the captions and cartoons; they were told nothing about the gender of the caption writers. Another group (twelve men and ten women) was told the caption writers were female. A third group (twelve men and fifteen women) was told the caption writers were male. All participants were asked to give self-ratings on a "sense of humor" scale. After they rated the captions, all participants were asked to write in free response their answers to the question of whether there were differences in the sense of humor of females and males. After they had finished rating and writing I talked with them about what I thought I was doing with the exercise and they offered questions, comments, and suggestions, some of which I include in the discussion below of the study results.

In general, males when they were in ignorance of the gender of the caption writers thought that male-written captions were funnier than did the females, while males and females did not differ in their overall ratings of the female-written captions. Self-perceived sense of humor was almost identical for males and females. Since the ratings for individual male-written captions (five captions for each cartoon) and for individual female-written captions (five captions for each cartoon) were summed, it is difficult to determine what specific captions accounted for the higher male ratings for male-written captions. However, some indication of the probable process at work can be given. A check of the ratings by women and by men for a male-written caption for cartoon no. 5 (which shows a woman driver talking to a policewoman ["Hey, sweetie! When was the last time you had a big bust?"]) reveals that the mean score for men was 3.5 while the mean score for women was 2.46. Cartoon no. 6 showed a man speaking to another man about four women marching with placards. Most of the students who wrote captions for this cartoon in the initial stage of this study treated it as a Women's Liberation cartoon. In their response to the open-ended question concerning whether men and women have a different sense of humor, a number of women made reference to this cartoon, writing that women are not as likely to laugh about Women's Liberation cartoons. Several women wrote that women are more likely to be suspicious, cautious about cartoons and jokes since so many are directed at women. Quite possibly women who wrote the captions for this cartoon and perhaps the other cartoons were writing captions according to the perceived usual content and form for such cartoons. (Most professional cartoon caption writing is, of course, done by men.)

Of the 114 students who responded to the question of whether women and men have different senses of humor, 104 thought there was at least some difference. Both men and women respondents referred often to women's dislike of crude or sexual jokes, and to differences fostered by social conventions. One man wrote: "Insofar as they have different areas of interest or commitment—whether individual, social, or biological—men and women will differ in what they *can* laugh at." Several men wrote that males are more aggressive in their joking. Said one, "Women tend to have sympthy, love, and affection toward the outside world. However, men are more aggressive and tend to lack the affection that women have. Men in nature have to be tough and able to face any difficult situation."

Several women wrote that women enjoy situational humor more than jokes on people. One woman wrote: "It seems that males get into more of a cut down type of humor whereas women get more into situation humor." Another wrote: "Oftentimes men's humor is more people-oriented (i.e., someone tripping, etc.) whereas a woman's is situated-oriented—funny things that occurred during the course of the day"; while another woman wrote, "Females tend to think of funny things they have experienced or seen in everyday life." Several women wrote responses similar to this one: "Men think it is much funnier cutting down the females, etc. whereas women find humor in different things."

Unexpectedly, given the popular beliefs about the difference between women's and men's sense of humor, the varying information given the participants about the sex of the caption writers did not produce significant differences in caption ratings. (The cell sizes were small for two of the conditions. A further study with the cooperation of larger numbers of participants might be useful, especially if other suggestions, below, could be incorporated into the study plans.)

Working with the muted group theory, I had predicted that women would rate the captions written by women as funnier than would the men, that men would rate the captions written by men as funnier than would the women, but that women would rate the captions written by men as funnier than men would rate the captions written by women. Men not told the gender of the caption writers did rate male-written captions higher than did the women. But there were not significant differences in the men's and women's overall ratings of female-written captions.

Possible explanations for the study results, observations in harmony with the muted group theory, include the following: First, four of the cartoons (no. 1, no. 2, no. 4, no. 5) showed apparent confrontations between the characters portrayed; one of the characters in each of those cartoons appeared rather angry with the second character. Cartoons that encourage responses to situations involving other than hostile interpersonal relationships would help provide a test for the belief mentioned by a number of the participants that women are more ready than men to see humor in situations that do not involve conflict among people. Second, the cartoon seen by most as a Women's Liberation cartoon (no. 6), required, as several of the women and men who participated in this study pointed out, women to rate captions that were perceived as anti-women and not merely anti-woman. In the initial stage of the study women were also required, if they were to participate completely in the study, to write captions to that cartoon. Third, the participants who were asked to write captions were not given a choice of cartoons with which to work. Letting women and men choose, from a number of cartoons, those for which they want to write captions might provide information about the pictorial representations that are viewed by women and by men as possible sources of humor. Finally, the mode of expression was determined by me rather than by the women and men. While none of the participants in the study had ever tried writing cartoon captions before, and while both women and men have received exposure to cartoons in newspapers and magazines, most professional cartooning has been done by men, and many cartoons portray women as silly, peculiar people. Quite possibly, women did not feel as comfortable working with cartoons as did men—perhaps cartoons are considered part of the male code. Women did rate the female-written captions as high as they rated the male-written captions, but perhaps women did not rate the same-sex captions higher because they reflect not female models of the world but male-determined concepts of what a cartoon should be.

The study results do illustrate, I think, both the importance and the difficulty of trying to make *explicit* a subordinate or a muted world view.

WORK FOR THE FUTURE

Much of past inspection of laughter and humor has focused on fairly ritualized insults. More attention to playfulness of people in daily dealings with each other will get us closer to seeing what world views women and men work from. We know quite a lot about what men think worthy of inclusion in joke books. However, Deanne Stillman and Anne Beatts (1976), the editors of *Titters: The First Collection of Humor by Women,* write that

> ... after years of telling our favorite jokes, witticisms, funny ideas, satirical remarks, and boss slashes to men, and having them respond, "I just don't think that's funny"—notice, no corollary statement about lacking a sense of humor here—we begin to get suspicious. How many people have to think something's funny before it's funny, we asked ourselves. (p. 3)

Stillman and Beatts continue by pointing out that since women's culture has been subordinate to men's, women "know far more about what the guys really talk about in the locker room than they know about what any four women . . . say to each other when there are no men around" (p. 4).

The past focus on men's humor and on men's speech in general is part of the customary research focus on men. As Edwin Ardener points out, no researcher could come back from a study of any culture having talked only to women and about men and be considered an authority on that group. Yet the reverse happens frequently. Models of the world that women can provide are not considered as acceptable or as "true." Yet ironically, it is likely that women are more aware than men of the world models of both groups. We will all know much more about people once women are included in any discussions of humanity.

NOTE

1. Certainly women know that they share storytelling and laughter in many group discussions. Barbara Westbook Eakins and R. Gene Eakins (1978) in informal observations have found that men appear to have no trouble with the role of humorist in either predominantly male or predominantly female groups, but women do not easily recount anecdotes in predominantly male groups (pp. 75-76).

IV

LANGUAGE
AND PRESCRIBED PLACE

What I am calling the reconstructed psychoanalysis approach is a variant of a long line of discussions based on the writings of Freud, the French structuralists, and the lectures of the Swiss linguist Ferdinand de Saussure. The theory introduced in this chapter is a psychoanalytic theory—but a psychoanalytic theory with a difference.

The difference comes (1) from the challenge several feminist theorists make to the psychoanalytic conception of women as "lack of"—that is, as a mere complement to men, and (2) from a stress on men's and women's different relationship to language.

In this chapter I discuss the work of Cora Kaplan, an American literary critic now living in England, and Luce Irigaray, a French psychoanalyst—both of whom are criticizing, modifying, and expanding the psychoanalytic writing of Sigmund Freud and his reinterpreter, Jacques Lacan. Kaplan's work is discussed at greater length because her paper, although based on theoretical writing coming from the Continent, also draws on her experiences in English and American culture; because the essay in which she develops her argument is not yet readily available in the United States; and because her discussion, which places less emphasis on biological differences than does the Irigaray challenge, seems more closely associated with the social and the psychological arguments many other feminists in the United States and Great Britain are making.

In a single chapter on this material I can do little more than introduce the analytical framework and point out the relationship I see between the Kaplan and Irigaray material and other language and gender research. I mention Freud's recent reception in the United States, Lacan's (enigmatic) writing, the Lacanian account of the centrality of language to our understanding of the world, Irigaray's challenge to Lacan, Kaplan's reading of and elaboration of Lacan, language and gender studies that seem related to the Irigaray and Kaplan descriptions of women's and men's relation to language, and my questions about the content of this psychoanalytic theory.

SIGMUND FREUD AND JACQUES LACAN

Freud is viewed by many feminists not as an understanding, empathic, perceptive friend of women, but rather as a phallocentric, repressive, would-be Father, whose writings have had grave consequences for women. Or, in the more forgiving view, as a skillful theoretician, perhaps a genius, but one whose views on women were determined by the particular social conditions of his time. According to this view of Freud as culture-bound, he did not make the division, thought necessary by many feminists today, between the social and the biological. Some of the widely read critics of Freud include Betty Friedan, Kate Millett, Shulamith Firestone, Germaine Greer, Eva Figes, and Simone de Beauvoir. These are the critics Juliet Mitchell (*Psychoanalysis and Feminism*, 1975) answers as she writes of the value of Freud's work "to an understanding of femininity" (p. xvi).

Mitchell recognizes some of the reasons why Americans have portrayed Freud as "one of the greatest misogynists of all time" (p. 297). "Particularly in America the cult of pseudo-psychoanalysis became another way of maintaining the repression of those aspects of mental life which it was its real task to uncover" (p. 297), that is, advocating adaptation to the status quo. But while she decries such patriarchal practices, Mitchell also argues that Freud's work itself provides an important and rich theoretical framework for our understanding of the meaning of sexuality and gender differences.

As Jane Gallop (1975) points out, Mitchell is advocating a Freud "virtually unknown to American feminists" (p. 19). One American feminist finds the writings of Freud and of Freudians on "the female" of little utility in developing contemporary feminist theory:

As a child of the 50's in the US, I lived in a milieu where I interpreted all personal relations and most literature I read in Freudian terms, where psychoanalysis promised the middle class solutions to the identity problems and angst, and where vulgarised Freudian concepts were part of daily life in the child bearing advice of Spock and Gessell, the advice columns of Dear Abby. . . .

In the 60's one of the first victories of the women's movement in the US was to liberate ourselves both academically and personally from the Freud trap. (Julia Lesage, 1975:77-78)

Another writer, in a review article on occupational segregation, writes that the Freudian theory has served as the "mortar" that holds the structure of male dominance in place (Jean Lipman-Blumen, 1976:31).

Although as members of a western culture Americans share with Europeans many similar notions about human life, we have had different political and intellectual histories. The theory described below, originating mainly in France and filtered through translators and other people primarily interested in film or literary criticism, may not seem as "natural" a structure for the discussion of language and gender work as the other frameworks presented. However, recent psychoanalytic developments are having an impact on many feminists' discussions of language and gender.

Jacques Lacan, the French psychoanalyst (born 1901, founder of the École Freudienne de Paris), who presents his work as a return to Freud, argues repeatedly that the unconscious is a language and thus psychoanalysis is linguistic analysis. Through the acquisition of language we are located (as female or as male) into a social structure. In learning our language we learn dichotomous opposition: speech/silence, science/poetry, logic/intuition, author/reader—masculine/feminine. This psychoanalytic approach, which stresses symbolism over cognitive development, offers a quite different method of looking at language and gender relationships, one which is receiving increasing attention, especially from people in France, Great Britain, and the United States.

Below, I outline very briefly, first the sources of some of the difficulties readers have with Lacan's work and second a few of the principles of Freud's work, as presented by Lacan. While some of Lacan's writings are available now in English translation (in, for example, *Ecrits* [1977]), much of the critical scrutiny of Lacan is based on work not yet available in English. And some critical explanation and evaluation of Lacan's writing is not available in many libraries in the United States. For this reason I include a number of sources where introductions to Lacan's texts can be found. I do not try to summarize Lacan's argument (which has been developed over the past forty years). Here I extract only a few of his concepts that seem especially pertinent to Kaplan's work and to other current language and gender research.

Lacan is not as clearly directive a guide as one might hope for. While many American feminists in particular have difficulty accepting the intellectual framework within which Lacan works, every reader has difficulty with the writing style Lacan employs.[1] Lacan's style is, at least in part, a conscious effort to call attention to the structure of language. Language, he says, makes knowledge possible. It is *the* symbolic order and through it we are told our places in the social order. Lacan deliberately "joyces" language (he has acknowledged a debt to James Joyce). Lacan wants to dismantle language in order to obtain knowledge about it. Yet he realizes that having learned to speak language, he has submitted to the knowledge and order of language. He rejects the possibility of a metalanguage; one cannot get outside language to talk about it. One does not control language but is rather the victim of it; the child is constituted through language and bound to the distinctions, divisions, and laws of culture through language learning. "Joycing" the language can, Lacan believes, illustrate some of its constraints and possibilities.

Lacan and others involved in the study of the relationship between language, texts, and society are thus deliberately concerned with the effects of language. Their style is not intended to be "easy." A second reason their work is sometimes difficult to comprehend is that Lacan and colleagues are concerned that their writing not *seem* to be easily assimilated. They feel that Freud's writing was too familiar in style and that it encouraged, especially in the United States, quick (mis)readings, evaluation, and adaptation. They believe that a deliberately "difficult" style will encourage, even require, rigorous study of their theoretical work.[2]

Another initial difficulty some American readers may have with Lacan's work is that it does not come alone. His work is usually discussed in the context of the investigations of, among others, Claude Lévi-Strauss (anthropology); Michel Foucault, Louis Althusser, Julia Kristeva, and Jacques Derrida (philosophy); Roland Barthes (semiology); and Ferdinand De Saussure, Roman Jakobson, and Emile Benveniste (linguistics). These theoreticians are in disagreement on many issues but in general they reject a notion popular in our society (at least among the academic portion of that society) that ideas are the property of individuals: they believe, rather, that entry into the world of ideas is made through language, which is there before the individual.[3]

In "The Insistence of the Letter in the Unconscious" (1970), Lacan writes of the manner in which we become individuals. The subject of psychoanalysis is the unconscious and the discourse of the unconscious. We have access to the unconscious only through its linguistic manifestations. Through the acquisition of language we become human and social beings. The language code represents and authorizes social hierarchies, and the ideological superstructure (the system of ideas of the culture). Language is not a collection of words each with its own meaning. There is no one-to-one correspondence, no fixed exchange, between the word (the signifier) and the concept (the signified)—although speakers may *believe* their speech to be representational. Rather, signifiers have meaning only in relation to each other; each is not the other. To follow Lacan we have to abandon the notion of fixed reality and the notion of spoken or written words as containing individual meaning. A child learning a language learns a pre-existing structure which embodies the laws of the culture, and becomes aware of the places she or he can occupy. For example, as we learn about the biological categories important in our culture we learn about our gender identity. We learn our places as social beings by learning our language—including learning the polarity masculine/feminine and how it functions in our culture.

Lacan bases his account of the acquisition of sexual identity on the central role of the phallus, not the anatomical organ but the symbolic importance of its presence or absence.[4] For a girl, entry into the language/culture entails recognition that she does not have the phallus (i.e., the power it signifies). Through learning the language code, which embodies the social laws, the child learns that "the Phallus is the signifier of the social order—implying with it the concomitant idea, and reality, of the rights to authority and supremacy in men and the 'inherited tradition' of subservience—passivity-masochism in women" (Elizabeth Gross, 1976:22).

The developmental process by which the infant first recognizes itself in the mirror (around the age of six to eighteen months) as a unified being while yet feeling itself a fragmented being (the mirror phase), through the stage during which the child works through the Oedipus complex is, of course, laid out by Lacan, colleagues, and critics in much detail. What I stress here is that language has, for Lacan, the central, all-informing role; the human is formed by language.

The language code gives individuals their construction of reality, and their location in that reality, including their gender identity.[5]

LUCE IRIGARAY AND CORA KAPLAN

Luce Irigaray, a practicing psychoanalyst who once taught in the Lacanian École Freudienne, quarrels with Lacan—although not mentioning his name in the text—in her book *Speculum de l'Autre Femme* (1974).[6] As does Lacan, Irigaray feels that linguistic analysis is central for psychoanalysis and for understanding the way by which the human animal becomes a social creature. However, she believes that Freud and Lacan, by emphasizing discussion of the phallus, ignore women's actual *difference*. Femaleness is described in Freud and Lacan as an absence, as a lack, as a subordinate negativity to maleness, rather than as a difference. The masculine/feminine opposition is, as presented by Freud and Lacan, not a balanced duality but primarily a concern with maleness. As long as power is in the hands of males and as long as femaleness is thought to be only an absence, language and culture and thus relationships are male-determined.

Irigaray (1977)—in a discussion that can also be considered relevant to the muted group theory—says that women do not participate in the elaboration of social norms. This exclusion places all women, whatever their unique experiences, in the same "sexual, social and cultural situation" (p. 67). Lacan, she says, has taken a needed step in expanding Freudian work on language. But Lacan needs to take one further step—that is, to question a basic tenet of his linguistic theory itself. While Lacan talks of the structure that exists before the individual—and by which she or he is placed—as *a* language, Irigaray thinks we need to talk of languages with the one maintaining "the alienation and exploitation of women in and by society" (p. 62) and the other a repressed language of the women. Women's language is not simply oppressed, it is silenced. Lacan, she says, writes of the universality of language, ignoring both the necessity of and the present impossibility of an audible female language.

Irigaray is critical, then, of a male-centered psychoanalytical theory in which women are considered merely the "other." Of course, such a theory reflects the structure of the everyday world and incorporates traditional misogynistic stereotypes. Yet, as she points out, the theory does not deal with the ramifications of male domination or the relationship women have to (male) language.

Her critique is, perhaps necessarily, abstract. She says it is difficult to describe the language of the female other than to say it is not governed by an Aristotelian type of logic. It is not admitted by men and therefore cannot be adequately described or defined.

Her own argument has been criticized by two editors of *Ideology & Consciousness* (Diana Adlam and Couze Venn, 1977) and by Monique Plaza (1978) as a return to a Freudian emphasis on the female anatomy since she stresses the biological differences of women and men. (She suggests that instead of thinking of women as "no sex," as lack of penis, we use a term such as "two lips" which connotes not lack of, but definite and different. This non-unitary, two-lipped imagery is carried into her discussion of female language. She writes that there is a "plurality" in female language; there are always at least two meanings.) At times she uses *language* to mean the spoken word, at times to mean a structure that constitutes reality.

Her critique of Lacan and her own assessment of the relation between language and culture are less than clear. She seems to say that women have the same relationship that men have to their language; yet she presents women as also having something more. Further, Irigaray does not indicate her own relationship to language. If female language is repressed, from what position is she speaking? In her critique of Irigaray, Shoshana Felman (1975) queries,"Is she speaking *as* a woman, or *in place of* the (silent) woman, *for* the woman, *in the name of* the woman?" (p. 3).

However, in challenging Lacan's presentation of *a* language, Irigaray (1977) questions what was given in Lacanian theory: the unity of language and culture. She suggests that what Lacan thought was universal—the relationship of female, male, and language—is, rather, an historical phenomenon. For, she writes, if each woman becomes conscious that her own experiences are shared by other women, together they can "upset the whole set of dominant values—economic, social, moral, sexual" (p. 68). Irigaray is critical of traditional psychoanalysts for being unwilling to rethink their system, for being unable to see it "as one historical construct amongst others" (p. 70). While Lacan writes of the importance of the "forgotten language" of the unconscious, Irigaray would have us also look at the ignored language of women, ignored in everyday discourse, ignored in the elaboration of socio-cultural norms, and ignored in the construction of language theory.

Cora Kaplan (1976), like Irigaray, argues that theoreticians such as Freud and Lacan are too ready to claim universal application for their theories. Kaplan, like Irigaray, believes that women by re-understanding language can begin to see how their relationship to language and culture could be changed. Both are concerned about Lacan's presentation of women's entry into language as "negative" (since, he writes, the phallus has privileged meaning, and women "lack" the power it signifies). Irigaray writes that the imagery of women might be better termed "two lips" than "no sex," and Kaplan also suggests that the girl's access to language and culture is *different* from the boy's, rather than negative. But while Irigaray, the psychoanalyst, is concerned primarily with revising the formulations on women and on language proposed by Freud and Lacan, Kaplan, the literary critic, is primarily interested in applying the formulations to a study of the "high language"—the literature—of women and men in order to see what insights this theoretical approach offers for literary criticism.

Kaplan accepts Lacan's description of the child's entry into culture. In the mirror-stage (sometime after the age of six months) the child sees itself as a whole, although an alienated entity reflected in the mirror, while at the same time feeling itself a fragmented being, not in control of its caretaker or its food. The image in the mirror is perceived both as self and other and is thus open to the possibility of symbolizing. As the child learns language she is able to mediate the opposing images; she learns through the language to differentiate self from others and learns her relationship to others. The "truth" of life is contained in the abstractions of language. For Lacan, and for other structuralists, the meaning of a word is determined by its relationship to other words in the same language. As we learn how to form sentences, and learn how to speak, we learn underlying relationships. As Kaplan puts it, "Language only exists through individual speech, so in each speech act the self and the culture speak simultaneously or, to put it another way, each time we speak we are also spoken" (p. 23).

As boys and girls are located in linguistic abstraction they are located in a patriarchal culture. Kaplan summarizes, "Our individual speech does not . . . free us in any simple way from the ideological constraints of our culture since it is through the forms that articulate those constraints that we speak in the first place" (p. 22). Women's different relationship to language and culture is determined, Kaplan suggests, during two developmental states, first the Oedipal stage when the female acknowledges the phallus as the right to authority and supremacy within the family and, second, puberty, when the appearance of adult sex differences firmly distinguishes girls from boys in the wider culture. The males, but not the females, then begin their entry into public authority.

Kaplan (1976 and conversation) concentrates on two aspects of this approach to language. First, she is interested in the structural analysis (originating in the linguist de Saussure's work) that views language as having two dimensions, or two modes of arrangement: the *combination*, as each linguistic element is considered in its relationship to preceding and following units; and the *selection,* as each element is considered in its relationship to other elements that might have occurred in its place.[7] Speaking and writing require making choices concerning both combination and selection. Drawing from psychological tests, verbal art such as songs and poetry, and studies of aphasia, Roman Jakobson (1956) concludes that

> In normal and verbal behavior both processes are continually operative, but careful observation will reveal that under the influence of a cultural pattern, personality, and verbal style, preference is given to one of the two processes over the other. (p. 76)

Kaplan argues that "metonymy [concern with selection] is a dominant trope [figure of speech] in women's poetry, since it is a way of referring to experience suppressed in public discourse" (1976:36). This line of work may provide a valuable methodology for the analysis and comparison of, particularly, the written work of women and men, since written work is likely to be more self-conscious than spoken words.[8]

Here, however, I am more concerned with Kaplan's second type of elaboration on Lacan's work—her discussion concerning the prejudice against women as speakers. This prejudice, Kaplan writes, is intra- and trans-class; it is built into language which is the embodiment of cultural laws.

Women's everyday speech seems very similar to men's everyday speech. Empirical studies that compare, say, the number of adjectives or adverbs in men's and women's speech, or the particular words used, do not usually find significant differences. Also, in general, girls do as well or better than boys when tested on, for example, vocabulary, spelling, and comprehension of written material. Girls learn the language well. The major differences come, according to Kaplan, not in females' understanding of the language or their ability to speak, but through the restrictions placed on their speech and their speaking. When girls learn the language they also learn the laws of patriarchy.

As males mature physically, they are gradually allowed more freedom to speak. The females, however, learn that men control public speech. In becoming social beings, that is, in learning language, they accept the limitations on their speech (or they become schizophrenic). They learn the many English diminutive, fruit, sexual, animal, and other terms used to describe the lowliness and incompetence of women—such as baby, girlie, doll, bit of fluff, peach, tomato, skirt, cunt, hen, bird, mare, cow, bitch, shrew, blonde, and petticoat. This process, Kaplan writes, "places them in a special relationship to language which becomes theirs as a consequence of becoming human, and at the same time not theirs as a consequence of becoming female" (1976:29).

Where can we look for confirmation or "proof" of these abstract ideas? Psychoanalysis is a theory and a therapy. The methodology associated with psychoanalysis is not that of traditional academic disciplines and hence psychoanalysis is often criticzed for not being "scientific." Yet North American empirical researchers have been accused (by other North Americans as well as by many Europeans) of being too behavioristic, too ready to dismiss statements that cannot be validated "operationally."[9]

Some of the major theoretical analyses of linguistic structures (e.g., the analyses by L. S. Vygotsky and Noam Chomsky) have been developed primarily from personal perceptions about cognitive, nonobservable phenomena. What constitutes data, proof, and analysis will differ, of course, from culture to culture, from discipline to discipline, and from time to time (which is why we are not going to find or develop a Grand Theory suitable to all). As I think the material collected for these chapters indicates, merely tacking gender as a variable onto empirical language studies may result in the accumulation of data but in little information about the relationship of women and men within communicative events. On the other hand, some of the early essays on gender and language structure and language use—early in context of the recent interest in this area (Robin Lakoff, 1974, 1975)—have been criticized for the categorical statements based only on individuals' perceptions. (See, for example, the critiques provided by Betty Lou Dubois and Isabel Crouch, 1975, and Penelope Brown, 1976.) Some of the early observations about gender difference in language have not been supported by later empirical tests.

The use of a variety of methods to explore the relationship between language and gender can give us enriched information about the language of women and men. One of the attractions of the psychoanalytic approach taken by Kaplan and Irigaray is that this approach has received much attention and elaboration through the years. For my discussion I have extrapolated from a large body of literature some of the material which deals with the relationship of women and men to language.

From my reading of Irigaray and Kaplan as they write of men's and women's different relationship to language, I set forth the following hypotheses for study—only a few of those that could be derived from their work—which may have implications for understanding language and gender.

1. Women do not have as ready access as men to public forums. Women's speech will be heard primarily at home and will be suppressed especially in public. Women's writing will rarely be considered "high" language.

2. At puberty females will become especially conscious of restrictions which discourage women's speaking, except among themselves.

3. Women who do attempt to speak and write publicly—especially about their concerns as women—will often show an awareness that in so speaking they are challenging would-be male monopoly.

Public language

One proposition coming from the Kaplan and Irigaray analysis is that women will not have as ready access as men to public forums. Information about social structure is embedded in language. Females learn their place as they learn language. Kaplan (1976) writes that since "women have spoken and learned speech up to and through adolescence" they will continue to speak—but primarily to women and men in homes, private places. Women are segregated and relatively few are allowed to speak or write publicly.

There is no human experience "free" from accompanying language. The separateness—and inferiority—of women is inextricable from the language we learn while absorbing the values it embodies. (That the relationship between language and values is mutable is, however, evident in permutations according to social class, education [formal rather than "given" culture] , and the like. Kaplan writes that women who do break the "taboo" against women speaking publicly, especially to men, are likely to be those women who have first been freed from constant reproduction, are educated equally with men, are in the labor force, and/or have wealth to give them leisure. So in this analysis social class is a factor which helps determine the degree of restriction women experience.)

In her study of English and American women poets, Kaplan (1975) details some of the poets' expressions of their desire to write and speak, a desire they recognize has been socially constrained. As she writes later (1976) of the material in that collection, "To be a woman and a poet presents many women poets with such a profound split between their social, sexual identity (their 'human' identity) and their artistic practice that the split becomes the insistent subject, sometimes overt, often hidden or displaced, of much women's poetry" (p. 22).

With few exceptions, political speakers are male. Margaret Thatcher, British Prime Minister, was astute enough to realize that in campaigning and speaking publicly she violated social norms. I saw a news film of her, walking with her husband to her Chelsea rowhouse gate: as he walks out and on, she calls after, asking him when he will be returning home. She is acknowledging, for the benefit of the audience of the film, that she knows the societal expectations of her activities as a female and wife. (The bobby assigned by the government to guard her house because she *is* a public person is not shown in the film.[10]) The restrictions on women as political speakers and as publishing authors have received some attention in recent years. And books such as that edited by Josephine King and Mary Stott (1977) have documented the ways women have been, for the most part, prohibited from writing and speaking for the mass media.[11] Women are not often the presenters of radio and television news, nor are they the "authorities" who produce or comment on news. The national networks employ fewer female correspondents than male correspondents (in 1977 CBS had fifty-three male and eleven female correspondents) and the female correspondents are less likely to appear on news programs (U.S. Commission on Civil Rights, 1979:28-29). Barbara Walters' appointment to an anchor role on a news program created much excitement and hostility in the press. A research team monitoring all British national television news broadcasts found that in the first twelve months of 1975 only sixty-five of the 843 named interviewees (7.7 percent) were women. Women infrequently speak public news (Glasgow University Media Group, 1976:14). Nor are women heard frequently on panel programs. The reason that a top official of the British Broadcasting Corporation (the BBC) has given for including only a token woman on talk programs is that the ratio of one woman to four men "represents the participation of women in public life" (King & Stott, 1977:24). In 1977 there was only one woman newscaster on British national television stations; the employment of a second woman newscaster on British national television in 1978 prompted much discussion in the print media about the phenomena of female public speakers. King and Stott write that "until recently it was almost Holy Writ that women couldn't read the news, much less be *seen* to read it" (p. 1).

My own present reservation is that these examples can be more usefully discussed through an examination of social structure rather than language structure. Yet, the way the cultural rules and laws embedded in language may restrict women's public speaking deserves more attention.

Identification with restrictions

Another suggestion Cora Kaplan (1976) makes is that at puberty girls will identify themselves as the objects of the restrictions against female speaking, especially speaking outside the home to males or to groups of males and females. Kaplan writes that while the child learning the language has had to acknowledge gender differences and has learned that women's speech is restricted, puberty "further distinguishes girls from boys by the appearance of adult sex differences and access to public discourse for men" (p. 26). As their identity as female is made absolutely clear to them at puberty, girls become particularly conscious of the restrictions on their talk.

Support or challenge to this suggestion should be offered in literature concerning the interaction outside the home of pre-adolescent (before puberty) boys and girls and of adolescents. We have available (relatively many) childhood studies and (fewer) adolescent studies, but very few studies spanning childhood through adolescence that indicate whether girls or boys, or both genders, change their conception of themselves as speakers during their pre-adolescent and adolescent years.

Several difficulties inhere in efforts to assess Kaplan's suggestion. For example, most of the studies of differences in language use of boys and girls that are mentioned in Maccoby and Jacklin (1974) have involved paper and pencils rather than tape recorder, and listening to the speech of individual youngsters rather than listening to discussions of groups of boys and girls. When youth group interaction *is* made the focus of a study, researchers have shown far more concern with male adolescents than with female adolescents or with male/female interaction. Most adults who are recognized or labelled "researchers" are male and perhaps these males see more importance in the study of males than in the study of female groups. Or they may feel that they as males will be more readily accepted into or on the fringe of male groups.[12]

Several writers have indicated that a researcher's sex is an important factor in determining the responses of the boys and the girls in mixed-sex groups when there is an awareness of the researcher's presence (John Elliott, 1974; Angela McRobbie and Jenny Garber, 1975). One group of (female) researchers concluded from a preliminary investigation of girls' groups in Birmingham, England, that "girl culture . . . is so well insulated as to operate to effectively exclude not only other 'undesirable' girls—but also boys, adults [in general], teachers and researchers [in particular] " (McRobbie and Garber, p. 222).

As just these considerations indicate, statements about the interaction of youths must be very tentative because the methods of obtaining information on the interaction is quite problematic and because the interaction of girls, as of women, has been largely ignored, considered unimportant or nonexistent. (William Labov, who has studied male adolescent peer groups, writes that males are the chief carriers of the vernacular culture. Who has bothered to do extended studies of girls to hear what they are saying, and how they are saying it?) Girls have been absent in most classic studies of youth groups, ethnographic studies, "pop" histories, and journalistic surveys (McRobbie and Garber, 1975:209). Furthermore, while researchers have shown little concern with developing conceptual models for adolescent activities, what is available has a distinctly masculine cast. Female development is presented, partly through omission, as more mysterious than male development. (See Judith Gallatin's [1975] detailing of this problem.)

However, the following tentative observations, based on a variety of observations and readings, can advance the discussion on possible differences in the ways boys and girls feel they can and may control public speech.

1. Girls of pre-adolescent and adolescent age get together in smaller groups than do boys and thus may have fewer chances to talk to large groups. Boys belong to same-gender *flocks* and girls to same-gender *small groups* (Lee Rainwater, 1970:282; Maccoby and Jacklin, 1974). Researchers indicate that this difference in group size comes at the time of adolescence (McRobbie and Garber,

1974:221), although Maccoby and Jacklin say they cannot determine from their review of the literature on group size just when girls develop "chumships" and boys "gangs." Their review states that such differences are reported (from several countries) as emerging several years before puberty (p. 207).

The setting for a particular study may account for some of the differences found in the age at which girls begin playing in smaller goups and boys in larger groups. One research team found that in an "open" nursery school children spent 42 percent of their time with others of the same gender while in a "traditional" school the figure was 69 percent (Roger Bakeman and Barbara Bianchi, 1976). Quite possibly the school program affects the size of single-gender groups.

Maccoby and Jacklin believe the girls' smaller group sizes is related to the relative reluctance on the part of girls to enter into dominance hierarchies. So far, such an argument is not antithetical to Kaplan's presentation, but while Maccoby and Jacklin argue that male eagerness to compete for positions within their groups possibly has a biological basis, Kaplan would stress the way the children acquire knowledge of their relations to others as they learn language and thus learn their gender identity.

Of course the fact that boys spend more time in larger groups does not mean they necessarily do more "public" speaking. Boys are said to engage in more rough-and-tumble play and in less talking than do girls. And perhaps within the larger group much of the interaction occurs between smaller groups. Perhaps a very few boys in any group do most of the talking.[13]

Girls and boys do seem to work out quite different social organizations. Status negotiation was continual in the conversations of the black urban boys, ages eight through thirteen, recorded by Marjorie Harness Goodwin (1978). However, coordination of activities through hierarchical organizations was uncommon in the conversations of girls from the same Philadelphia streets. In fact, Goodwin heard the girls, even those as young as four and five, participate jointly in group decision making. The girls used proposals (and mitigating "maybe's") rather than commands. The process of disputes differed also. The boys stated their grievances much more directly than did the girls, who were more likely to work out complex alliances with each other, against another. The arguments among boys were usually over quickly. Those among the girls could last for weeks and tensions often led to realignments within the social groups. I have talked with many women who remember the intense, elaborate, and extended discussions about relationships among the girls in their school classes and neighborhoods.

In short, girls do get together in smaller groups, in general, than do boys. However, the girls' focus on more intense relations is evident several years before puberty and does not appear to change dramatically at puberty. The boys may have more opportunities than girls to speak to larger groups of peers.

2. Girls at puberty appear more likely than boys to talk with each other in the setting of private homes. At ages twelve and thirteen, adolescents are still interacting, according to most studies, primarily in single-gender groups. While boys are more likely to gather on the street or on playing fields, girls are more likely to get together in homes; they talk together more in private than in public

settings. "Requiring only bedroom and a record player and permission to invite friends" (McRobbie and Garber, 1975:220), groups of girls may thus appear invisible to researchers. These more private meetings in homes with walls and doors as protections against interruptions may allow girls to avoid public "humiliation or degradation" (McRobbie and Garber, p. 220). For whatever reasons (and the reasons may include parental restrictions), girls likely do not do as much talking in public locations.

3. By adolescence, girls (and boys) know what behavior, including speech behavior, is expected of women and men (Carole Edelsky, 1976a; Cheris Kramer, 1977). Usually the assumption is that youngsters become *gradually* aware of what "masculine" and "feminine" talk should be as they approach adulthood (Gallatin, pp. 248-252), rather than experiencing intense awareness at puberty. Edelsky, in her study of the ability of children to interpret language correctly as appropriate to one sex or the other (with "correctness" determined by adult responses), found "a gradual approximation to adult norms" (p. 51). However, that study involved first, third, and sixth graders, and adults, and hence does not clearly indicate whether or not the ability to recognize the sex-linked (according to adult responses) language items increases dramatically for girls at puberty. (Her study tested for the "correct" assignment to males or to females of words and expressions such as "Damn it," "Oh dear," and "Won't you please," not beliefs about where and when women and men "should" speak.)

John Elliott (1974) believes that their understanding of appropriate speech behavior for females (that it should be passive especially when the subject matter is perceived as belonging to males) prevented female students of about fifteen years of age from participating in group discussions as individuals with personal points of view. But here again we have no comparable material from younger girls and boys to use to determine when girls clearly identify themselves with the restrictions against female public speech.

Several other researchers, while not referring specifically to increased awareness and identification with restrictions on public speaking, do suggest that girls at puberty feel their roles outside the home more and more restricted. A study of American women holding middle management positions reveals that they remember becoming acutely aware of their gender and of the restrictions which are a part of their gender at the ages of twelve to thirteen (Margaret Hennig and Anne Jardim, 1978). In their book *On Becoming a Woman,* Fay Fransella and Kay Frost (1977) mention a study of London children which found that while young boys want a man's life and young girls, a woman's, by twelve years of age about half of both the boys and girls were undecided. But by age fifteen only twelve percent of the boys desire a woman's life compared to forty percent of the girls who want a man's life (p. 69). Fransella and Frost further report that girls do not start to "underachieve" until about the time of puberty, the sixth grade; up until then the girls do slightly better than the boys in school work (p. 72).

Perhaps, as Cora Kaplan (1976) argues, most pre-puberty girls, while knowing about the speech restrictions for women (because they acquire such knowledge as they learn the language), do not closely identify with such restrictions. Research that includes pre-puberty children *and* adolescents may help us understand when and how we acquire "feminine identity." (Such stress is needed, for most theoretical models seem to work better for explaining "masculine identity" than "feminine identity." As long as our society acknowledges firm gender-appropriate behaviors we will not be able to assume we can talk realistically about only *one* process of gender identity.) We do not yet have the necessary materials to knit together an explanation of how or when females come to understand the restrictions on their speech.

4. Girls tend to engage in fewer public displays of verbal competition—at least according to available studies. Here again there are more questions than answers. Young black males seem to give more demonstrations of rapping, signifiying, the dozens, and other competitive verbal performances, although black girls know the techniques involved (Rainwater, 1970:277, 284). (However, primarily boys and not girls have been listened to by sociologists and linguists.) Other regular public speech activities seemingly equally available to males and females include debating, writing contests, volunteering in class, and initiating talk with adults other than parents. More knowledge of male and of female participation in these activities before and after puberty would give us indication of whether or not puberty causes a sharp confirmation to females of the restrictions on public speaking.

The hypothesis that puberty in particular makes females aware of the restrictions on their public discourse is not strongly supported by material I have found in my reading. However, the review prompted by the hypothesis does reveal the paucity of studies that "cover" this stage of physical maturation. Researchers have frequently used puberty as a distinguishing event and have studied values, beliefs, and linguistic competence either before or after. Puberty has seldom been seen as a possible key event for determining, for example, how males and females perceive themselves as speaking subjects. Carole Edelsky (correspondence) suggests from her teaching experience that girls at about the sixth grade change in their interaction with boys from being straightforward, perhaps dominant, to being coy, seemingly allowing the boys to control the conversation.

Women comment on restrictions

Another hypothesis suggested by the writings of Irigaray and (particularly) Kaplan is as follows: Women who do attempt to speak and write publicly, especially about their concerns as women, will show an awareness that in so doing they are challenging would-be male monopoly.

Some support for this statement is included above in the chapters on the muted group theory. Kaplan (1976), herself, offers further examples. She states that women writers "from the seventeenth century onwards (when women first entered the literary ranks in any numbers) comment in moods which range from abnegation to outright anger on the culture's prohibition against women's writing, often generalizing it to women's speech" (p. 29). Kaplan comments specifically on such works as Elizabeth Barrett Browning's *Aurora Leigh,* a long poem about a woman who like Browning herself defies society in purposely working to become a major poet, and on Emily Dickinson's "They shut me up in Prose / As when a little Girl / They put me in the Closet— / Because they liked me 'still'—."

In her collection of poems by English and American women, Kaplan gives other examples, as well as illustrations of the manner in which male reviewers, even when they do write favorable comments, often mention their disapproval of most "female poetry."

Marguerite Duras, the French novelist, dramatist, and film-maker, talks (interview and translation by Susan Husserl-Kapit, 1975) of her conversation with a male friend. She asked, "Now, can you imagine being a woman?" When he answered, "Sure," Duras told him, "O.K., keep quiet" (p. 431).

With the exception of a very few contemporary women (perhaps most notably Julia Kristeva, the French philosopher and writer on semiology), women have not been centrally involved in the debate (at least as it takes place in widely distributed and discussed sources) on the relationship males and females have to language. The "alternative" ideas mentioned here are available primarily in feminist publications. Men's theorizing about language will itself suffer from a *lack* until these concerns of women are at least acknowledged.

QUALIFICATIONS

Lacan, many critics repeatedly state, is the dominant force in French intellectual life. In France, discussions of psychoanalysis are an important part of discussions about the concerns and impact of the Women's Liberation movement. For these reasons and because the use of this theory raises some interesting questions about the language and the speaking rights of females and males, the study of psychoanalytic ideology can be of great value. To those of us accustomed to looking at humans primarily as either individuals or the products of a socialization process, looking at women and men as constituted by language can encourage, at least, a reassessment of former positions. Some of my own ambivalent feelings about much of the Lacan psychoanalytic theory (as I understand it) have been stated. Psychoanalysis, like any theoretical position, develops out of particular socio-economic considerations. It is neither universal nor a-historical. Lacan, in returning to Freud, did not avoid his patrocentrism and phallocentrism. What is lacking in the work of both is what Anthony Wilden (1972) calls a critical understanding of the oppression of women which the theory incorporates.

Some problems come from the central tenets of language in Lacan's model for the study of language. His theorizing is based on de Saussure's statements about language as a system governed by its own laws; signs define each other through their differences from each other. De Saussure thought that all forms of human communication could be considered as systems (of, initially, arbitrarily designated signs). Following de Saussure, Barthes and Lévi-Strauss have posited that people's clothing and people's preparation of food—indeed, all human interaction—can also be considered as languages, as systems of mutually defined relationships; the autonomy of the individual (who becomes human only by use of the language whose structure has been determined prior to the individual) is limited to understanding that the language she or he uses determines what "truth" she or he knows. Work on structuralism in the past few years has raised some, to me, very important questions about the generalizations that de Saussure once thought could be made about all forms of human communication. Critics have pointed to the limits of the sign approach to language. For example, while phonemes, morphemes, and words can be counted—are finite—sentences are not. The idea of language as a system of signs appears to break down when we go beyond the level of the sentence; works of literature, for example, possess so many possible elements, so many systems of signs that it is difficult to think of them as a closed system of social signs. Edmund Leach (1976), while agreeing with the structuralist position that language cuts up our world into meaningful objects and puts "things and persons in relationship to one another" (p. 33), and agreeing that at a very deep, abstract level all nonverbal dimensions of culture—music, clothing, food, physical gestures, for example—are organized in a manner similar to the organization of sounds, words, and sentences, also argues that "the syntax of non-verbal 'language' must be a great deal simpler than that of spoken or written language" (p. 11). Is it accurate or useful to say that nonverbal forms of communication have a formal structure that is equivalent to spoken or written language or to say that nonverbal and verbal language are expressive in equivalent ways? The psychoanalytic approach of Lacan not only pays little attention to nonverbal behavior, but also fails to indicate how the nonverbal might be studied in relationship to the verbal.

The concept of language in Lacan often seems to ignore communication; he focuses on code rather than on actual speech. Certainly much contemporary work under such headings as, for example, social evaluation of speech, phenomenology, ethnomethodology, and language functions seems to provide a much "fuller" account of human interaction. The emphasis on psychological "interiority" and on the construction of the "subject" or individual, does not deal with the whole of communication.

For these various reasons, while appreciating portions of the Lacanian theory, I have difficulty with some aspects of it. However, this theoretical approach has interested many, provoking much discussion from feminists, particularly in Europe. These feminists are talking in study groups about its value and are suggesting interventions necessary to make the theory less patrocentric (especially since it has had an increasing impact on psychoanalytical practice and popular values). With all that is dubious in his theory (as it has been expressed in Lacan's difficult prose) it is still interesting and important, and I think, deserves some attention by language and gender researchers. As Wilden (1972) points out, we can reject portions of the theory while finding some tenets insightful and useful. What others, especially women, say about women's and men's relationship to each other and to language should be a part of an ongoing evaluation of any theory concerning these relationships.

NOTES

1. One woman who attended Lacan's lectures writes: "One understood nothing, if by understanding is meant the discursive exposition of arguments which one had been taught to

practice. Nothing, for several years; but a familiarity began to form in the ear, by necessity, nonetheless" (Catherine Clément, quoted in Jane Gallop, 1976:31). Colin MacCabe (1975) refers to Lacan's "enigmatic teaching" (p. 8). Jean Roussel (1968) writes that while Lacan's style is methodical, very much a conscious effort to exhibit the structure of language, the style, paradoxically, "is often attacked as obscure, meretricious, idiosyncratic, and quite inappropriate in a 'man of science' " (p. 63). Another writer refers to the "inscrutability" of Lacan's diction that makes his writings "difficult, if not ultimately impossible, to fully decipher" (Gross, 1976:12-13).

2. Another view is that Lacan is just unable or unwilling to write clearly. For example, his use of the word *language* is often critically ambiguous. See Trevor Pateman (1980) for a critique of arguments that humans are necessarily controlled by language.

3. Short bibliographies of the people who work together with, around, or in opposition to Lacan are included in the Spring/Summer 1973 *Screen* (pp. 227-241), a British film journal devoted in part to discussions of Lacan's theory of language. Other introductions to the writings of Jacques Lacan (and bibliographies of his writings) are in Anthony Wilden (1968, 1972), Jacques Ehrmann (1970), *New Left Review* 51 (1968), *Yale French Studies* 48 (1972), Sherry Turkle (1978), Richard Wollheim (1979), and Stephen Heath (1978). Carolyn Greenstein Burke (1978) has written a valuable report of French women's examinations of their language during the 1970s.

4. Critics have pointed out that only sometimes does Lacan make this distinction between phallus and penis. His lapses in this regard are, in part, responsible for the charge of patrocentric bias made against him by several feminists. (See Elizabeth Gross, 1976:20.)

5. See Juliet Mitchell (1975) for an account of the social production of females according to Freudian theory.

6. She lost her job after the book was published. She writes, "The meaning of this expulsion is clear: only men may say what female pleasure consists of. Women are not allowed to speak, otherwise they challenge the monopoly of discourse and of theory exerted by men" (Irigaray, 1977:71).

7. The combination dimension is often called the syntagmatic, or predictive, or metaphoric dimension. The selection dimension is often called the paradigmatic, or substitute, or metonymic dimension.

8. Trevor Pateman has commented to me that while it is *trivially true* that all speech involves selection and combination (except one-word utterances), without further explication Jakobson's "preference" is quite meaningless. Similarly, without a standard of reference Kaplan's statement is not clear. All poetry is hyper-metonymic. However, Kaplan (1976) argues that the poetry of women often has more metonymic force than the poetry of men since women in their poetry can express desire and experience usually censored in patriarchal culture. She quotes Lacan on metonymy as a way "to bypass the obstacles of social censure" and adds, "Perhaps that is why so much of the most resonant female poetry has been written with a full and bitter self-consciousness of the resistance of all patriarchal culture to the female voice" (p. 36).

9. For example, *The* [London] *Times* (June 1977) ran a second-page news report of the "inevitably" American effort requiring "many years of research funded by innumerable foundations, the combined efforts of the Johns Hopkins University in Baltimore and Harvard University," and the "incomparable" profile-of-nonverbal-sensitivity-test in order to test for the existence of female intuition. Presumably *The Times* would have been more receptive to a theoretical discussion than to this laboratory report. (Although in this particular case I wonder if the male reporter is also concerned that one of his beliefs about sex differences is receiving close scrutiny in a laboratory. He begins his report with a Rupert Brooke poem, "But there's wisdom in women, of more than they have known, / And thoughts go blowing through them, are wiser than their own.")

10. Trevor Pateman (conversation) suggests that news films of male politicians drinking beer in a pub might be considered comparable to the Thatcher film. The men also think it necessary to show that they are regular males.

11. The newsletter *Media Report to Women* provides a continuing discussion of the discrimination against women in radio, television, and print media.

12. If, as several researchers have stated, the male adolescent peer groups and the female groups are quite different in size, activities, and gathering locations, these two types of groups are not equally available for either adult male or female researchers. Adult females are the norm in primary school rooms and perhaps can move less obtrusively in these classrooms. Female researchers hanging around groups of adolescents, boys or girls, are less likely to arouse suspicion and anxiety from youth club organizers, school officials, parents, or police (Janet Lever, 1976). Barrie Thorne (conversation), in school playground and lunchroom field work, found that the girls welcomed her into their groups more readily than the boys did. Boys tend to congregate in larger groups than girls, and male groups may therefore be more open to the male researcher.

13. Trevor Pateman (conversation), who has worked as community center youth program coordinator in England, believes that gangs often have a group leader—but in addition, an "intellectual" leader who conducts questioning and arguments with adults.

V

DREAMS FOR TEENS

The reconstructed psychoanalysis framework discussed in the previous chapter posits a division between male and female speech, especially public speech, that is dramatically—and traumatically—confirmed for females at the time of puberty, when their social identity as females is sealed. While males after puberty are gradually released from the checks that have limited their speech as children in adult company, females grow up only to learn more about restrictions on their voices. Restrictions on many speaking rights accompany sexual maturity—for females but not for males.

The meaning of puberty for males and for females is culturally defined, and it changes somewhat over time. In a history of adolescence in America, Joseph F. Kett (1977) writes that although youth has usually been seen as a problematic period of life, the specific economic and social relationships between youths and adults have changed a great deal during the past 200 years. For example: in contrast to current thinking, in the nineteenth century the onset of puberty in males was not considered an important cue for one of the stages of life. Rather, adolescence customarily was linked more closely to social status—whether the male was, say, a student or a paid worker—than to physical changes accompanying puberty. Thus, ministers and other youth counselors directed much of their attention to individuals in their late teens and early twenties, the years of significant challenges, perils, and decisions (at least for those white males of the more highly educated middle- and upper-classes).

However, in discussing the attention that was paid to those in their later teens and their twenties, Kett (1973) presents almost as an aside the information that "There was one notable exception to the lack of interest in the middle teens; paradoxically, the years around puberty were thought to be extremely critical for girls" (p. 107). Girls were thought to experience trauma at the onset of puberty. For boys the physical changes were not thought to determine, immediately or later, life's direction. The common sexual changes were more important for girls; the individual status changes were more important for the boys.

While there have been many changes over the years in the experiences and expectations of young females and males, in the second half of the twentieth century we note that the early teen years still appear to be more traumatic for girls than for boys. For example, girls in junior high school are reported as experiencing more dissatisfaction, anxiety, and tension than boys—although teachers are more attentive to the dissatisfaction of boys than to the dissatisfaction of girls (Daniel Linden Duke, 1978). Repeatedly, studies of IQ scores of individuals over time have found that females' scores on the tests become lower between the ages of ten and sixteen while males tend to increase their scores. One researcher found that girls whose IQ scores dropped were more likely than others to express belief in the importance of stereotypic masculine and feminine behavior (Patricia B. Campbell, 1976).

We need more information about when females come to know their relationship to the various sanctions on women's speech—against joke telling, assertiveness, obscenity, public speaking—and about when boys come to know their relationship to the sanctions on their speech—against crying or public display of affection for other males. Carole Edelsky's (1976a) article indicates that an individual's process of learning the stereotypes of women's and men's speech is gradual, continuing through elementary school. However, quite possibly, females and males may learn *about* these differences but not accept this segregation of men's and women's speech as applying directly and finally to them until puberty, when they must align themselves with adult men and women.

Attention has been paid to the comparative reading and writing skills and the verbal fluency of males and females in the schools. Not as much attention has been given to the students' perception of their speaking rights and restrictions and of the evaluation of their speech in actual social interaction with their friends and with adults. High school males and females perceive the speech of men and women as differing on many accounts (Cheris Kramer, 1977).

The material in the preceding chapter indicated something of the complexity and elusiveness of the work by Jacques Lacan on the centrality of language to thought and identity, and of the suggestions by Cora Kaplan on the importance of puberty for females in making clear to them the restrictions on their talk. In the discussions here I do not pretend to deal with the many different kinds of relationship the study of language and maturation can offer. Rather, I take a very exploratory look at some of the reading material American girls and boys look at as they go about discovering the social laws concerning their behavior as girls and boys and, eventually, as women and men.

Certainly females and males have many opportunities to learn about what speech is expected of them. Many of their school texts give them such information, for example. The texts used in elementary school, junior high school, high school, and college are receiving increasing scrutiny from many researchers who are calling attention to the sexism of many of those books. In this section I look very briefly at another kind of publication—the popular magazines addressed to teenagers in which distinctions are made between what can and should be read and spoken by males and females.

TEEN PUBLICATIONS

Most publications for the very young (e.g., *Jack and Jill, Highlights, Humpty Dumpty*) are for children of both sexes. Most journals for teenagers are primarily for either females or males (e.g., *The American Girl, Flip, Ingenue, Tiger Beat Magazine, Seventeen, The American Newspaper Boy, Boys' Life, Model Railroader, Hot Rod Racers*). The subject matter, terminology, and style of the magazines for young females differ in great part from those of the magazines published for young male teenagers. Males and females are talked to differently in these publications and are presented as talking differently.

The descriptions of the magazines indicate the sharp differences in the topics discussed in the publications for males and the publications for females. *True Confessions, Sweethearts, Teen Age Love, Romantic Story*, and *Love Story* are all classified in *The Standard Periodical Directory* (Leon Garry ed., 1973) as "Romantic fiction touching upon some of the social and personal problems faced by today's teen." *Teen Age Hotrodders,* and *Hot Rods* and *Racing Cars,* are described as "authentically written and drawn tales of the world of wheels. For the boy who is looking forward to his first car." *Texas Rangers, Outlaws of the West,* and *Wyatt Earp* are listed as "shoot-em-ups and showdowns in the old romantic West" while *Judomaster* is "set against the background of World War II." *Army Attack* and *War and Attack* are "set against combat-zone backgrounds from World War I to Viet Nam." All of the above are listed as having circulations of 115,000 or more.

Tiger Beat Magazine is described in one reference work (Lavinia Dobler and Muriel Fuller, 1970) as for "chiefly girls," in elementary grades and high school; its contents provide "leisure reading about the young entertainment world." *Fave,* "chiefly for high school girls," includes "fan-type interviews" (Dobler and Fuller, p. 26). *Hot Rod Magazine* is listed as "symbol of speed and status . . . probably the most popular of the automotive magazines for young men" (Dobler and Fuller, p. 27). *Teen* is "for young active teen girls" and is "devoted to fashion, beauty guidance, plus special features on entertainment, records, movies, fiction, and service departments for teenage questions on dating, etiquette, beauty, problems, fads" (Garry, p. 1688).

Clearly the interests of adolescent females and adolescent males are thought to be different. While material in magazines for children younger than twelve may make some similar distinctions in the activities of males and females, the material written for young teens is evidently thought to be different enough to necessitate or make desirable separate publications, thus emphasizing gender as a factor in information gathering and dissemination. How much the publishers establish the interest in separate journals and how much the journals reflect the interests established by other factors in the culture is clearly a very complex (and important) issue.

There *is* interest; the journals do sell, most of those discussed here by the hundreds of thousands each issue. They are widely exchanged among teenagers, although the fan magazines for girls are considered contraband in some households, according to junior high and high school students I talked with who said their parents were concerned about the "shallowness" of the articles and the emphasis on boy-girl relationships.

Some participants in a language and gender class I teach at the University of Illinois have looked at what messages some of the teen periodicals contain about how females and males talk, are talked about, and are talked to. It seems that rather than treating young women as if they are on pedestals, the publishers treat them as if they are in highchairs.

In a detailed look at a *Tarzan* comic (April 1978), Robin Wright found 176 drawings of men and 28 drawings of women (there were more of apes than of women). Men spoke 108 times and women 15. Wright notes that throughout the story Jane is pictured leaning against something—a rock, a tree, or Tarzan—and is usually pictured as disheveled, tired, and frightened. She is frequently acted upon by men: she is kidnapped, saved, comforted, held, threatened, saved again. She also watches, waits, rests, and hides. She screams in fear and cries from fear and pain.

Tarzan is a match for his environment. Wright states: "He speaks at least three languages (English, Greek, and Ape), outwits the enemy, fights and kills both men and animals, and saves Jane without a scraped elbow or a torn loin cloth."

Meanwhile in the April 1978 issue of *WONDER WOMAN* the heroine saves *her* man. However, Wonder Woman is an aberration, not like Tarzan who is only a super specimen of his gender. She lives in a community that is dominated by women; however, there are no men living on her island. Even on the island, the queen is given insight, wisdom, and knowledge by two men from another world. All the women except Wonder Woman are spectators to the action of the story.[1]

In a close inspection of a fan magazine Rebecca Moehnke found a happy and humble consideration of everyone, especially fans and their idols. While an editorial in the (boys') *Hot Rod* (June 1978) dealt with the restrictions imposed by "powermad federal and state bureaucracies" (p. 4), the editorial she read in the (girls') *Teen Beat* (July 1978) was quite different: "Spring is here. It's a time of rebirth. The sun is shining. Flowers are in bloom. Everyone happily sheds woolens for spring time pastels and prints" (p. 6).

In general the girls' magazines contained words of dreaminess not found in the more "worldly" journals for boys. As Betsy Kay found, the editorials, letters to editors, and articles in the magazines for females were concerned with love, with relationships with people, while those in the magazines for males were concerned with people and things not assumed to be intimately related to the reader. The fan magazines for girls give hints on how to become intimate friends with idols. For example, the July 1978 issue of *Teen Spectacular* had an essay from singer Shaun Cassidy entitled "You Can Be My Dream Girl, If—" and an article entitled "Spend a Day at the Beach with Leif Garrett, Singer." In her analysis of this issue Denise Sukkar writes of the many ways Leif is presented as in control during this day. He "expertly" tools his car; he "knows exactly where he's heading"; he "lets you catch up to him"; meanwhile, "you hestitate," you are "managing to keep up," and at the end of the day you say "thanks." Henry Hertz found the titles used in the auto and cycle magazines have tougher-sounding words (such as *truckers, rambling, bleeding, superbowl, dragon, street beast*), while journals such as *Teen Beat* use words with less aggressive connotations (such as *secret dream, reveals, love, nice, personal, good, fairy-tale*).

In an analysis of two articles in an issue of *Fighting Stars* (August 1978), a magazine that features celebrities who participate in the martial arts, Susan Wagner found that Bo Hopkins (always referred to in the story written by Nancy Frizzelle as "Hopkins") and Cheri Caffaro (always referred to in the story written by Stuart Sobel as "Cheri") were given quite different treatment. Hopkins is pictured ten times in his article, always fully clad. Cheri five times, twice with skimpy tops and pants. What is said about Cheri primarily concerns her good looks and overall physical appearance and demeanor. Hopkins approaches everything "with lots of dedication"; Cheri thinks "life is like a present which she enjoys opening each day." Hopkins was quoted in 90 lines out of 184 in the article about him; Cheri, in 61 lines of 196 in the article about her. Hopkins often depersonalized his comments. For example:

> "... if you have a bad temper, it [karate] keeps you from losing it.... It's because you *know* you can walk away from a fight," he explains. There's no point in fighting anymore because you don't have to prove your manhood." (*Fighting Stars,* August 1978, p. 33)

Cheri was more likely to use "I" rather than generalizing to "you" (e.g., "That was fun for me"; "I love the challenge of trying new things"; I love to write"). Wagner adds that the propensity Cheri had of expressing herself in joyous words as *love, wonderful, favorite*) was contagious. The interviewer also used those words in discussing Cheri's activities.

Studying journals written for older teenagers or young adults, Pam Quaggiotto noted that letters to the editor in *Seventeen* are very short and not answered whereas letters to the editor of the auto magazines are longer and are answered in detail. (*Seventeen* does publish letters to the beauty editor which receive detailed responses.) She commented on the contradiction within the journal; while the articles encourage attention to personality, the advertisements emphasize physical appearance.[2] Comparing issues of journals for females and male bachelors— *Gentleman's Quarterly* and *Cosmopolitan*—Laura Horian found *Cosmopolitan* editors more likely to use conversational language (e.g., "Well, it's all quite riveting" and "... but never mind!"), to emphasize togetherness (e.g., use of *we* and *us*, meaning women), to use rhetorical questions, and to use more, and stereotypically female, adjectives, e.g., *fabulous, lovely, fascinating, delicious, dreamy, divine...*).

The emphasis of the journals for males appears to be on acquiring and displaying physical and mechanical skills, while the emphasis of the journals for females appears to be on improving appearance and personality. Erving Goffman (1976) suggests that in advertising photographs the girls are pictured as naturally like their mothers. Girls merely "unfold" into womanhood while boys have to "push their way into manhood" (p. 107). This distinction, of presenting boys as having to work harder to become men, is also expressed in some of the writings of men who are discussing and critiquing the acquiring of masculinity in our culture. A boy becoming a man "must become inexpressive," must learn skills, "to *control* a situation . . . and to maintain his position" (Jack W. Sattel, 1976:471, 472). The analysis by Kaplan would also indicate that males leaving childhood learn how to work in, speak during, and control a greater number of situations, while females' growth and change is primarily biological. Women, according to this analysis, are encouraged to continue to obey many of the restrictions imposed on children's speech. Not as much change is involved.

Yet, as Esther Newton (1972) in an account of female impersonators in America points out, many of the components of "women" are culturally determined:

> It seems self-evident that persons classified as "men" would have to create artificially the image of a "woman" [in order to become a female impersonator], but of course "women" create the image "artificially" too. Note that the only item listed [in an inventory of the female impersonator's props] that is intrinsically more "faked" for a male is the bosom. But what of padded bras? (p. 5)

Discussing the teen magazines, Pam Quaggiotto (conversation, 1978) says that these journals indicate that girls as well as boys must learn to acquire womanhood. In fact, the material in the magazines for females is more clearly stated as *advice*, as directions, than is the material in the magazines for males. The "you should's" are more frequent in the beauty and fan magazines.

Undoubtedly many young males and females in the United States never or seldom see the journals discussed here. And the impact of the material on the teenagers who do read them is not known. In class Henry Hertz suggested that most of the readers of the girls' journals likely consider the text superfluous. He thinks most teenagers read the pictures and the advertisements, and the analysis should center primarily on the nonverbal messages and on what readers say about the journals.

At the time my class was studying the journals I asked two sisters, eleven and thirteen, about the fan magazines. The younger said she would rather read James Herriot, a veterinarian who writes about his experiences with people and animals, than fan magazines: "James Herriot is funny and his books are not full of fluff like those magazines." Her older sister reads fan magazines borrowed from a girlfriend. I asked about her interests in the magazines. Her responses may not be typical, but they do suggest that listening to the statements of boys and girls can suggest valuable lines of inquiry about the impact of the journals on the readers and about the reading interests of those passing from what is defined as childhood to what is defined as adulthood.

"I like the posters. There's no information—except on recording stars. Yes, I read the magazines but they are really stupid. But not as stupid as the ones written for women. Every time I go to the drug store I look at the other stupid ones. How to keep your husband happy and how to keep him from running off with some movie star. They are always giving advice on how to keep husbands. And the population of unwed mothers with star fathers seems to be dense in Hollywood. The magazines are so stupid. I think they are written for people who are jealous of Hollywood but who can read the magazines and can then say, 'Well, anyway, my husband isn't running off with Cheryl Tiegs like all those husbands out there.' "

Are those magazines written for women? "Yes. You can tell because of the stereotype of women being dumb and liking dumb things. Those magazines have unbelievable stories with dumb language."

But you read them. "I don't know why. I think boys read them also. They read their sisters' or they buy them saying they are for their sisters. It's okay for girls to read *Tiger Beat.* Boys are ashamed to admit reading it. It's sissy to read fan magazines because it's stupid for boys to be going 'Oh! Marie Osmond is just fab!' For the past 100 years, starting about 1950, girls have been getting hysterical about stars. But if boys get hysterical about Christy McNichol people would say 'hardy-har-har.' Boys read *Sports Illustrated*; but some of them buy it just to show off. It's considered tough to be in sports.

"I don't know why I read those magazines. I think it's pretty sad to like them really. Maybe I like them because I like the posters. Maybe because I like a laugh. They can make a story out of nothing. And they even write ads for restaurants right in the copy. And they really build stars . . . how marvelous the stars are, how they love animals and people; they are the good people next door. But then they tell you how perfect those stars are—*not* just like the people next door. I think it is stupid and crazy and dumb to be so crazy about people we don't know. About how I can be 'Sean Cassidy's One and Only.' Boys aren't allowed to moon about."

She considers herself a feminist but confided, "It's not easy to be a feminist in junior high." It is not, of course, a difficulty limited just to some junior high students. But her statements suggest a dissatisfaction about the roles of girls and women presented in the magazines that are designed to tell her what growing up is all about. I talked with several of her friends; they said that they did not really read the magazines. Well, just for laughs. *Other* girls were serious about the magazines, they said, but they found that hard to understand because the magazines were so stupid. They each offered quotes from misleading cover headlines (e.g., "Eric [of the Rollers] Wants to Quit!" Inside, Eric is quoted as saying that he can't quit smoking). They had all been misled many times by these titles. The girls I talked with all had language skills which were not challenged by the prose of the journals. The readers are portrayed as followers of the stars, needing help in winning recognition by the stars. This literature suggests that the males are the leaders of females in most activities. Not surprisingly, at least some of the readers have ambivalent feelings about admitting that they read these magazines.

The pictures and prose of these fan magazines do suggest that for girls their appearance, and their relationship to others—female and male—must change for them now that they are teens. The journals for adolescent girls appear to concentrate more on advice about appearance, about the interests of males, and about what girls should say to males to win their attention and approval. The magazines for boys concentrate, in general, more on athletic skills, and automobile knowledge, and on rough and tough male life apart from females (in war zones, in the Wild West).

These differences in topics correspond in part with the differences in the way female and male adolescents are evaluated. Clothing and popularity with the other gender group are important factors in boys' and girls' evaluation of the status of girls. Athletic skill is an important determinant of the status of boys but not girls (Philip R. Newman and Barbara M. Newman, 1976:272).

These remarks about the context, the readers' perception, and the impact of the content of journals written for young adolescent males and females are speculative, based as they are on the observations of a total of thirty middle-class adolescents and adults. Yet this initial exploration, prompted by interest in Kaplan's thesis that girls at puberty become especially conscious of the restrictions on their public speech, does suggest that these magazines deserve our attention as we consider the formation, types, stereotypes, and evaluation of language differences between females and males.

NOTES

1. This is not to belittle the strength, magic, courage, independence and Amazon powers of WONDER WOMAN. For an essay of appreciation of the WONDER WOMAN comics of the 1940s, see Gloria Steinem (1972).

2. Barrie Thorne (correspondence) thinks that in contexts that stress gender differences and sexual objectifying (e.g., beauty contests), "personality" is sometimes a euphemism for physical appearance.

VI

SPEECH STYLES APPROACH

The relationship of females and males, as described in the "reconstructed psychoanalysis" and the "muted group" discussions, has been viewed by theorists as changeable yet basically unchanging. However the relationship is thought to be established—through an unconscious development, training, social interaction, or a combination of these—the relationship is, in general, presented as embedded in, and a basic feature of, social structure. Women and men are presented as acting, reacting, but only within a set gender asymmetry. The theorists have been interested in possibilities for change and in evidence that changes are being made: Shirley Ardener (1975) states, "It is important to remember that the relationship [between the dominant and the muted groups] will not necessarily be a constant one" (p. xxi); Cora Kaplan (1976) writes that while she gives an account of how women become segregated speakers she is not justifying the process; she encourages "invasion and subversion by female speakers" (p. 36). Yet in both cases the primary interest is in accounting for and describing the frequently occurring and long-enduring dominant-subordinate relationships between men and women.

This chapter provides a theoretical framework for examining the dynamics of the intergroup speech behavior of women and men, including change in that behavior. This discussion is based on several essays concerning language behavior between ethnic groups (Howard Giles, Richard Y. Bourhis, and Donald M. Taylor, 1977; Henri Tajfel, 1974) and an essay concerning the changing relationship between women and men (Jennifer A. Williams and Howard Giles, 1978). These essays (by present and past members of the social psychology department at the University of Bristol, England) propose a general framework for understanding the relationship between linguistic groups: the authors do not argue its use specifically for language/gender study. Yet material from their work can be extrapolated to provide a valuable approach for studying and explaining the linguistic behavior of women and men as members of subordinate and dominant groups, and for discussing the degree to which their language is central to women's and to men's sense of themselves.

The speech styles framework offers a method for studying the following topics:

1. The possible analogy between women and men as linguistic groups and other comparison groups (e.g., white/black, Welsh/English, young/old).

2. Political, historical, economic, and linguistic variables involved in an analysis of the vitality of the linguistic group *women*—how likely that members of the group will behave as and remain a distinctive, active, collective entity.

3. Shifts in speech styles—"convergence" and "divergence"—as women and men accommodate or not to the speech of members of the other group.

4. Methods by which members of a subordinate group (women) modify speech style in order to derive positive social identity.

5. Women's challenges to male hegemony and to men's arguments intended to keep women in a subordinate linguistic position.

Many studies of language and gender—like most sociolinguistic studies—have been conducted in a theoretical vacuum. In much of the work the unstated, but implicit, assumption about the relationship between language and society is that people who are in certain social "slots" and in particular social situations speak in certain ways which can be documented. The focus is on correlations—on the way language use varies with social position—rather than on causes or on social constraints on speakers. Correlational sociolinguistics assumes that social structure and language variation are independent yet, in inexplicable ways, systematically related. In correlational sociolinguistics women are considered a subgroup of people who use language a bit differently from other subgroups.[1]

The speech styles theorists also work from the premise that particular linguistic forms and genres of speech are differentially associated with social groups and thus serve as indicators to the group membership of individuals. For example, distinctive speech style is considered an important distinguishing characteristic of whites and blacks, and of Scots and English people. However, these theorists transform the static model into a more intricate and dynamic model by emphasizing (1) the ways that distinctive speech can be used by members of a group to create solidarity and to exclude members of outgroups from some interactions; (2) the ways that dominant group members use the distinctive features, actual or perceived, of the speech of subordinate groups as a focus for ridicule; and (3) the ways that speakers manipulate their speaking styles to emphasize or de-emphasize particular social identities.

The relationship between language and intergroup interactions is influenced by many psychological variables, as well as such social and situational variables as the group status, the size and distribution of the group, and the institutional support (for example, from churches, schools, unions, and other important agencies) for the group and its language. The speech styles approach recognizes that relationships between groups change as, for example, members of a subordinate group work to assert the value of their language, and the dominant group reacts by making it difficult for the subordinate group to re-evaluate and develop their linguistic distinctiveness.

While Robin Lakoff (1973) has written of the existence of a "woman's language," and I, in an essay (1975c), considered the possibility of "genderlects" (or systems of co-occurring, sex-linked linguistic signals), the results of many empirical language/gender studies of the past few years encourage caution now before making generalizations about extensive differences in the way women and men talk. Yet even if the linguistic differences already located or hinted at by past investigations are not extensive, a theory that deals with the social and psychological factors involved in the relationship of "linguistic" groups is useful for our studies. And as the several books and many essays on language/gender research attest, the *beliefs* concerning differences between men's speech and women's speech *are* extensive. Giles, et al. (1977) argue against taking too restrictive a view of "language," suggesting that two competitive or frequently compared social groups will likely have some speech style distinctions and that the members of the two groups will surely *think* there are group-specific speech differences (p. 21). They suggest that a distinct speech style (whether discernible or not to outsiders) is one of the most important symbols of a group. They also argue that group members will be most conscious of the distinctiveness of their speech when they live in proximity to members of the contrasting group.

As in the preceding chapters, I am not attempting here to write a précis or summary of the theoretical papers I use as base point, but rather to put forward some of the principles that seem to me to provide particular potential for analyzing past language/gender research and for suggesting a framework for future work. In this chapter I discuss material related to the first three of the five topics listed above. In the next chapter I mention some of the very recent changes in the way feminists are talking about and changing their speech, and reactions to the changes feminists advocate. While numerically relatively few women are involved in this reassessment, what they are saying about women's speech may have a major impact on women's status in the future.

WOMEN AND MEN AS LINGUISTIC GROUPS

We can usefully, at least in a provisional fashion, say that women and men constitute two linguistic groups, and that the speech styles approach provides a starting base for intergroup analysis. This seems a fair conclusion based on (a) consideration of past discussions by other researchers who indicate that the intergroup situation of women and men is similar to that of other groups linked by a subordinate/dominant relationship, and on (b) consideration of the importance of the prevalent belief that women and men speak differently.

Recently many people have compared the relationship of women and men to the relationship of blacks and whites, and to that of children and adults. (Arlie Russell Hochschild [1973] calls this approach the "minority perspective" [p. 256].) For example, women, like blacks (both men and women) and children, are more restricted in their movements outside the home, earn proportionately less, are not represented proportionately to their numbers on governing boards, and are more dependent upon the actions and evaluations of others.

The perceived intellectual capabilities, efforts, and speech of black men and women and white children and women, have been subjected to prejudice and discrimination by dominant groups, according to studies of these "minorities" (minorities in terms of power, not necessarily of numbers). Such comparisons have been provocative, in positing that a minority—white adult males—are in charge of a social structure based on many economic, political, and social inequalities.

Several people have made language comparisons along these lines, pointing out that women's and blacks' speech has been described by white males as emotional, intuitive, involving much verbal subterfuge, and employing some words not used, or used infrequently, by the dominant group. Additionally, both of these subdominant groups are said to use touch more, and in general to make more extensive use of nonverbal communication patterns. Playing dumb, dissembling, expressing frequent approval of others are said to be strategies common especially to white women and blacks (Hochschild, p. 256). Women, like children, are interrupted frequently (Candace West and Don H. Zimmerman, 1977); the descriptions of conversational interaction between adults and children also seem to apply in good part to at least stereotypical male and female conversation.

However, there are dissimilarities also. For example, black speech in the United States contains more systematic grammatical and phonological variants (in comparison to white speech) than does women's speech (in comparison to men's speech). Also, when males interrupt, females typically remain silent, while children more often continue to speak (West and Zimmerman). The differences among the groups in the continuance of membership, the demands made of the dominant group, the living arrangements, the numerical balance in the population, and the sociopolitical history provide difficulties in setting forth extensive, neat similarities between the groups.

Comparisons such as these have had limited success in both examining women's position in society *and* accounting for social change, and thus hold only limited promise for future work on language/gender. Nevertheless, the essays from Bristol suggest that a refocusing on certain political, historical, economic, and linguistic, as well as psychological, variables can lead to more helpful comparisons.

THE RELATIVE VITALITY OF WOMEN'S AND MEN'S SPEECH

The Bristol writers propose several situational variables that affect the likelihood that the paired linguistic groups will continue to survive as distinctive and active entities. The most important such variables (see Figure 1) are named as Status factors (economic, social, sociohistorical, and language evaluation), Demographic factors (for example, proximity to other members of the same group and to members of the contrasting group, and mobility), and Institutional Support factors (for example, representation in and recognition by business, cultural, and state policy bodies). These are the factors that need to be considered if we are to

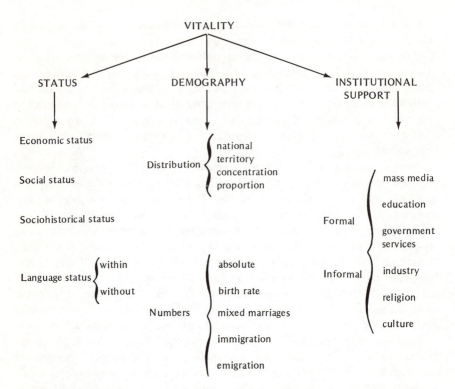

A taxonomy of the structural variables affecting linguistic vitality of groups. Howard Giles, Richard Y. Bourhis, and Donald M. Taylor (1977:309)

determine the vitality of the group—the group solidarity, and likelihood that the group members and others will continue to consider themselves, and be considered by others, as a distinctive linguistic entity.

At first glance, the Bristol group framework provides useful headings for the discussion of the vitality of men's speech. But by itself, it does not seem to explain how women's speech has survived as a perceived distinctive style. Also needed is a discussion of men's interests in the maintenance of something called women's speech—to increase the vitality of men's speech. I will discuss these matters in turn.

Status

In brief, women in the United States and Great Britain, in comparison to men, have relatively low economic and social status. Their supposed speech style (i.e., stereotyped speech style) is often ridiculed and is not considered an acceptable style for either men or women in public affairs. However, women do have a history—although it is not well recorded or publicized—of some collective efforts to present themselves as a separate, and in some ways superior, group.

As the many analyses of women's economic and social status make very clear, women have little control over their economic (mis)fortunes, and their social status is more often tied to their fathers or husbands than to their own responsibilities or achievements. As evidenced by inequitable incomes, advancements, and opportunities, the qualities and activities associated with males are more highly valued by the administrators of businesses and institutions than are the qualities and activities associated with females. Women are not able to bolster group morale by pointing to a period in which they have experienced control over their economic or social situation (although, for some, discussions of anthropological data and hypotheses about women's activities and importance in collecting/hunting societies, and stories about long-ago Amazon sisters may fulfill in part this function).

Evaluation

The evaluation accorded the language and its history is another factor suggested by Giles as important in assessing the status of a linguistic group. Much of the material in the preceding chapters is evidence that women's speech has not been highly evaluated, at least by men. One of the more eminent linguists of this century, Otto Jespersen (1922), presents women's speech as an aberration of men's speech. Women's vocabulary is, he claims, less extensive, their sentences are not as complex as men's, they talk more rapidly and with less thought than do men. According to Jespersen, women chatter, while men speak more analytically after greater reflection. Many authors have cited material from his 1922 chapter "The Woman." I found Elsie Clews Parsons' chapter "Sex Dialects" (in her 1913 *Old-Fashioned Woman*) quite by chance while searching library stacks for other material. Parsons, an anthropologist, discusses women's and men's differing use of swear words, exclamations, slang, adjectives, overstatements, and salutations, and differing control of vocabulary, topics of conversation, and verbal behavior in general. She discusses the control men exercise over women's speech, and some verbal strategies women use to lessen men's criticism.[2] (The "new" concerns of people working with language and gender are remarkably similar to those presented in Parsons' chapter; we could have profited in the early 1970s with less of Jespersen and more of Parsons.) Although Parsons became well-known and respected for her publications on Pueblo Indian cultures, I have not seen many citations to her early feminist books dealing with the relationships between women and men and with the topics and words that were considered "tabu" for women. (Her book, *Religious Chastity* [1913b], in which she describes the treatment of women as chattels in religious practices, was published under a male pseudonym, John Main.)

Etiquette books for the past 200 years have cautioned women about their gossiping, their often sense-less and excessive talk, and their high-pitched voices (Connie Eble, 1976; and Kramer, 1975a). (Statements about the speech of women and of men have remained remarkably constant for those 200 years.) Yet many of those guides also refer to the way women's speech reflects their natural goodness. Eliza Farrar (1836) wrote, "Women are happily endowed with a quick sense of propriety, and a natural modesty, which will generally guide them aright in their intercourse with the other sex" (p. 290). The comments of Richard Wells (1892) are typical of those found in many etiquette books of both the nineteenth and twentieth centuries:

> Women observe all the delicacies of propriety in manners, and all the shades of impropriety, much better than men; not only because they attend to them earlier and longer, but because their perceptions are more refined than those of the other sex, who are habitually employed about greater things. Women divine, rather than arrive at proper conclusions. (p. 34)

Women's speech, from this point of view, reflects women's innate frailness, modesty, and irrationality. The authors of many of the etiquette books and of the contemporary "true womanhood" books do argue that, although there is much to be deplored in women's speech, there is also something of special value;[3] not to the world of reason, but for the maintenance of smooth relationships between people.

High school and college students (women and men) have also indicated that, although they believe men's and women's speech differ in many aspects (Kramer, 1977), they do not perceive women's speech as further from that of the "ideal" speaker. In fact, women's speech was rated "more ideal" on more items (the characteristics rated were those listed by students as differentiating male and female speakers) than men's speech (Kramer, 1978). These results do not necessarily represent accurately people's feelings about women's speech during actual interaction, and they do not tell us about the saliency or significance of the individual speech characteristics—that is, which qualities are to be preferred in different sorts of conversations. Perhaps it would be more effective or more noticeable in many social situations for a speaker to use, for example, a low voice pitch than to use an open, self-revealing speech style. (Men receive more positive ratings for their lower pitch, women more positive ratings for their more "open" speech style.) While few people claim that women's speech is esteemed, most people probably do not give it the low evaluations that cartoon and joke writers would have us believe it has.

Yet, as many writers have pointed out, male speech *is* the norm (see Barrie Thorne and Nancy Henley, 1975; Dale Spender, 1977; Nancy Faires Conklin (1974); women's speech is seen as a deviation from "real speech"—just as black dialect is "non-standard" since it does not conform to white dialect norms. Although in the past individual women from time to time have spoken or written of the specific values of women's speech (e.g., Charlotte Perkins Gilman, 1911),[4] until very recently there has been no concerted, sustained campaign by women to gain recognition of their speech as valuable precisely in its *difference* from men's speech. Only very recently has men's criticism of women's speech itself been a unifying force for women (as now they are organizing, for example, convention programs and study groups on the topic of linguistic oppression), and still probably only for a relatively small number of women.

In sum, women have relatively low economic, social, sociohistorical, and language status. But they have never been as unadventuresome, untrying, untalented, and unsuccessful in their work in the "real" world as our history books would lead us to believe. The media coverage of women's activities often supports the view of women having only recently begun to show expertise in anything other than the traditional "women's tasks." The media are interested primarily in dramatic "firsts"—for example, women appointed or elected to offices.[5] (As I started collecting the many "first" articles in newspapers and magazines during the past several years I came to understand more deeply just how many ways women have been excluded from public activities.) The emphasis on these "firsts" (1) fosters a belief that women's public role is changing and deflects attention from the overall (basically unchanging) employment locations and wages of females relative to those of males, and (2) fosters a belief that only traditional "men's" positions and activities are important. As shown by recent government reports comparing women's employment over the past fifteen years, women are, in general, still directed into the same jobs at, in general, the same relatively low status and pay (Jane Bryant Quinn, 1979).[6] As historians such as Mary Ritter Beard and Gerda Lerner make clear, women have been important participants in history. However, females are not yet born into a sense of a rich history illustrating proud collective efforts.

Distribution and numbers

Demographic factors are also usefully considered in an analysis of the strength and stability of a group, according to Giles et al. The more numerous the members of a group, the higher the birth rate, and the more members concentrated in the same geographic area—all in relationship to the demographic features of the contrast group—the more vitality the group will exhibit. The initial observations concerning male-female demographic features are obvious. In actual numbers, females just outnumber males, and barring interventions such as war this ratio remains constant. Except in a few locales (e.g., mining towns that have experienced a severe accident, or frontier towns) geographical areas seldom have marked male or female concentrations.

Yet, considering only sheer numbers and general geographical distribution of women ignores the specific locations of women—millions of whom live in private households with men. (This isolation in private houses is not, of course, equally prevalent for women of all races and social classes in the United States and Great Britain. Carol B. Stack [1974] discusses, for example, the strong bonds among black ghetto women.) Information on the daily movements of women within their communities and their interaction with each other is very limited because it has just not been considered relevant to an understanding of the social structure.

However, Susan Ervin-Tripp (1976) suggests that study of the speech of people who live together but who differ in gender and in the amount and type of interaction they have with other women and men can give us important information about speech diversification and about social structure. Unlike racial or class groups, women and men seldom experience residential segregation; their daily lives are more intertwined.

In a study of black women in a rural area of South Carolina, Patricia C. Nichols (1976) found that those women who travelled frequently within and outside their communities and who had opportunities for upward mobility were more likely to adopt "standard" forms of English grammar than were women who had more restricted social experiences and opportunities. Nichols (1978) argues that we need to study the differing experiences, opportunities, and goals available to women and men in order to explain any diversity found in the speech of women and men: "First and foremost, women are members of small face-to-face speech communities, and it is in the context of these relationships that they speak."

Institutional support

In addition to status and demographic factors, another major factor proposed as affecting the stability and longevity of a linguistic group is the institutional support, formal and informal, it receives. Pressure groups, organized from within a language group, provide informal support and help safeguard the group's interests, according to Giles et al., who suggest that the existence of such groups is a source of vitality for the represented language group. Support comes through recognition of the group members and their language from such institutions as mass media, and state and national government.

Although women are not as conscious of themselves as a separate linguistic group as are, say, the Welsh, women have in the past, sometimes, organized themselves to put pressure on officials to recognize that women *are* speakers. One example: women of the Fawcett Society in London worked to encourage the BBC to hire women as radio and television announcers. Their efforts were not very successful; they did, however, call the public's attention to the bias of the BBC officials and to their inconsistent arguments over the years on why women are not desirable as news announcers. Men in the past have often worked through institutions to segregate women and their language. (Mr. A. Stewart was the BBC official interviewed by a London *Daily Herald* reporter [22 June 1937] following an announcement that women commentators had been banned by the BBC from programs covering the visit of the King and Queen to Edinburgh. The news account stated, "No woman has been found who can come into line with a male commentator on a serious or symbolic occasion" and Mr. Stewart explained to the reporter that women are quite suitable for "frivolous" occasions.)

Women are not well-represented on the policy-making level of institutions. Although there has been in the past few years a very slight increase in the percentage of women workers employed in management jobs, most of these women "executives" have relatively little say in important corporate decision-making (Quinn, 1979). One of the reasons men give for not wanting women to hold jobs in mass media, government, armed forces, law, and religion is that women cannot speak in appropriate ways. Women do not have, according to many men, authoritative voices. But of course until women are in positions considered important, their voices will not carry authority.

Considering men and women as two linguistic groups, and evaluating the groups in terms of status, demographic, and institutional support factors, give us a useful perspective on the relationship between men's speech and women's speech.

Working just from the framework offered by Giles et al., one would probably conclude that women's speech is not an entity with much of a sparkling past. Women do, of course, steadily constitute fifty-one percent of the population, and do have frequent interaction with other women. However, women are low in economic and social status, and their language is not considered the medium of technology, business, politics, or science. Women have little representation at decision-making levels of state, business, and cultural institutions. This situation has existed for many years. Why, then, has there remained a concept or a speech style called "women's speech"?

Maintenance of women's speech

It appears that in this case the dominant group is safeguarding the existence of the speech style of the minority group. For example, while the speech of blacks and other ethnic minority groups is at present virtually ignored by the advertisements and commercials in the mass media in the United States and Great Britain, the stereotype of the speech of women *is* represented in the media. Women in advertisements often express uncertainty, and talk in stereotypically (i.e., nonserious, and nonrational) ways about topics considered trivial by men. For example, a woman with small (uncertain) smile, biting a fingernail, says, "I wonder if I'm pregnant." A woman, frowning, hand to her face, says, "I switched from clay litter to _____ when my granddaughter said, 'Grandma's house smells like a kitty box!' " A smiling movie star, touting a shampoo, says, "Try _____. You'll love your hair." Another woman, praising *her* shampoo, exclaims, "I was flat [-haired, -spirited] til I went fluffy with _____." (Examples are from advertisements in *Family Circle*, 15 December 1978.) School readers seldom represent people speaking in ethnic or regional dialects. But as numerous studies have indicated, girls and women portrayed in school readers do often speak in stereotypical female ways.[7]

This brief discussion of the factors proposed by Giles et al. as important in an analysis of the relations of various linguistic groups, and the possible application of these factors to an understanding of the relationship between women and men, is only intended to be suggestive. Any theoretical approach abstracts, of course, and the speech styles framework as it is used here may put too much emphasis on *differences* between the way men and women talk. Further inquiries into factors involved in intergroup situations may make clearer the similarities and differences of the male-female speech dichotomy to those of other contrast groups, as well as offering an explanation of the differences. Quite possibly the degree to which the speech styles of the contrast groups are mutually understandable is an important factor in determining the actions that the dominant group take in dealing with the speech style of the subordinate group. Men can insist that women have a different speech style and can encouarge a separateness (by, for example, discouraging women from learning the lexicons of politics, law, finance, philosophy, and other specialized fields of discourse) without being themselves excluded from knowledge of the women, without losing business, and while safeguarding their own jobs and status—because the speech styles are similar in a way that French or Welsh are not similar to English.

The preceding sections of this chapter were concerned with the relationship of the two (linguistic) groups, women and men. They were analyses at a macrolinguistic level. In the following paragraphs, I am interested in the way knowledge of the intergroup relationships may affect actual speech practices when individual members of the contrast groups, males and females, converse. The assumption of much of the past work on the presentation of women's speech in mass media is that the evaluation of women's speech as expressed through the (primarily) male institutions has an important, pervasive effect on male/female communication. The authors of the many recent studies of the manner in which dictionaries and textbooks often present males and their language as the norm, and females and their language as aberrant trivialities, usually argue that these presentations both reflect and strengthen the day-to-day evaluation men make of women (Candace Helgeson, 1976; Casey Miller and Kate Swift, 1976). The widespread use of the generic masculine pronoun perpetuates the male-is-norm viewpoint. Experiments by Wendy Martyna (1978a; 1978b) and by Donald G. MacKay and David C. Fulkerson (1979) demonstrate that listeners and readers do not consider the "generic" *he* as neutral, referring equally to both men and women. The assumption, sometimes explicit and sometimes implicit, of these studies is that the evaluation of women and of their speech, as represented for example in the media, is linked to the way women are evaluated and talked to on the personal level.

WOMEN'S SPEECH ACCOMMODATION

The theory of speech accommodation proposed by Howard Giles (1977), combined with the intergroup theory just discussed, provides a conceptual framework for studying the role of language in group relations and in interpersonal relations. It, like the other theories discussed, is a theory very much in-progress: Giles and others are exploring its possibilities, learning its advantages and disadvantages. It is an attempt to explain how language can be used to express one's relationship to and distinctness from others. Within this framework, language and gender study is not a matter, as in some studies, of matching up various verbal behaviors of females and males to an undefined structure of male dominance, but rather an inspection of the interplay among members of social groups and of the motivations that underlie changes in speech style between and among individuals.

Individuals are seen, as in the work of Henri Tajfel (1974) and George Kelly (1955), as continually active, categorizing and defining themselves and the rest of their environment. For many people, among the more stable of core categories used to understand the world are such categories as blacks and whites, female and male. People's knowledge of their own membership in particular categories or groups and of the value of that membership as assessed by themselves and members of the contrast groups determines people's social identity. Our actions even on the interpersonal level are, then, related to our perceived membership in various social groups of people, for as we interact with others we are concerned with evaluating, and being evaluated by, others as members of social groups (Tajfel, 1974).

Giles proposes that people continually adjust speech style to reduce or accentuate the linguistic differences between speakers—in order to communicate social similarity, difference, approval, disapproval, or desire for approval. A shift toward the perceived speech style of another he terms *convergence*; a shift away is called *divergence*. According to this theory of speech accommodation, in most cases the more a speaker wants the approval of another, the more that speaker will attempt to converge—that is, to match the speech of the person whose approval is desired. Convergence and divergence involve both how a message is transmitted and what is said. Convergence toward a high prestige language variety is called "upward"; toward a low prestige variety, "downward." When both speakers desire approval the higher prestige speaker may shift downward while the other moves upward and mutual speech convergence occurs. An elaboration of the theory is contained in Howard Giles and Peter F. Powesland (1975) and Giles et al. (1977).

The motivations for people's differing speech styles in any one situation are not always self-evident. For example, divergence between two individuals may mean, among other possibilities: (1) that the speakers belong to different social groups and in their speech are trying to maintain distinctiveness; (2) that the speakers do not have repertoires that allow for convergence; (3) that one or both speakers are attempting to speak what she or he thinks is a style admired by the other (for instance, a young male talking to a female whom he wishes to impress may use many characteristics of stereotypical male speech, to gain approval and emphasize distinctiveness); or (4) that one speaker is trying to help the other or others learn another speech style (for instance, a parent or a teacher may use a grammatical complexity not used by the child). Clearly divergence cannot be explained simply by citing hostility on the part of one or both speakers; in fact, it cannot be explained simply at all.[8]

The measurement of speech style (let alone its perceived effectiveness), over the course of any one interaction, is problematic. What are the salient speech elements for the participants? Are they the same for both (or all) the participants? How can these elements be measured? (What the linguist hears may not be what the participants hear.) These problems and questions will necessitate further investigation. The analysis of speech style or of conversation is not easy: however, the purpose of a theoretical model is to help us handle, that is, "understand," the complexities of the phenomenon. The present form of the accommodation theory gives us ideas of the number of variables that may be relevant to various interactions and some tentative ways the variables may be related.

What is of special interest for our work on language/gender is that the argument chain that Giles et al. (1977) propose links discussion of intergroup relations and interpersonal relations through speech: (a) Humans are from birth actively trying to make sense of their environment by categorizing themselves and their world. Gender is a basic organizing category of our social structure. (b) People's social identity and self-evaluation are derived from knowledge of their perceived membership in social groups and from the perceived evaluation of those groups by the contrast groups. The language variety associated with a social group is usually a highly salient dimension of a group's identity. (c) Through speech style shifts, individuals work at establishing and communicating their distinctiveness.

As this material makes so clear, what speakers say to each other is a function of many factors. Simon N. Herman (1961) suggests that background situations, personal needs, and the immediate situation are important variables. Giles and Powesland (1975) list the following as involved: emotional factors (temperament, mood, cognitive functioning), motivations of the speakers, the topic, the formality of the situation, as well as the speakers' and hearers' perceived membership in social groups—for example, age group, ethnic group, and gender group.

The difficulty of weighing the importance of these various factors in various situations makes it seem virtually impossible to set forth generalizations about the speech of women and men in mixed-sex interactions. But some researchers, although recognizing the complexities, have made some generalizations—if not about speech style shift, at least about some overall qualities of speech style. For example, J. L. Dillard (1972) writes:

> There is a complex interaction of these sociological factors [age, class, status-grading, and peer group influence]. There are also probably some personality factors which make for a kind of individual variation. But we can be sure that an upward mobile female Negro past the age of about fourteen will speak something relatively close to Standard English; on the other hand, a six-year-old ghetto resident (male or female) will usually speak something which is amazingly different from Standard English. (p. 239)

Several writers (e.g., Roger Abrahams, 1973) have suggested that black women are more likely than black men to have fairly frequent verbal interaction with white middle-class speakers, to talk more "sweet" and to use convergent speech tactics both with speakers of black dialect and speakers of what is called by many educators and linguists Standard English (i.e., the style sanctioned by the education system).

Describing and analyzing male/female conversations of either blacks or whites in terms of the speech styles theory is more difficult. Giles and Powesland (1975) note that we will have difficulties in describing and explaining male/female conversation, even if we know that each speaker is seeking the approval of the other. Attempts at approval may not always involve trying to match speech styles but may involve trying to set up "complementary" speech styles. Courtship speech may involve exaggerated "macho" and "femme" speech styles. Take, for example, the tough male football player interested in receiving approval from a relatively unathletic young woman:

> One might suppose that he would not advance his courtship by modelling his manner on hers but would be wiser to maintain or even exaggerate his own virile and masterful style of speech and behavior. This is not to say that no accommodation is likely to take place in heterosexual encounters. . . . The point is that there may be a conflict between accommodative tendencies and constraints to behave according to sexual norms and stereotypes. These norms may be acknowledged and subscribed to by both parties. (p. 167)

As they conclude: "The outcome as far as speech is concerned is not easy to predict" (p. 167).

This courtship example indicates that the dynamics of speech differentiation between females and males is not parallel in all respects to the dynamics of interaction between members of other paired linguistic groups such as black/white or Welsh/English. The ritualized relations of females and males (in dating and in "courtesy" customs, for example) seem designed to stress gender differences to win approval. Women and men who join campus sororities and fraternities may want the same-gender bonding in order to elevate their status as desired females or males and thus facilitate cross-gender approval. Barrie Thorne has suggested (personal correspondence) that the ritualized sharpened divergence—the exaggeration of gender differences—in these and other segregated youth organizations might be seen as extensions of the strong female/male segregations and ritualized relations (e.g., the name calling and the chasing) between groups of girls and boys on school playgrounds.

The difficulties of applying the speech styles theory to predict and explain female/male interaction are endemic. Every speech exchange is governed not only by a matrix of the sort of sociological and demographic factors that Giles et al. write about, but by the personal capabilities and felt needs taken into a conversation by each of its participants. Every conversation constitutes its own phenomenological reality as it proceeds. Use of the speech styles theory, although focusing on gender differences, also involves a certain reduction of the theory, as would the focusing on any one or several of the multitude of relevant factors.

Recognizing the difficulty of trying to explain, let alone predict, speech diversity in any female-male encounter, I set out below only a few indications of how the speech style model might be usefully employed in language/gender study.

SPEECH STYLE ADJUSTMENT

First, although Eleanor Emmons Maccoby and Carol Nagy Jacklin (1974) conclude from their review of studies of gender differences that *girls* are not more "social" than boys and not more motivated to receive social rewards, many researchers—both "naive" and professional—believe that *women* do have a greater need for social approval than men. Giles and Powesland (1975) hypothesize that people requiring a relatively great deal of social approval will do more accommodating than those who have a low need (p. 159). Robin Lakoff (1975) writes that girls of ten "retain their old ways of [childish] speech" but that "most women who get as far as college learn to switch from women's to neutral language under appropriate situations (in class, talking to professors, at job interviews, and such)" (p. 6). She thinks that women, at least those who stay in formal educational settings for many years, are more likely than men to shift speech styles frequently. Women are expected to accommodate to men's speech style in more settings than the reverse. (In the past few years mass circulation magazines in the United States and Great Britain have carried articles on the clothing and speech style options and recommendations [e.g., "mother earth" and "businessman-like"] for women employed outside the home.) So we can hypothesize that women will do more accommodating to the speech of men than vice-versa, at least in formal situations.

Research by Lewis Levine and Harry J. Crockett, Jr. (1966) indicates that women are more likely than men to change phonetic speech patterns as the formality of the speech context changes. (Patricia C. Nichols [correspondence] calls this "linguistic flexibility.") They made their analysis by examining tapes on which respondents were asked to perform various speaking tasks, not by examining tapes of "natural" speech in various locations. Jenny Cheshire (1978) taped the conversations of teenage boys and girls, first as they interacted on a playground and later as they talked in a classroom, and found that girls made more pronunciation changes toward Standard English than did the boys as they moved from the informal setting to the more formal classroom setting. She was concerned in her study only with phonological comparison between the boys and girls in the two settings and not with a wide range of stylistic elements or with comparison of talk between the same individuals in the two settings.

Obviously a study designed to measure and compare the ways males and females possibly alter speech style in several settings when talking with several people would present the researcher with a number of mechanical and methodological difficulties. If radio microphones (as used in the study of the conversation of a married couple [William F. Soskin and Vera P. John, 1963] and between parents and children [B. Woll, L. Ferrier, and Gordon Wells, 1975]) could be employed to "track" the speech of individuals as they speak in various physical settings, on various topics and/or to various people, the resulting data body would likely be both daunting (in amount of data to analyze) and valuable (for our understanding of speech style shifts).

More limited studies may also be useful in determining whether in male/female conversations women are more likely to shift speech in order to match the nonverbal and verbal behavior of men than vice versa. Shirley Weitz (1976) found gender differences in shifting in a carefully controlled study in which the videotaped nonverbal behavior of unacquainted women and men was coded by raters who saw only one of the interactants at a time—and so did not know the gender of the other person in the conversation. The women in the female/male conversations adjusted their nonverbal responses to the males' nonverbal responses. The women were rated as more submissive when conversing with dominant men and as more dominant when with submissive men. Men did not make such adaptive responses; nor did women in the female/female interactions. Review of other studies that suggest that women make more adaptive nonverbal responses to men than vice versa can be found in Nancy Henley (1977) and Marianne La France and Clara Mayo (1979).

Jacqueline Sachs (1975), and John R. Edwards (1979), found that prepubertal boys and girls, that is, children with vocal tracts of similar size, can be identified as boys or girls from their voices, suggesting that females and males may modify their voices (smoothness, intonation patterns, pitch) in order to make themselves more easily discernible as female or as male—or perhaps for other reasons such as to be heard as more polite or more independent. (Sally McConnell-Ginet [1978b] reviews intonation research.)

Focusing on the use of address terms by males and females may give some indication of whether, in general, women are more sensitive to, and/or more ready to adjust to the speech of males. (Accommodation theory predicts that low status groups will adapt their speech style to receive approval from high status groups.) In a study (Cheris Kramer, 1975b) of the forms of address used in literature, I found that fictive men frequently in first meetings—before a high intimacy factor could be considered to be operating—address young women in very familiar and often slighting terms (for example, *lovely, ninny, lady, slut, honey, baby,* and *bitch*). Fictive women did not frequently address men with whom they had little acquaintance—perhaps because in reality the subordinate status of women and their language restrict them when speaking to men from taking the liberties in speech that men can take when speaking to women. Men perhaps are more likely to use the same terms of address for many people in many situations. In fiction at least, women are more likely to wait until they have been addressed before they address, and to use an address "correct" for the situation even if they have not been "correctly" addressed. Here is another possible instance where a person desiring approval may not try convergence in speech style since, as McConnell-Ginet (1978a) points out, addressing someone is "locating the addressee in a social and interpersonal space relative to oneself" (p. 23).

We could look for evidence that women may accommodate more than do men by checking to see how, in initial conversations, women and men attempt to determine the interests and the speech style of the other. For instance, we might check such variables as which speaker asks more questions and/or which does less talking and more listening. Here also several explanations would be possible if women were found to talk more. Women are often said to be "conversation smoothers," to talk in times of perceived tension or uncertainty in order to help put other participants at ease. Also, Mercilee Jenkins has suggested to me that women show more interest in the social function of talking than men do. Talking with others (not just *to* others) is a more important, satisfying activity for women, perhaps.

We could listen for women's use of questions, both in all-women groups, and in mixed-gender groups. That college women, working in problem-solving groups, used questions more frequently in presence of men (while the men's rates did not change much from the same-gender to the mixed-gender groups) suggests that women may feel more need to be supportive and show their subordination, when they are with men (Julie R. McMillan et al., 1977).[9]

We might consider the values women and men assign to the speech of working-class and middle-class speech of women and men. Peter Trudgill (1975) and William Labov (1966) have found that men associate positive masculine values with working-class speech. In another study, middle-class women and men guessing the gender of children heard on tape misidentified more working-class girls than working-class boys, while for middle-class children, more boys were misidentified. The researcher, John R. Edwards (1979), writes, "the working-class voices were perceived as being lower, rougher and more masculine than the middle-class voices" (p. 125). Future work with the speech styles framework—and thus a focus on the social identity of speakers and their intergroup relations—should lead us to additional investigations of the intersections of class, race, and gender.

The speech styles theory might be used to study the verbal behavior of the lone man or woman in a work situation. Will, for instance, the women holding "men's jobs" attempt to win approval from their colleagues by accommodating to their speech? Will they, as Phyllis Chesler and Emily Jane Goodman (1976) suggest, shift speech style by at times dropping their voices (to emulate males) and at times using flirtatious giggles (to show their distinctiveness)?

Does the entrance of a woman into a previously all-male gathering increase the number of swear words and other "male-group" words or jokes, as some feminists have suggested?

VALUE OF SPEECH STYLES THEORY

This framework draws attention to the relationships of intergroup evaluations, personal social identity, and speech style. A plenitude of possible factors and relationships involved in any encounter have been suggested. Formulating specific explanations and predictions based on the theory will not be easy.[10] Yet an adequate account of the relationship of gender and language must include recognition of many if not all of the variables discussed by the Bristol group.

A further value of the approach of the Bristol group is that it is not based only on traditional linguistic variables. While some phonological differences have been consistently found in the speech of males and females of varying ages and in various locations in Great Britain and the United States, researchers studying, for example, syntactic usage, lexicon, and intonation have not found extensive or consistent differences. Studies that have focused on *interaction* have produced observations that suggest that gender differences will be found not in, say, word counts but rather in patterns of conversational assertiveness and supportiveness, and in verbal and nonverbal gestures of dominance and submission (Pam Fishman, 1977, 1978). Barrie Thorne and Nancy Henley (1975) argue that "Language helps enact and transmit every type of inequality, including that between the sexes [, and] helps maintain the larger political-economic structure" (p. 15). If we want to deal with the language of comparison groups within a political-economic structure, a theoretical framework designed to explore those interrelationships deserves our attention.

NOTES

1. Not all sociolinguistics can be defined in this way. For example, Dell Hymes in publications spanning many years has consistently advocated the study of meanings that speakers themselves have for social contexts and uses of language; that is, the study of the functional importance of language for speakers. He is interested in studying the claims people make on and for their language, the skills and interests of the linguist as they are related to

the language skills and interests of the members of the speech group studied (1972), the integration of linguistic and social features in a systematic theory (1974), speech "as a mode of action," not as a static abstraction (1971:67), and language as a structure which transmits values and which does not serve all speakers equally well (1973). Hymes has made references to men's and women's ways of speaking an integral part of some of his discussions, as when he argues that it is impossible to adequately deal with linguistic competence apart from a discussion of social structure; in illustration he writes that the forms of competence expected of and allowed women are often quite different from the forms expected of and allowed men (1974).

2. For example, Parsons writes:

Women . . . are apologetic about using certain words to men. "Is that the right word?" or "Is that the way you pronounce it?" is a kind of self-deprecatory question they are apt to ask in using unfamiliar or technical terms. It protects them against an anticipated charge of pedantry, recognizing the fact of their trespass, but disarming male criticism by its appeal. (1913a:155)

3. The contemporary "true womanhood" authors continue this tradition. In her book *Fascinating Womanhood,* Helen B. Andelin (1975) writes about the power of women's speech to heal their husbands' wounds inflicted by others. She argues that by using "childlike mannerisms" such as pouting, putting hands to face and saying "Oh dear!" women ease tension in their marriage (pp. 294-295). Oleda Baker (1975) writes that "women were created to be nurturers" and to listen to their husbands (pp. 29-30). Women, both of these authors argue, are not inferior to men, only wonderfully compatibly different. In each case, however, women are advised to accept any perceived imperfections of their mates, while at the same time advised to work hard to become in the eyes of their husbands "complete" and perfect wives in speech and other deeds.

4. Gilman writes in 1911 of "our androcentric culture" in which the male "assumes his influence to be normal, human, and the female influence to be wholly a matter of sex" (p. 154). Our language structure helps reveal this androcentrism:

The adjectives and derivatives based on woman's distinctions are alien and derogatory when applied to human affairs; "effeminate"—too female, connotes contempt, but has no masculine analogue; whereas "emasculate"—not enough male, is a term of reproach, and has no feminine analogue. (p. 22)

In an article published in 1938, J. M. Steadman, Jr., reports collecting a list of words college men and women thought affected or effeminate—and the students made little distinction between the two, Steadman writes. Most of the words they disliked were associated with descriptions of females or with the stereotyped speech or activities of females. None of the words were classified as masculine. (Examples of words listed as effeminate: darling, dear, delicious, divine, doily, giggle, lovely, luncheon, and stunning.)

5. Discussing these media "firsts," Louise Kapp Howe (1978) writes:

Very often when you check back through history you will discover that what has been labeled a "first" is really not one at all. Very often when it *is* unprecedented, you find that the numbers following after turn out to be disappointingly small. And . . . even when there is a substantial dent made in a formerly "male" occupation, the odds are enormous that you are still talking about only a tiny fraction of the female workforce . . . and that within that occupation the highest levels continue to be reserved for males. (pp. 4-5)

6. Relatively few women earn "men's" salaries. In the United States, only five percent of those earning more than $15,000 are women; but sixty-nine percent of those earning between $3,000 and $5,000 are women (Quinn, 1979). The median income of white males is the greatest, followed by that of black males, white females, and black females. Again, contrary to the commentary in many media stories, the difference between the average income of black families and white families has increased in recent years. Approximately four out of every ten black families are headed by a female, an increase from a decade ago when the ratio

was one in four. The comparable figure for whites is one in ten. While a few women have been hired for showcase jobs, in general the economic and social standing of women relative to that of men has not improved much during the "affirmative action" years (Alfred L. Malabre, Jr. [1979], of the *Wall Street Journal,* quoted in *The* [Urbana-Champaign] *Morning Courier,* 18 March 1979, p. 33).

7. The textbooks, the advertisements, and other fiction help create and support the stereotypes of female speech. In other words, many of the jokes men make about the way women talk are based on a myth men have themselves created.

8. Discussion of convergence is no more clear-cut. Giles, who read an earlier version of this chapter, made a marginal note "Love it!" on one page of the manuscript. Was he (1) modifying his writing style to express himself in a more "feminine" way to this female writer, and/or (2) expressing approval in a way that is conventional for him in many situations, and/or (3) showing sarcasm by mimicking "female" talk and emphasis? *My* interpretation (1 and 2) of that note was based not only on the form of the other marginal notes (the context) but also on my background knowledge concerning such factors as his regular speaking and writing habits, his past verbal behavior toward me and other women who talk and write to him about language/gender research, and my need to believe that he was making a positive comment. Of course, face-to-face interaction provides nonverbal and intonation cues to help listeners evaluate people's comments (and much diverging and converging probably involves matching or not of gestures, pauses, accent, and speech rate). Yet these examples indicate some of the complexities involved in analyzing the ways people may modify their speech to others in order to stress or minimize linguistic and social differences between them.

9. The strategy theory (Chapter VIII) might be a more useful framework for this investigation as we listen not only to the ways women may "acknowledge" their subordination, but also to the ways men attempt to control conversation. Zimmerman and West (1975, 1978), recording two-party conversations in a variety of places, found that in mixed-gender interaction almost all interruptions and overlaps were by male speakers. Barbara Eakins and R. Gene Eakins (1978), studying tapes of university faculty meetings, noted that females (especially those with low departmental status) took fewer speaking turns, but were interrupted proportionally more than the males (69).

10. Giles et al. (1977) do discuss the "likely linguistic strategies" used by speakers of dominant and subordinate groups when dealing with members of the outgroup, depending upon whether or not speakers perceive alternative ways of seeing the existing intergroup relationship. For example, if members of a subordinate group perceive no cognitive alternatives to the present intergroup situation, they are likely to consider their low status as resulting from the inferior characteristics of their group. Some speakers may accept the inevitability of their inferiority. Others may try to disassociate themselves from their own group, adopting the speech patterns of the dominant group in an effort at individual social mobility upward. However, when subordinate group members do perceive alternatives to the intergroup situations, they are likely to advocate social change, to blame the dominant group for their oppression, and to stress the distinctiveness of their speech. It is important to recognize, then, that not all group members will react in the same way to the intergroup situation. These ideas are discussed in the next chapter.

VII

SPEAKING OUT
AND SHOUTING DOWN

Women and men as social groups are seldom even mentioned in academic discussions of intergroup attitudes and relationships. Other groups are thought to be formed at least in part by social, economic, and political processes, but the gender groups are usually seen as universal and permanent. Men and women are seen as so intermixed that we do not often think of them in large group terms. A change in the relationship of other groups is often considered a possibility (and so people discuss the benefits, evils, or dangers of ghettos, and of intermarriage among, for example, blacks and whites, Jews and Gentiles, English-speaking and French-speaking Canadians).

White women (and blacks) are defined unequal at birth, for life. Yet while it is increasingly becoming "improper" to ask, on questionnaires and application forms, about the race of respondents, asking individuals whether they are male or female is still acceptable. I think it is now generally assumed that social scientists and public officials should have a socially acceptable reason for asking questions about people's race. The whiteness or blackness of a person's skin is no longer said, at least in "polite" or "official" talk, to be a factor that tells others how that person should be categorized, explained, and treated. One's gender, however, is still considered by many as a primary, stable, permanent characteristic, which can be used, without apology, to predict and explain behavior.

In the last chapter I discussed some of the political, historical, economic, and linguistic variables involved in an analysis of the stability and strength of the paired linguistic groups, women and men. In this chapter I explore the consequences of considering these not as stable linguistic groups, but as groups whose identities are mutually connected and in flux.[1]

An essay by Jennifer A. Williams and Howard Giles (1978) suggests that a theory of intergroup behavior (Henri Tajfel's [1974]) can be utilized to examine the *changing* relationship between women and men. Their essay, although not concerned specifically with language, can provide a framework for a brief discussion of some of the strategies feminists are advocating and putting into effect in their own speech, and for a discussion of the responses of others to the increasing number of suggestions and demands for changes in sexist language.

The Tajfel approach which Williams and Giles utilize posits that categorization is one of the cognitive tools we use to define both ourselves and the world. Our social identity, part of our self-concept, is derived from our knowledge of the social groups we belong to and the values we believe are attached to other groups. Tajfel is particularly interested in "inferior" groups—that is, groups that are often negatively evaluated—and in the methods group members employ to achieve a positive self-image.

One method is to accept the "inferiority" of the group and work to achieve a positive position by individual means. If, however, many members of the group believe their low status is unjustified, they may employ group-oriented actions in order to achieve a positive social identity. These actions will be responded to by the dominant group, members of which will use strong social action in order to try to maintain their group's superiority.

Williams and Giles suggest that today one strategy some women are using to change their status is to collectively refuse to accept the negative definition of themselves that has been organized and perpetuated by men. One method women particularly concerned with the effects of language are using is to cull dictionaries, fiction, and conversation for the terms used to define women, in order to document the type and extent of the linguistic put-down of women. This is the technique used by, for example, Alleen Pace Nilsen (1977), Varda One (1970), the Bristol [England] Women's Liberation Group (n.d.), and the editors of the *Feminist English Dictionary: An Intelligent Woman's Guide to Dirty Words* (1973). In the introductory commentary to that dictionary Ruth Todasco writes that while the old dictionaries cannot be rewritten at once "a general awareness of their sexism must weaken their authority" (p. iii). She argues that talking about words that have been men's property (e.g., the many epithets for women) exposes and destroys some of the power that the words have had over women. The women studying and writing about traditional dictionaries are questioning the way that language and women have been treated by those who have determined the paradigms for the study of language and women.

In addition to pointing out and analyzing the manner in which women have been set aside and negatively defined by men, a number of women are also concerned with defining themselves and their interests. Early in the contemporary Women's Liberation movement, many feminists were consciously developing a vocabulary to deal with their concerns. (For example, an article in the *Long Island Press*, 21 November 1970, p. 8, lists thirteen new expressions—including *sexist, male chauvinism, sexegration*—in use by feminists.)

Additionally, many women are currently determined to keep their own names when they marry, or to give themselves names of their own creation. The legal restrictions and the hostility that have made it difficult for women to obtain nominal rights led to the creation of the Center for a Woman's Own Name in Chicago where women can obtain advice about how to determine their own names regardless of their marital status (Gary Wisby, [Chicago] *Sun-Times*, 1979). Of course many women in past decades also tried to convince others that women should have the right to keep their own names after marriage. Although Lucy

Stone never won legal recognition of her own name after she married Henry B. Blackwell in 1855—except when she paid her taxes—her name and her crusade have received much attention in the twentieth century. The Lucy Stone League was formed in 1921 to change social and legal restrictions involving women's names (Una Stannard, 1977:102, 193). However, members of the League received little general approval for their activities, especially during the years after the Second World War, until the early 1970s.

Stannard points out that when the National Organization for Women was formed in 1966 the right of a married woman to her own name was not one of the rights demanded. It did become a demand of the organization in 1970 as an increasing number of women worked to challenge social and legal restrictions that required them to be labelled as Mrs. Man when they married. Others are changing their patronymic last names given them at birth (Julia Penelope Stanley and Susan J. Wolfe [Robbins], 1978). An increasing number of women are working for nominal equality as a part of their interest in becoming involved in the entire naming process.[2]

Books challenging men's right to establish the naming system for everyone are receiving a lot of attention. For example, Mary Daly's *Gyn/Ecology: The Metaethics of Radical Feminism* (1978), a book about women's redefinition of the world, sold thousands of copies in the first few months after publication (Ann Marie Lipinski, 1979).

Women are not limiting discussions about language to their own groups. Another strategy women are using is to assert themselves in previously male-dominated spheres. They have pressured publishing companies into establishing guidelines for writers, suggesting ways to avoid sexist terms. Feminists have published their own dictionaries. An entry in "A Woman's New World Dictionary" (1973) reads:

MAN. [Generic] 1. An absurd assumption still accepted by some that both sexes are included when the word "man" is used. 2. A mis-statement of fact. 3. An egotistical male distortion, legitimized in the language, that "man" could/should represent both sexes. 4. A false hope. See WO/MAN.

Some feminist groups are publishing their own journals and in some cases financing their own presses. They are also discussing language and gender questions in women's studies courses. They are making public recommendations about how labelling should be changed. For example, in a *New York Times* essay Ethel Strainchamps (1971) suggests that instead of discussing the alteration of the titles of women (e.g., using Ms.), editors should, for once, consider that men might make an adjustment and begin to label themselves according to *their* marital history. These women are speaking of things and in places which have been traditionally controlled by men. Working within the structures of their professional organizations, women have organized caucuses in order to speak more readily and clearly their concerns to their colleagues, through professional programs, legislative boards, and newsletters.

The Women and Language programs at the 1978 Modern Language Association meeting attracted hundreds of listeners and participants, as speakers talked about what women's equal involvement in language study, publication, and literary criticism would mean—to the paradigms used in these fields and to women and men. Of course, these discussions are still usually set apart on "women's pages" and "women's programs" and women public speakers are not listened to by many men. Yet, through these collective actions women are increasingly working toward greater access to public forums for their ideas; not just to talk with or to men. This collective effort has resulted for many women in an increased appreciation of friendship among women. Women's increased amount of public speech is perceived by both men and women as changing—or as an attempt to change—the relationship of women and men.

Additionally, some women are creating new dimensions on which they may compare themselves favorably with men, another strategy discussed by Williams and Giles in their analysis of the changing relationship between women and men. For example, instead of comparing the syntax of women's speech and men's speech and finding women's speech slightly different and thus strange, instead of comparing women's and men's performance as leaders of groups and finding women's performance weak, some women are reconsidering and re-evaluating the elements of communication among women and among men. Jean Baker Miller (1976) writes that "the parameters of the female's development are not the same as the male's . . . the same terms do not apply" (p. 86). She argues that although men need affiliation, "for them it can *seem* an impediment, a loss, a danger, or at least second best. By contrast, affiliations, relationships, make women feel deeply satisfied, fulfilled, 'successful,' free to go on to other things" (p. 87). Many women are talking and writing about the existence, and of the desirability, of cooperation rather than competition as the prime pattern of interaction within many women's groups (e.g., Susan Kalčik, 1975; Lee Jenkins and Cheris Kramer, 1978). In the past, women's greater willingness to reach agreement and to avoid conflict has been evaluated as a weakness by many men who have concluded that women are more persuasible and thus less stable (see Wayne N. Thompson [1967] and Alice H. Eagly [1978] for reviews of some of this literature). The women who now discuss the "very 'male' pattern of relating to each other"—vying with each other for individual attention ("A Continuation . . . ," 1970:9)—are challenging the value of showing primary concern with maximum productivity, "objective" facts, and competition, the standards used by many men to evaluate both men's and women's interaction.

These are some of the techniques women have used in their attempts to call into question the stereotypes and the evaluation of women's and men's speech. The techniques are discussed in greater detail in Chapter IV.

Counter-reactions have emerged along with women's efforts to combat stereotypes about women through alteration of certain language structures and practices. Deep-seated, even unconscious, feelings about the order of life are implicit in the structure and use of language, and such counter-reactions can be no surprise.

Following Tajfel's work, Williams and Giles (1978) propose that strong action from a subordinate group will be met with strong action from the dominant group attempting to maintain its superiority and control. Their discussion appears valuable for an analysis of the opposition many people are making to women's proposals for alleviating sex bias in language (a topic discussed briefly in an earlier chapter). Williams and Giles mention several responses that might be made by members of the dominant group and by those who identify with the values of the dominant group.

One strategy is to accept, seemingly, the changes women advocate but then to redefine the situation so that the meaning of the change is diminished or lost. Such a strategy has been used by critics of women's proposals to change the language structure. One instance of such a redefinition: the acceptance of the label *chairperson,* but the use of it only in reference to women. Thus *chairman* and *chairperson* have become gender labels.[3]

Williams and Giles mention another strategy to counter strong threatening action by a subordinate group: the use of humor or ridicule. Julia P. Stanley (1972) in discussing changes in language structure writes that laughter is a response many men use to avoid considering viewpoints that are inimical to their interpretation of reality. However, the analysis at the intergroup level suggests that laughter and ridicule can also be seen as a response members of a dominant group use to defend its threatened social identity. Especially in the early 1970s many columnists and writers of letters to editors played with the feminists' complaints about the so-called generic *man* and *he* by writing essays in which "person" is substituted for each "man" resulting in strings of sentences like the following: "It was interesting to see how a group with obviously persongled egos were able to personipulate an organization the size of ours into looking like a pack of fools. 'Chairperson' indeed!" (Edmund Shimberg, 1971:2). The over-extensions of the suggestions women have made for language change are, as Maija S. Blaubergs (1978a; 1978b) suggests, one way to try to discredit the original proposals.

Another strategy, also listed by Williams and Giles, is to accuse women who behave in ways that threaten the status quo of having sexual, emotional, or physical defectiveness, i.e., as being deviant from "real" women. Women who write and speak publicly are by those actions alone considered at least slightly deviant. As many feminist critics have noted, women writers are often split off from "writers" and reviewed separately, with their sex and their marital status often a prime consideration in the evaluation of the book. For example, the (London) *Sunday Times* (1 May 1977, p. 41) reviewer concludes his comments on Erica Jong's novel *How to Save Your Own Life,* "It is not so much a case of Women's Lib as Women's Glib," and continues:

> So it was that when I took up *The Golden Honeycomb* I suffered some misgivings to find it was by another woman author, Kamala Markandaya, but my uneasiness quickly vanished, for soon after I began the book I realised I was reading a novelist of rare quality. Her insights are not prejudiced by her gender; her art is to report the truth and life of things. (Ronald Harwood, 1977)

(That is, in her historical saga she is not advocating changes threatening to the male reviewer.) Another reviewer writes of the homage he believes many Western women pay "to the howling, rampageous and brazen-voiced Militant Lesbian" (Paul Johnson, *The Daily Telegraph*, 16 September 1976, p. 12).

The Williams and Giles list of strategies used by those who reject new definitions of female and male behavior can be enlarged. Women who implicitly or explicitly recommend change in the relationship between women and men are often accused of intellectual deviancy. They are said, for example, to be making "childish war" on language (Jacques Barzun, 1974:18), or to write "from a very subjective point of view" (review of *The Women's Directory* in the [London] *Sunday Times*, 3 October 1976, p. 43). One man suggested to the editors of the *Feminist English Dictionary* that they include a male adviser to provide an "objective view" (reported in Alice Klement, 1974). The Macmillan Publishing Company guidelines for more egalitarian standards in the representation of females and males in children's stories have been described as "a willful exercise in intellectual dishonesty" (James J. Kilpatrick, 1976:85). The British feminist publishing house, Virago, is accused of "contemplating social follies and injustices from an arbitrarily feminist point of view which makes its literature not only non-serious but, worse, humourless" (*New Society*, 27 January 1977, p. 164).

Another strategy used by those who oppose changes to alleviate sexism in language is to argue that such changes are not "natural." As Jessie Bernard (1973b) and Dot Griffiths and Esther Saraga (1977) have noted, the kinds, extent, conclusions, and explanations of sex differences research vary depending upon what issues are politically and socially useful for the dominant group at any particular time. Seventeen members of Harvard's Department of Linguistics wrote a reply to those students who were asking for a ban on the use of *man* and masculine pronouns to refer to all people, a reply which stated in part: "The fact that the masculine is the unmarked gender in English (or that the feminine is unmarked in the language of the Tunica Indians) is simply a feature of grammar. . . . There is really no cause for anxiety or pronoun-envy on the part of those seeking such changes" (quoted in Casey Miller and Kate Swift, 1976:76). Stefan Kenfer in a *Time* essay entitled "Sispeak: A Msguided Attempt to Change Herstory" (23 October 1972, p. 72) warns that the Women's Liberation movement has "a touching, almost mystical trust in words" but the feminist "attack on words is only another social crime—one against the means and the hope of communication." Frequently, the approach is one of seemingly sympathetic interest. John Condon (1975) questions the wisdom of the women who are talking about male bias in language:

> Sometimes blaming language habits is a rhetorically effective way to alert us to and dramatize a social problem. But also, sometimes attempting to change some conventional habits is not very effective in changing the attitudes and behavior which are at fault. We must be careful that our efforts are not misguided and wasted. (p. 68)

What none of these critics acknowledges directly is that when women change the language structure and their language use, they are in fact taking action to change their status in society. They are challenging the legitimacy of the dominant group. By calling the challengers and their proposals for language change silly, unnatural, irrational, and simplistic, the dominant group tries to reaffirm its social identity in the face of a threat.

An understanding of the strategies employed by women affiliated with the liberation movement and concerned with language use and structure, and a look at the types of responses by their critics, provide a means of interpreting the perceptions people have of women's and men's speech. The long tradition of male control of language, determining both the symbols that are developed and the norms for usage for women and men, means that women's speech will not be evaluated the same way as men's speech. If it is believed that women naturally do and should use language in a way different from men, even when women and men use similar words, pronunciations, and intonation patterns, the speech may be interpreted differently. In other words, our understanding of what women say, what men say, is dependent in part upon our understanding of the limits to what women do/should/can say and what men do/should/can say.

Recognition of traditional restrictions on what women can do to and with their language can help explain the finding of several investigators: different labels for similar or same vocal behavior. In a study involving the same child, identified for some observers as a boy and for some as a girl, John Condry and Sandra Condry (1976) report that the child's crying was labelled "anger" if the infant was thought to be a boy, and "fear" if the infant was thought to be a girl. D. W. Addington (1968) found that the changes in the tone of voice of males affect the evaluation of their personalities differently than do similar changes in female voices. Meredith D. Gall, Amos K. Hobby, and Kenneth H. Craik (1969) found that for women verbal fluency is negatively evaluated but for men it is positively evaluated.

A woman manager of a delicatessen in a grocery store, made the target of much verbal and physical aggression by male co-workers, responded in kind—and was fired. The director of management testified in court that her inappropriate language was a major reason for the firing (*The* [Lansing, Michigan] *State Journal,* 19 November 1978, Section B, pp. 1, 3). A woman construction worker in London was dismissed because her language was "too strong." In bringing her case to a tribunal she argued that her boss would have tolerated the same language if spoken by a man. In a British Broadcasting Corporation television program, "The Tongues of Men" (8 April 1977), the linguist George Steiner showed films of what a reviewer of the program called "fascinating things . . . the strange clicking speech of Zulas, a Turkish language of whistles, [and] the intonations, body movements, speech rhythms of a very expressive fat American lady" (A. S. Byatt, 1977:18). The woman was talking on the telephone about a car accident. Steiner asked listeners to "Note the pitch, the speech, the volume and intonation patterns of the language as it pours into the receiver." Working from a tape of the program I clocked Steiner in his thirteen-second introduction to the film clip speaking at approximately three words per second. The woman in her twenty-three-second discourse about an upsetting experience talked at the rate of approximately three and one-half words per second. I found, in this case, that the tongue and pen of the men were as interesting as the speech of the woman. Researchers at the University of Michigan's Institute for Social Research found that contrary to stereotype, the men working at jobs outside the home "spend" an average of fifty-two minutes of every day on snack breaks and socializing, while women "fritter away" thirty-five minutes this way. The verbs in quotation marks are those used in the news report of the study in *Family Weekly* (5 February 1978, p. 27). Whether used satirically or not they indicate that women's talk is not evaluated in the same way as men's. Women may talk less, but they still talk too much.

Any discussion of the intergroup attitudes of males and females should include recognition that while we can talk about general evaluations made by each group of the other, individuals will each have different orientations to and acceptance of their group membership. As Williams and Giles point out, women gain positive identity in a number of ways. Some women, for example, accept the interpretation that women's talk is basically trivial—but consider their own speech as better than that of other women. Others call attention to the limitations of men's talk. Some others question the interpretation of the dominant group, and work collectively to redefine the descriptions of women's and men's speech and to incorporate their concepts of the world into the conventions of writing and speaking.[4]

This collective action to redefine relationships has been met with differing responses by members of the "superior" group. Some may individually express support for the statements about sexism in language and about the evaluation of women's and men's speech. (It is also accurate to say that individual attitudes might not be linked to behavior. Some men may believe that present linguistic inequities are unjust, yet still not speak against them. Other motives such as safeguarding their own interests may operate.) The changes advocated by women may be redefined so that the meaning of the changes is lost. Women who demand changes in the linguistic relationship between women and men may be called deviant, and offered pity, help, or contempt by the "superior" group. These responses can be viewed as methods to maintain dominance. Tajfel (1974) stresses that a "superior" group must constantly work at preserving its distinctiveness and superiority.

This analysis of the speech of people from different social groups can aid us in viewing their relationship as dynamic, rather than unchanging. The feminists who are advocating a reworking of the social regulations of language code and use are suggesting a reorganization of a social classification system. Their efforts at influencing word making, word meaning, and decisions about who can say what, where, and to what effect have been met—not surprisingly—with opposition from those who would rather women not become acknowledged interpreters of culture.

NOTES

1. Another version of this discussion appears in Sally McConnell-Ginet, Nelly Furman, and Ruth Borker (eds.), *Women and Language in Literature and Society,* New York: Praeger Publishers, 1980.

2. Descent is traced only through male names. Men have been, Stannard (1977) points out, the mother of us all. Naming is a way of controlling pedigrees. A child whose mother, but not father, is known through community records is often called illegitimate. The father's

name must be certified before a child has a legitimate place in society. Some judges today will not let divorcees (what label do we have for men who are divorced?) reclaim their pre-marriage names if they have child custody, arguing that all members of the family should have the same name. However, the judges do not complain if the mother remarries and changes her name to her new husband's, even if the children do not (Wisby, 1979).

3. Nancy Henley (correspondence) points out that *person* (as in *chairperson*) has come to mean *female* and has begun a process of pejoration, the traditional fate of words used to refer to women. Muriel Schulz (1975) discusses this "repeated contamination of terms designating women" (p. 71).

4. Members of a group will not, during times of redefinition of intergroup relationships, all express the same views or take the same actions. During the Civil War some Southern blacks fought against the Confederacy. But others remained loyal to their white masters, volunteering to put on fund-raising concerts, and serving the Confederate Army in a variety of jobs. The reaction of the whites to the blacks who were loyal to the South during the war was also not uniform. Some did not trust the blacks who expressed an interest in being allies in the Confederacy. Some whites did not *want* the involvement of blacks. Many others were glad for the help of slaves and free blacks (J. K. Obatala, 1979).

VIII

STRATEGY MODEL*

Speech is socially situated action. The speakers' understanding of the particular situation, the particular relationship of the speakers, the shared speech norms, and the speakers' strategies—all are a part of the patterning and meaning of interaction.

In the framework discussed in this and the following two chapters, this view of speech is linked with a description of women's position in our industrialized society as separated spatially and ideologically from men's. The division of labor—with more value given to men's activities—means that women and men have different resources and different amounts of legitimate power, and will thus use different strategies to obtain their goals.

The idea that women work in devious ways to control men is a part of Western folklore. During the 1970s a number of anthropologists and historians studied the position of women in Western societies in order to determine why women lack access to legitimate power, how they do exercise power, and when.

These scholars theorize that the rise of industrial capitalism in the eighteenth and nineteenth centuries brought about a pattern of two spheres as work became wage-earning and separated from the home. While a division of labor within the family based on gender was common in pre-capitalist and early capitalist societies, the sharp division between the world of commodity production (public world) and that of the family (domestic world) did not emerge until the nineteenth century (Eli Zaretsky, 1976). This spatial division—which is at once actual and metaphoric—involves a sexual division of labor; it involves a separation in location of activities; and it involves the emergence of highly specialized public institutions of economy, religion, and politics. The separation is spatial—but also ideological. Nancy Chodorow (1979) writes that as the family lost its role in production, the home became "the place where people go to recover from work, to find personal fulfillment and a sense of self [and where children are cared for]" (p. 89). More accurately, home has become the place *men* go to recover from work; women, even those who hold jobs outside the home, are responsible for domestic work. From the analyses offered by several anthropologists and historians I have extrapolated a framework for the study of language and gender which I label "the strategy model."

Briefly, the reasoning is as follows:

1. Industrialized capitalism has sharpened a division between the labors of women and men, and a separation in the location of their activities. Men are more visible in, and ideologically defined by, the public sphere while women are relegated to the domestic sphere. Women have always been—and are increasingly—among the wage laborers, but even employed women are primarily defined by their family roles.

2. Authority (legitimate power, authorized power to command) is associated with the public sphere and men have clear monopoly of this. Men have greater access to the valued resources of the larger social units whose total workings we think of as society—income and valued roles in production, education, political office, religious leadership, and control of prestigious rituals. This public sphere, at least in capitalist societies, generates social value and power. As a social class (or caste since their basic status is, like that of Hindus in India and blacks in the United States, fixed at birth), women are treated as if they are essentially irrelevant to the publicly important tasks. The structural opposition between domestic and public spheres is discussed in great detail in the essays in Michelle Zimbalist Rosaldo and Louise Lamphere (1974), and in Rosaldo (1978, 1980).[1]

As a result of this differentiation between their roles and activities, men and women have different relations to power. Men have more direct access to authority, or legitimate use of power; women are more likely to be limited to indirect access to authority.

3. As a consequence of the division of labor, the separation of spheres, and the differential allocation of resources and legitimate power, women and men will use different strategies to influence others and shape events. Although women are denied legitimate access to many important economic and political activities and resources, they nonetheless work in structured ways to have a say in events that affect them and others around them. The speech of women can best be studied not merely as ineffective and "other"—the most frequent approach taken in the past by professional and lay sociologists and students of language—but as rational, creative behavior. The proposal here, as in the other sections of this book, is that women's and men's speech can be most usefully studied within the context of the social formation of the classes *women* and *men*.

4. The concept of strategy provides a link between the social structure and the actions and interactions of individuals. The definition and explanation of verbal strategies used in this framework come from the work of Penelope Brown and Stephen Levinson (1978), who have training in both linguistics and anthropology. (Both of them have studied and worked at the University of California [Berkeley] and the University of Cambridge, England.) They believe that interaction is the "expression of social relationships . . . built out of strategic language use" (p. 61). If we can discover the principles of language usage, they argue, we will at the same time discover principles of social relations.

Currently many linguists are studying speech as rule-governed behavior, constructing descriptive codes to correspond to the social knowledge that speakers hold in common. For example, adults know speaking conventions about taking turns and speaking only one at a time (Harvey Sacks, Emmanuel Schegloff, and Gail Jefferson [1974] discuss turn-taking rules). These rules provide the base for listeners' evaluation (conscious or unconscious) of interaction.

Brown and Levinson argue, however, that a search for and listing of rules specifying speaking formulae will not go far toward describing and explaining "the flexible and indefinitely productive strategic usage" which we witness in interaction (p. 91). The word *strategy* usually implies conscious manipulative action. The Brown and Levinson definition is more inclusive. They use the word to refer to "(a) innovative plans of action, which may still be (but need not be) unconscious, and (b) routines—that is, previously constructed plans whose original rational origin is still preserved in their construction, despite their present automatic application as ready-made programmes" (p. 90).[2]

They believe that speakers are rational, able to reason from ends to the means that might achieve their goals, and—also—that speakers possess and protect "face," their self-image presented to the public. This "face" includes the desire for freedom of action and the desire that the self-image is approved of by interactants (pp. 63-69). In general, speakers cooperate to maintain the "face" of each other since if someone's "face" is threatened that person is more likely to defend self by threatening the other's "face."

However, we do not all have equal rights to peace and to self-determination. Consider the affronts to children, to blacks, to women both black and white. Brown and Levinson reason that the seriousness of a face-threatening act in any situation involves (in the perception of the interactants) the following factors: the social distance of the participants, their relative power, and the ranking of impositions in the culture. So, the speakers' perceived rights, obligations, and reasons to impose upon the individuality of others, and the amount of pain or pleasure the imposition brings to the others, are factors involved in the evaluations people make of face-threatening acts.

Brown and Levinson's analysis recognizes the complexity of interaction, and recognizes the connections between the larger social structure and the daily interactions of individuals.

Women who are relegated to the domestic sphere, and *men* who have greater access to the authority and resources associated with the public sphere, do not have the same "rights" to impose their plans on others. Yet Rosaldo (1974) suggests that "it is necessary to remember that while authority legitimates the use of power, it does not exhaust it, and actual methods of giving rewards, controlling information, exerting pressure, and shaping events may be available to women as well as to men" (p. 21). Women, like men, will act to seek personal gains. But since women do not have the same status or the same resources as men, women will often use different means in order to have an influence on their own and others' lives.

Rosaldo and Lamphere caution that although by the standards of male norms women's actions "may appear to be idiosyncratic, disruptive, unimportant, or undesirable," to ignore the forms and purposes of women's actions means ignoring an important part of the structure and processes of social life (p. 10). Jane Fishburne Collier (1974) argues that "women are social actors whose choices affect the options open to politically active men"; if we are to know the actual pragmatic strategies of a society we must look beyond normative rules and develop models of social life that recognize the strategies—the employment of plans and actions toward specific goals—of all human participants (p. 96).

Again, the use of the word *strategy* in descriptions of verbal interaction should not limit us to thinking of individual behavior only in terms of how people obtain control and power. While power relationships are increasingly seen by researchers as important to discussions of social arrangements between women and men (see Epilogue), we have many motives in our interactions other than obtaining power. In fact, dissatisfaction with an emphasis on individualist, profit-maximization assumptions in such interaction models as George C. Homans's (1961) exchange theory is one of the reasons feminists are working out alternative theories which more accurately reflect our own experience.

Specific contextual factors enter into the participants' actions and assessments of the interaction in any situation. However, the preceding analysis suggests some very general hypotheses concerning women's and men's speech:

1. Women, who in general lack culturally valued authority, will use different verbal strategies than will men.

2. Norms for women's and men's speech, and the structure and use of the language, including allowance for language change, will be under the authority primarily of men.

3. Conversation in the home will be perceived as a different genre from talk in public places.

4. Married women will be considered responsible for providing emotional support to family members, both by verbal and by nonverbal interaction, to a greater degree than will married men. In work situations, also, women will be expected to be nurturers and emotionally expressive.

5. The speech directed to boys and girls in the home will differ; mothers' talk to daughters (but not that to sons) will encourage affective relationships with others and encourage identification with maternal behavior.

6. As subordinates, women will be more conscious than men of "proper speech" and of speech strategies, working from a recognition that they do not have the same access to language control, do not have an equal share in determining speech norms, and do not speak from the same power base.

In this and the next two chapters I take a quick look at types of research and types of findings that can contribute to an exploration of these and other hypotheses that can be derived from the strategy model.[3]

PROVERBIAL KNOWLEDGE

The idea that women do not talk like men and yet do have some unobtrusive, indirect influence is certainly not completely new. Most adults have heard about, and many adult males talk about, feminine wiles. The power of women may not be thought to be very crucial, logical, consistent, or even intended. But, behind every great man is a woman. Never quarrel with a woman; you will never win. Trust your dog to the end, and a woman to the first opportunity. (The seemingly general "you" appears related to the seemingly generic "he" and "man.") Tell a woman a secret and you tell the world. A man must ask his wife's leave to thrive. A woman's tears are a fountain of craft. The cunning of women is equal to their obstinacy. A woman will always have her way. While there's a world it's women that will govern it. Women will have the last word. Women are strong when they arm themselves with their weaknesses. A little girl can twist her dad around her finger. Women have tears at command. A woman's advice is a poor thing, but he is a fool who does not take it. Man is the head, but woman turns it. A woman's strength is in her tongue. Women's instinct is often truer than man's reasoning. Women and their wills are dangerous ills. A woman's counsel is not worth much, but woe to him who ignores it. Trust not a woman when she weeps. A woman can do more than the devil. He is mad who quarrels with women. Women are wasps if angered. Only the foolish man thinks he is the head of the family. There is no mischief but a woman is at the heart of it.

These proverbs all reflect and reinforce the common belief that women are not always subordinate and supportive in their relationships with men. Of course, they exist alongside other sayings attesting the goodness (read "submissiveness") of woman, and attesting her ineffectiveness when she tries to reason or when she steps outside the domestic domain. A virtuous woman is a crown to her husband (Proverbs 12:4). A good wife is worth gold. A hundred men can make an encampment, but it requires a woman to make a home. Woman, fairest of creation, last and best. Woman is the fairest work of the Great Author. A woman's place is in the home. A woman's mind and winter wind change often. Women in state affairs are like monkeys in glass shops.

However, the very existence of such contradictory statements about women indicates that what they say and do has had some impact on how men run their lives. Women's activities cannot be easily forecast, men complain. Women cannot be totally ignored even if (or especially because) their behavior often seems to men to be idiosyncratic and illogical rather than carefully planned.

We do not have a similarly rich store of proverbs and sayings about men's subtle control of women. Men's control need not be subtle. They have direct, legitimate, "natural" authority. Women who exercise power over public matters— that is, over "important" matters—are often called over-ambitious, deviants, or manipulators. Men who exercise power in these areas are more apt to be perceived as acting as men should—go-getters, high achievers, well-motivated. We do have some works that help to explain women to men so that men can learn how to better deal with them. These are often written from a "They're crazy in the way they differ from us in logic, but they're also rather wonderful" approach. For example, F. Lee Bailey and Henry B. Rothblatt in their handbook for lawyers, *Successful Techniques for Criminal Trials* (1971), present sections on how to deal with stool-pigeons and accomplices, stupid or illiterate witnesses—and female witnesses. There is no section on male witnesses. The authors suggest special courtroom techniques to deal with women, who, they write, are more prone to exaggeration, stubbornness, crying. The intelligent woman, they write, may be dangerously evasive. What Bailey and Rothblatt do not deal with are the *reasons* why men and women behave differently in the courtroom. Or why women are to be regarded as more problematic than men. (Because in a male-dominated context, women are an aberration?)

Men are encouraged to openly assume and exert power. Woman are usually forbidden power except, perhaps, as they "play the power game 'underground' by means of 'sneaky,' 'feminine' influence techniques" (Constantina Safilios-Rothschild, 1974:114). Women have easy, recognized control over only those areas which men do not want to control.[4] The social rules indicate that husbands are to dominate wives and children. An openly competent, authoritarian wife means the husband appears weak; both appear deviant. If a wife actually does more of the controlling, then, she also uses tactics that ensure that the husband has the illusion of power at least during public appearances. These are, at least, assumptions about decision-making that appear in fiction about middle-class, married whites.

Is there support from other sources for the statements about females exercising forbidden influence, through "subtle" speech? The value of the strategy theory is, in part, its promise as a guide into areas of language/gender research that have previously drawn less attention than they deserve as we search for guidelines to define and categorize similarities and differences in ways of speaking and their functions. Rather than trying to fit together material to "test" each of the hypotheses I have listed, in the next two chapters I will, rather, discuss the material from several areas of study that seem related to the hypotheses and suggest some of the problems and possibilities I see with that material.

Perhaps the most stimulating and potentially important possibilities in language/gender study using the strategy model lie in the study of communication patterns of families. Research into what is called "marital power" provides helpful indirect commentary on the issues of speech and gender differentiation. However, the models that have frequently been used in the past for family and marriage studies, including those of marital power, have not been based on the same assumptions as those developed in the strategy theory of female/male relationships. In the next chapter I take a brief, critical look at some of the literature about family codes and conventions, and at some of the conclusions about communication between wife and husband.

NOTES

*I am especially indebted to Barrie Thorne for her suggestions made on earlier drafts of this chapter.

1. The writers in the Rosaldo and Lamphere collection presented the domestic/public dichotomy as universal. This proposition has been criticized by many other anthropologists, including Eleanor Leacock (1975, 1977), Rayna R. Reiter (1975), Rayna Rapp (1979), and Ruby Rohrlich-Leavitt (1975) as being a-historical and as ignoring the wide range of cultural variability. Rosaldo (1980), while still believing that women's powers and privileges seldom equal men's, now considers that the basic domestic/public dichotomy may be more a product of industrial capitalism than a basic organizing dichotomy for all cultures at all times. However, for our culture the concepts of gender asymmetry in authority or "legitimate" power, male dominance in public affairs, and the "indirect" power women hold are familiar concepts, discussed especially by people involved personally and professionally in a reassessment of social structure and values. The arguments presented here can, I believe, usefully serve as an initial framework for discussing gender and differentiation of speech.

2. Brown and Levinson are specifically interested in explicating underlying universal principles of language use, particularly modes of politeness. To study these principles they set forth an explanatory account of the assumptions upon which people base their interaction. They give illustrations of verbal interaction from several cultures. Here I am interested only in the value of their account for explaining verbal interaction in the British and American cultures, so this brief summary does not indicate the richness of their discussion nor the details they provide concerning universal strategies of interaction.

3. Susan Harding (1975) in her essay "Women and Words in a Spanish Village" deals with many of these topics. The division of labor in the village determined the division of types of influence and the division in the use of language. She writes that the women and men have "distinct verbal roles that structure their use of language and assign to them distinct verbal skills and speech genres" (p. 287). Women do not speak with authority in legal and church affairs; women do not have formal power in the village. Gossip—the collection, exchange, and analysis of villagers' activities—is considered by the villagers as disruptive, wicked—and women's specialty. This gossip, conducted to aid the women in their, and their families' interests, is considered sinful, Harding says, because in gathering and selectively exchanging information about village households the gossipers are challenging the men's power over the village activities. According to Harding,

> The point is not that women are unique in their use of verbal skills for political ends, but that these skills must be uniquely developed by them in their exercise of power, given the absence of explicit, formal institutions to lobby for their desires and needs, their subordinate economic and political position in both the household and village spheres, and their lack of formal access to the decision-making processes in the society. (p. 305)

She concludes that, although the village women do have some power, "the role of women in the running of everyday life in the village is dwarfed by the role of men in running the structures that determine the conditions of everyday life" (pp. 306-307). The power women have does not extend to changing the basic hierarchical structure and plot that allow them only relatively minor speaking parts.

4. In general, women's pronunciation and grammar are more "correct"—closer to "prestige English"—than men's. (However, Patricia Nichols [1978] describes the complex issues involved. Women's use of prestigious speech varies depending upon such factors as amount of formal education they have, the kinds of job opportunities available to them, and their geographical locations.) William Labov (1966) and Peter Trudgill (1975) have written of hidden (i.e., not overtly stated) values men associate with nonstandard, working-class speech. What is good, even expected, for women is not so good for men. Too much concern for proper English is not manly—or boyly. Perhaps women would not be considered proper speakers if proper speech were highly prized by men. In an interesting essay on the speech of

women and men in an East African community, Elinor Keenan (1974) writes that men are considered the ones who speak according to the rules, and women are considered the "norm breakers." Unfortunately, her report does not make clear whose evaluation (the women's? men's? hers? everyone's?) this is.

IX

FAMILY — TIES THAT BIND

Most of us have intimate knowledge of at least one family. However, what each of us knows about families in our culture is quite limited. Our study, formal or informal, of the family is limited by our own experience in a particular family, in a particular culture, and by the privateness of family life in Western cultures. In general we feel we should not look too closely at the family life of others. The interaction between family members is usually considered to be the concern of only that family; probing into family affairs of others is considered prying, peeking, and in general, violation of their privacy. Parents have the "right," for example, to observe, and to ask teachers and principals questions about, classroom interaction. But parents do not have the "right" to observe or ask questions about the family interaction in the homes in which their children visit and play with friends.

Yet, although family affairs are thought to be private, many public laws affecting all of us are based on what is thought to be correct behavior of family members. For example, laws of marriage, divorce, alimony, child abuse, abortion, credit, and property control are based on voters', politicians', and judges' ideas about "normal" family life. Clearly, family relationships are part of the total economic and political structure of our society. These laws in turn help determine marital power.

Actually, there is no dearth of spoken and written words about some aspects of family life. We talk about our families, although probably not often with candor. We read Abby, Ann, fiction, biographies, and autobiographies for information about what the family life of others is and should be. Researchers *have* observed and asked. More than 10,000 research studies of marriage and the family were published just between 1965 and 1972 (Joan Aldous and N. Dahl, 1974).

Not only scholarly interest remains high. Marriage itself continues to be popular. In fact, in the 1970s the percentage of married people in the United States was greater than at the beginning of the century. Divorce was more frequent in the 1970s but the percentage of divorced people who were marrying again was larger. The pervasiveness of the family makes it seem a natural relationship. And indeed many definitions of family include the concept of naturalness. (For example, Arthur P. Bochner [1976] calls the family "an organized, naturally occurring relational interaction system" [p. 382].) The "natural" family is usually thought to be two parents and their minor children; most variations on this pattern are seen as unnatural or unfortunate (Arlene Skolnick, 1973:33).

Yet according to 1977 statistics of the United States government, thirty percent of households consist of married couples with no children or with no children living with the parents. Only approximately sixteen percent of households consist of a father as the sole wage earner, a mother working full-time as homemaker, and one or more children under eighteen (percentages reported in *Ms.,* August 1977, p. 43).

The difficulties with definition continue. The figures above are based on groups of individuals living together in "households." When people talk about family does their definition imply a common residence for a certain number of years? A *married* couple and offspring? Does it include aunts, uncles, grandparents? Relatives who have died? Close relationships not of blood or marriage? A sense of responsibility? A relationship that involves frequent interaction? Household sharing? How similar, how different are our individual definitions and assumptions about the family? How does the concept of the family differ depending upon people's regional, ethnic, or social-class identification?

Therefore, before we can discuss family communication patterns we note that the unit of analysis of communication studies is not necessarily the same in all studies. The theoretical approaches have also varied, depending in part upon how independent a unit the person doing the analysis thinks the family is. For example, some people view the family as an independent unit with shared, egalitarian norms based on affection. Others see the family as an institution under the regulation of people in control of such governing institutions as big business, government, and religious organizations which support male/female division of labor with women as the unpaid or poorly paid workers. Different questions about communication in the family and different interpretations of findings will result from such different approaches. What appears to be scientific fact to one researcher will appear as folklore or wishful thinking to another.

Most of the studies of the family have been devised and conducted by men, or through study questions and models devised by men. Most of the studies have been limited to marital power and have focused on conflict, real or hypothetical, between wife and husband. Most of the studies are limited to married couples. Little attention has been paid to children and how they interact with adults in traditional or other family forms—such as those with single parents, other relatives present, communes, or gay couples or groups. Few of the studies concerning marital power have been conducted by people primarily interested in communication. So what is actually said often is not recorded. Few of these studies are concerned with the individual's "power" in respect to "outside" legal and other social regulations. In many of the studies the adults in a family are often assumed to have equal resources and equal opportunities to influence family events if they wish.[1]

The strategy model of different female/male methods of obtaining power suggests other possibilities. That model states that humans are presently organized in sexual asymmetry, that women's social recognition is limited primarily to the private sphere, which is considered by the male-oriented accounts of social structure to be of less importance than the political and economic sphere. This discrimination affects the influence women have even within the domestic domain. Men have greater access to money, wider social contacts, public status, and formal education. Because their relationship to the total social structure is different—even if the husband and wife share similar tasks, share decision-making, and converse in an equitable manner—the meaning of the "same" activities may be interpreted differently depending upon the participants' understanding of what is legitimate authority, and legitimate behavior. That is, cultural norms and values about ideal behavior may affect the wives' and husbands' perceptions of reality.

The strategy model, as set forth in the previous chapter, does not deal with the specific amount of socially legitimatized authority that men have over domestic affairs, the sphere of activity that is in general recognized as belonging to women. Yet the arguments several authors (in Michelle Zimbalist Rosaldo and Louise Lamphere, 1974; Rayna R. Reiter, 1975) have used lead to the conclusion that men have determined what constitutes the boundaries of the domestic sphere and they have determined what types of authority women have in this sphere. That is, women are allowed decision-making control only in areas where men have relinquished control. And even then men keep ultimate control. In an important sense, then, men also control domestic activities even when women seem to exercise control. Obviously, individual families have made individual "adjustments," and various husbands and wives will have what can be seen as quite different patterns of interaction. (And social class, race, religion, ethnic background, employment, family size, and experience of family life as a child may also affect what is considered as legitimate power.) The concern here is to look at prevailing cultural norms and values as set forth by the strategy model and some of the implications they will have on the evaluation of what women and men say.

Despite these limitations of some of the past marital power literature, the studies that do explore the relative influence of family members provide some suggestions about who makes decisions involving the activities of family members, and about verbal strategies used by family members to achieve personal goals. A review of those studies reveals that more often than not spouses disagree as to who makes the decisions (Constantina Safilios-Rothschild, 1969); that in general the higher the husband's occupational prestige, income, and education the more power he has to make decisions (Robert O. Blood, Jr. and Donald M. Wolfe, 1960); that power relations between black couples and white couples are similar (Dair L. Gillespie, 1971), and that power is not based on individual contributions to the domestic unit, such as the number of children cared for during the day, over the years. If the relative power of wife and husband were determined by the contributions each makes to the family, the wife's power would be greater during the time she was caring for preschool-age children than before she had borne children. Yet the opposite is true (David M. Heer, 1963:137-138). In a review of marital power literature, Gillespie (1971) concludes that difference in power is not due to personal competence "but is related to questions of social worth; and the value of women and women's work, as viewed by society, is obviously very low" (pp. 456-457). The contributions within the home are accorded little value. "Husbands," she writes, "gain power in marriage as a class, not as individuals, and women are blocked as a class, not as individuals" (p. 445).[2]

REALITY FOR WIVES AND HUSBANDS

The verbal interaction of couples will presumably reflect the division of power. What topics are considered to be in the realm of debatable issues, the amount of time spent discussing problems, who initiates the discussion, the types of arguments presented—all will be influenced, I assume, by the relative power of the partners. Yet, very little information is available on these aspects of decision-making—except the evidence that spouses often do not agree on what has happened and who has said what during discussions. This disagreement between wife and husband has troubled researchers in marital power work. In general, they have been concerned primarily with finding the "truth," not with perception differences except as they interfere with the search for the "truth." George W. Brown and Michael Rutter (1966) write: "The process of communication is one of great complexity, and it is known that husbands and wives have considerable difficulty in reporting accurately more obvious aspects of the process, let alone its subtler components" (p. 259).

One researcher, considering the conflicting replies given by husbands and wives to questions about the amount and kind of talk by self and by partner, writes that one explanation

> may be the possibility of two "realities," the husband's subjective reality and the wife's subjective reality—two perspectives which do not always coincide. Each spouse perceives "facts" and situations differently according to his [or her] own needs, values, attitudes, and beliefs. An "objective" reality could possibly exist only in the trained observer's evaluation, if it does exist at all. (Safilios-Rothschild, 1969:291)

The strategy model offers an aid to the interpretation of the disagreements. Not only motivational incentives of the individuals are involved, but also the asymmetry in the authority and value of the activities of women and men. According to the strategy framework the evaluation of husbands and wives will be affected by other social factors; their individual resources are dependent in part upon their power, as a class, in the larger society.

Because most studies do not include even portions of transcripts of conversations between spouses, we do not have much evidence from marital power literature that the woman exercises indirect control through verbal strategies—for example, attempting to lead the man to believe that a suggestion she had made earlier in the discussion was actually put forth by him. Most researchers have been more interested in the end decision than in the process that led to it.

The strategies theory would predict that women are strategists who will find subtle ways of influencing relationships. Certainly, as indicated earlier, folklore reveals a popular belief that women are skilled in subtle manipulation of others;

and we have much literary evidence of the currency of the idea. These observations come from people's beliefs or wishes, and are important to our understanding of the perception and evaluation of female and male speech. Folklore, self reports, findings from contrived laboratory conflict situations, and concluding "facts" made by researchers are all helpful in the exploration of what is said between women and men. Additionally, however, naturalistic studies can yield valuable information about family communication and conflict, and about the way women and men may differ in the ways they attempt to influence the thinking and actions of others.

STUDYING DOMESTIC VERBAL INTERACTION

Recording crews from public television organizations in both England and the United States have experimented with filming family activity fairly continuously throughout the day over a period of weeks. (In the United States the televised interaction of the members of the Loud family became a national topic of conversation, as popular as many fictional family television series. In a *New Yorker* cartoon, a woman at an elegant dinner party says to the others, "I'm probably old-fashioned, but I felt much more at home with the Forsytes [of the serialized *Forsyte Saga*] than I do with the Louds.") The broadcasted segments of film from these experiments have prompted a great deal of discussion by people who viewed them—partly, I would guess, just because the domestic sphere is *not* public, because domestic activities are set apart from the rest of societal activities, and because, except perhaps for bang-up arguments, we have not usually considered the things that are said and the way they are said between family members to be very important or of theoretical interest.

Yet, increasingly, people *are* allowing observers into their homes to record, for example, dinner-table conversation (when often all members of middle-class families are together) and parent (usually mother)-child interactions during the day.

But proponents of naturalistic studies, who believe they should affect the situation studied as little as possible, have difficulty in obtaining the type of interaction data, such as conflicts, in which power is manifest. As one research team writes, "For practical reasons, it would have been difficult to follow couples in their homes, waiting for them to engage in different types of conflict in the presence of observers and recording equipment" (Harold L. Rausch et al., 1974:6). That research team studied families at several stages (when the couples were newlywed, when the wife was pregnant, and when the couple became parents) via interviews and, primarily, audio tapes of couples working through situations they were asked to enact (e.g., conflict resulting from the different plans the husband and wife had for their anniversary dinner). Although the situations were simulated and suggested by the researchers rather than arising from the life of the couples, and although the conflict scenes were limited in time in a way that many conflicts are not, the study is of interest here because the researchers began with the premise that marriage itself provides a context for conflict, with women and men differing in values, orientations, and authority (pp. 36-37), and because the researchers were explicitly interested in checking the validity of beliefs about "masculine rages and feminine tears, of male rationality and female emotionalism" (p. 37) in these specific types of situations. They were interested not only in the final resolution of the conflict, but also in the way that women and men spoke during the discussion, what kind of talk was used. Strategic maneuvers were coded into the following categories, which could be considered as various strategy acts, that is, the employment of verbal actions toward specific goals: cognitive acts (suggestions, rational arguments), resolving acts (designed to cool the conflict), reconciling acts (aimed at reconciling partners), appealing acts (asking for grant of one's wishes), rejecting acts (rejection of argument or person), and coercive acts (aimed at forcing compliance by power plays, guilt, disparagement of other).

Their conclusions do not provide immediate support for the strategy theory. They state, "Any supposition that men and women differ greatly in how they communicate and deal with conflict is clearly refuted by the data" (p. 140). Their analysis led the researchers to state that in the situations in which partners were asked to enact, "husbands and wives tend to respond in the same way to each other's acts" (p.140). Husbands and wives differed only slightly in the type and order of speech acts in these interpersonal conflict situations, but the trends that appeared ran counter to expectations based on folklore: newlywed husbands exhibited a greater proportion of positive supportive "expressive" acts and were more likely to try to resolve conflict and reconcile differences (p. 147) than were their wives.[3] The results of this study also conflict with the often-referenced sex-role differentiation theory of Talcott Parsons and Robert F. Bales (1955) which states that men are more instrumental (rational, abstract, cool) and women more expressive (emotional). But in the report of their findings the investigators in the marriage conflict-management study offer the following explanation for their findings: the men were more likely to engage in cooperation because they work from a stronger power base. Supportiveness and nonaggression toward women is expected from men, but women perhaps have to learn how to harass in order to change the behavior of the one who has the more power. The researchers write:

> The use of words as strategic devices for gaining an end have, it seems, been employed by women throughout history. A female's reputation as a scold, a shrew, a nag attest to the costs incurred from crossing her desires. We are not suggesting that the wives in our sample are nags, but we are pointing to the possibility that women, as a low power group, may learn a diplomacy of psychological pressure to influence male partners' behaviors. (Rausch et al., 1974:152-153)

Men, on the other hand, who belong to the public world, can, from positions of power, offer support and care for the women who are more dependent upon them than they are upon the women (p. 153).

In addition to the limitations of the study already mentioned (the interactions were *performances* given for researchers), clearly the improvisations studied did not allow the researchers to study many of the ways that women and men may influence each other by complex means—for example, by using knowledge of past behavior to make subtle comments, understood only by those involved, about the fears, wishes, skills, weaknesses of the partners. However, in (1) showing that, in these enactments of conflict at least, the interactive styles of husbands and wives are very similar, and in (2) arguing that when differences do occur they tend to indicate that men are speaking supportively from positions of independence while the women are more likely to be attempting to coerce and appeal from positions of weakness, the study illustrates that traditional assumptions about communication patterns of couples need to be re-evaluated and that a strategies approach may be useful in conceptualizing marital conflict.

However, relationships and influence are not established and revealed only through clearly conflict situations. The focus and results of one recent study involving the general conversation of couples (not only conflict/decision discussion) provide some evidence to support the hypothesis that women and men use different verbal strategies in their seemingly mundane, daily talk.

Pamela M. Fishman (1977, 1978), analyzing fifty-two hours of tapes made in the apartments of three middle-class couples between the ages of twenty-five and thirty-five (the tapes were made with the couples' permission), found that men controlled conversation partly through silence, i.e., through their refusal to take up topics introduced by the women. Women asked nearly three times as many questions. Women were more likely to encourage responses by prefacing topic introductions with remarks such as "This is really interesting" and "Do you know what?" (This latter remark is also used often by children [who have relatively little authority], perhaps trying to get not only a response but also a "What?" response—that is, a request for a reply that would ensure the child's right to speak.)

The women and men used minimal responses such as "Yeah," "Ummm," and "Huh" in different ways. The women were more likely to slip them in throughout the men's talk, demonstrating interest and encouraging the men's continuation of talk. The men were more likely to use the minimal response to fill longer pauses, when the women stopped talking so that the men could pick up the conversation. The men's uses of these monosyllabic responses seemed to discourage interaction.

The strategy model, based on the premise that women and men, because of the division of labor and differential access to valued resources, do not have the same powers and prerogatives, offers a clear challenge to other popular approaches to the study of marriage and the family. As I have indicated, a number of academicians writing about marriage believe that women and men do have the same power. Ronald Fletcher (1973) writes in the preface to his revised book on marriage and the family that feminists are "out for the family's blood" (p. 25). He writes that he has difficulty understanding much of the fuss made by feminists, because the human family is, after all, a "natural" grouping based on the free-choice union of a woman and a man. "Both," he writes, "are of equal status and expect to have an equal share in taking decisions and in pursuing their sometimes mutual, sometimes separate and diverse, tastes and interests" (p. 139). Fletcher writes that "the central core of concern in the *family* [his emphasis] is the having and responsible upbringing of children" (p. 142). But clearly the day-to-day core concern is to be expressed in different ways for the men and women of the family he has in mind, for he also writes, "If a woman has completed her education and secured qualifications for a career before marriage, when her children are over the age of early dependence she is in a position to undertake part-time employment, and, later, can participate as fully as she wishes to do in wider social activities" (p. 140).

His view of "equal status" is similar to that of Michael Young and Peter Willmott (1975), who write that in the families they studied in Great Britain husbands and wives have a "symmetrical" relationship, "opposite but similar" (pp. 31-32).

Clearly, research such as this, organized and analyzed under the assumption that men and women have equal status in a marriage, will not contain a lot of ready-made material to support the strategy model—or even to reject it. The "equal status" writers would, however, imply that women's speech, although perhaps differing from men's speech, will be as highly valued or nearly as highly valued as men's speech.

FAMILY COMMUNICATION AND RACE

Few researchers have concerned themselves with the relationship of power and value within the family to extra-domestic activities. (Ann Oakley [1974] is one of several exceptions. She not only has traced the development of the role of housewife concomitant with, and as a product of, the development of industrial capitalism, but also has taken the unusual step of talking to housewives about their work, activity usually considered too trivial for study.) The interest that the family structure has received has been restricted almost entirely to white middle-class families. There have been a few exceptions. Daniel Moynihan was a presidential adviser in the mid-60s when he made the highly publicized statement that black husbands have little power ("The Moynihan Report," 1965). He stated that while the husband's relative powerlessness is characteristic of all low-income families, it is particularly prevalent in the black social structure. Moynihan viewed black women (who have had higher participation rates in the labor force than white women) as responsible for a crushing burden on the black males. Bonnie Thornton Dill (1979) writes, "It is a cruel irony that the black woman's role as a worker has been used to represent dominance over and emasculation of black men" (p. 550). She points out that such a view ignores the meaning of work for blacks and ignores the complexities of the interaction of class and culture.[4]

And as usual, what women have to say about their interaction with others, and their relationship to domestic and public spheres of life, is considered less important than what men say. While linguists and ethnographers have made available much anecdotal data and many transcripts of conversational exchanges from black males, they have been slow to recognize that black females are also talking. Yet, according to Roger Abrahams (1975), the opposition of females and males is a constant theme of conflict in black communities. If this is true, future ethnography of communication should include careful consideration of the speech and perspectives of both the females and males. (Abrahams suggests that the autobiographies of black women are an excellent source of information on the evaluation of speaking in various public and private situations.) Further, Abrahams suggests that life in black communities is organized around a female/domestic and male/public division, the private home and the public street worlds, adding, "the two worlds become identified to some extent with the age [as well as the sex] of their citizens, the household world being associated with the very young, the old, and with women, the street with adolescents and young adults and primarily with men" (p. 67).

Surely social class will make a difference. Dill (1979) reminds us that "too often, social science researchers have sought to describe black women and their families as if they were a monolithic whole, without regard for differences in social class" (p. 551). And the domestic/public division is not absolute, of course, in either black or white families or communities; for example, some young black women and not all young black men learn to "fancy talk" (with Latinate words and elaborate delivery style) in public places. Yet "if a woman places herself in a public situation, she is in jeopardy of having to contend with men and their *jive*" (Abrahams, p. 75). If a woman's respectability is challenged by her presence in public she may use *smart talking* as a defense, as a way of maintaining distance and showing coolness. Abrahams writes, "Smartness may be found in the repertoires of men, women, and children, but it does seem to be especially important in women's talk both with each other and with men" (p. 76). This style can be used to "produce strategic advantage (and thus to modify the behavior of the man)" (p. 76).

The women's and the men's activities and status are tied to different domains. They are expected to have quite different, even opposite, concerns. Yet common to all is an interest in maintaining control of working toward desired goals and for approval from others. The different expectations of women and of men will mean the verbal strategies used to exercise control will differ or that similar strategies will be evaluated differently. Although limited, the literature on black women's varieties of speech indicates that a strategy analysis very similar to that suggested in this chapter has already been utilized in this area. In a book-length study of the black family and in particular of black girls, Joyce A. Ladner (1971) argues that the "sophisticated" black female, in her dealings with men, frequently "engaged in manipulative strategies as they became necessary in her interpersonal relationships." Furthermore, "she had learned the rules of the game and devised her own strategies to cope with what was often a hostile world" (p. 183). But "strategies" as used here and in many other sources does not distinguish between verbal and other types of strategies, and illustrations as to how these strategies differ from those used by men are not included.[5]

CLASS DIFFERENCES IN FAMILY RELATIONSHIPS

Housework is usually considered woman's primary activity, whatever else she does; it comes with being female. A white, middle-class friend of mine, Margaret, tells me of the time when she first consciously realized the absurdity and unfairness of this. She and her husband invited a male friend of theirs, recently divorced, to dinner. As Margaret, who in her adult life has always worked outside as well as in the home, served the meal, she heard her husband commiserating with their friend, "Gosh, it must be hard to work all day and then have to fix your own dinner too." He was evidently oblivious to the fact it is also hard for Margaret—who cooks for a family of four.

Housework is seen as a natural activity for women, both middle-class and working-class. Additionally, their work outside the home is often considered of lesser importance than that of men's. Several analysts have suggested, however, that working-class wives may gain more power by working outside the home than middle-class wives do because the money the working-class women make may be more vital to the family welfare (Fay Fransella and Kay Frost, 1977:125). Working-class women who take outside jobs do report that they are not as submissive in marital conflict situations (Lillian Breslow Rubin, 1976:176).

But working outside the home does not necessarily move working-class women and their husbands toward equitable and companionate relationships. The domestic/public dichotomy is sharper for working-class women than for middle-class women who are expected to be knowledgeable enough about community and world events to help entertain their husbands' professional friends. And middle-class women who attend more public events are "on show" more outside the home. Working-class men do not exercise as much public authority and thus are more likely to think of the home as the one place where their wishes can be carefully heeded. Rubin found that many working-class husbands of women working outside the home complained about the increased independence that women exerted because of their employment. For example:

"Look, I believe every woman has the right to be an individual, but I just don't believe in it when it comes between two people. A man needs a feminine woman." (p. 177)

"I'd like to feel like I wear the pants in the family. Once my decision is made, it should be made, and that's it. . . . Because she's working and making money, she thinks she can argue back whenever she feels like it." (p. 177)

Rubin writes that working-class couples "talk *at* each other, *past* each other, or *through* each other—rarely *with* or *to* each other" (p. 116). The women are trained to be emotional in their talk and the men to be taciturn, rational people who ignore feelings (pp. 116-118). Their different expectations and their different experiences produce many tensions. Rubin acknowledges that the situation is similar for middle-class couples. But their greater income gives them more flexibility in their leisure activities and more possibilities for activities outside the home. While we develop our understanding of the ways that women are alike in their relation to men and the domestic and public domains, we do well to also explore the types and extent of class differences.

As those who trace the evolution of the public/domestic dichotomy have made clear, relations between family members change as other social conditions change. The current discussions in the public media about the importance of expressing feelings and talking out problems with spouses will likely bring changes in what working-class and middle-class couples consider proper family interaction. Noting this, Rubin writes: "*Intimacy, companionship, sharing*—these are now the words working-class women speak to their men, words that turn both their worlds upside down" (p. 120).

Some women and men have argued that in addition to the variables discussed above, geographical location and its attending cultural values will be an important determining factor in the types of strategies women, including married women, use. The editors of a *Time* essay (27 September 1976) entitle their work on the Southern woman, "The Belle: Magnolia and Iron." That is, the woman who has the vapors at the dance also is capable of wielding a great deal of influence over those around her. In that article, many women refer to the good manners and smiles they use in order to draw attention from the firm control they often exert. One says that the advice she received from her mother was "Do, but don't be seen doing." Another writes of the way the behavior of the Southern white woman has been accepted as innate: "The rest of the country makes the mistake of seeing those [pretty and helpless yet strong behaviors] as ingrained ways of being rather than learned skills" (p. 73 [European edition]). Again, specific examples of "strategic speech" are not given.

LIMITATIONS AND POSSIBILITIES
OF FAMILY INTERACTION RESEARCH

As this discussion suggests, few studies of the family have focused primarily on communication patterns among family members or have dealt with family power relations. The literature on marital power, although often containing little information about actual interaction (focusing, rather, on who has influence over what types of decisions), nonetheless is of particular interest to a discussion of the strategy theory and study methodology.

Some of the marital power researchers acknowledge that use of questionnaires and recordings of couples' interactions during experimental simulation of conflict—two common research techniques—does not necessarily tell us much about actual interaction. Questioning husbands and wives about their own behavior and that of their mates usually does not give much indication of what was actually said during conversation; the couples' behavior may be artificially slotted into categories determined by the researchers; the answers given by the individuals may be a *part* of the strategies used by the women and by the men; and the descriptive labels used in the questionnaires may not mean the same to all individuals. For example, the phrase "give and take" might have different meanings for individuals depending on their understanding of normal/proper family interaction (Bruce R. Glick and Steven Jay Gross, 1975). Some of the problems with simulation methods have already been mentioned.

Researchers are also recognizing that, for example, high consensus between husband and wife on decisions does not indicate how consensus is reached; "the silent covert influence may be an effective way to reach a strong authority position without challenging the other's publicly recognized authority" (Alan Booth and Susan Welch, 1978:25).

Furthermore, there is a growing awareness among researchers that understanding interaction and power relationships between family members can be best accomplished by working to understand power relationships of the total society. While many people assume that the family is the smallest unit, the baseline, for a whole culture, the marital power literature suggests that the unit is further divisible; that the members do not necessarily share equally and do not necessarily wield the same amount of control over events that affect the entire family, and that the political and social structure is not only affected by but also affects the interaction within the family.

Children's interactions with brothers and sisters and with parents are seldom studied; looking at relationships among children; between parents; among parents, children, other family members, and friends of family members will help us understand what kinds of strategies are used as all family members work to shape their environment and to pursue their individual and collective goals.[6]

The analysis of adult-child talk has usually focused on the speech of mothers to young children. We know that markers of this speech include repetition, and adjustments in rate, sentence length, and complexity to the child's comprehension (Catherine E. Snow, 1976). (Since mothers do so much more child-care work than fathers, mother-child interactions are much more accessible by researchers and have been the focus of more study.) We know relatively little about parent-child verbal exchanges after the child is six or seven. Yet patterns of family interaction are continually changing, continually being negotiated as the children learn more sophisticated language usages and as parents perceive children as becoming more responsible for their actions. Furthermore, although many of us are aware that adult-to-child talk in public is often quite different from talk in the home, we have few recorded examples of this shift.

Muriel Schulz (1979)[7] discusses markers of adult-to-child domestic speech and contrasts it to adult-to-child public speech. She thinks that Motherese and Fatherese in the home includes many direct commands, and also an increasing use of sarcasm as the child becomes older. For example: "Oh, that's just *wonderful*; smart fellow!" spoken to the child who the parent thinks has misbehaved. In public, parents' talk seems to contain more indirect commands, less "yelling" and more terms of endearment. Schulz suggests that since mother's talk is usually located in the home, mothers feel uneasy and self-conscious when they talk to their children in public, that is, when they perform a domestic task in a public setting.

Jean Berko Gleason (1975) in a study of the adult-child interaction of two female and two male day-care teachers found that both the men and the women in this nurturing role used in general the same speech markers that have been labelled Motherese. This suggests that men in nurturing roles can become as sensitive as women can to the needs and wishes of young children. Yet we can not now generalize from this finding to the speech of mothers and fathers and say that when men are the chief caretakers their speech will closely resemble that of mothers. While both female and male teachers used fewer imperatives than mothers and fathers the difference between the proportion of imperatives in male teacher talk and in fathers' talk was dramatic. Day-care teachers, paid for their work, are *supposed* to be patient and attentive to their charges. Mothers are *supposed* to be "naturally" nurturing. Day-care teachers and mothers may speak under more constraints than most fathers. I have heard one father who belongs to a men's consciousness-raising group talk about trying to avoid use of demanding syntax or volume in his speech to his wife and children. He tries to listen to and understand the perspectives of the other family members. However, when he becomes really angry he resorts to direct threats—which obtain, he says, the desired results more quickly than the threats of his wife. He is, after all, the man.

One researcher (Esther Blank Greif, 1980) studying conversations between parents and preschool children found that fathers more than mothers interrupted their children. Both mothers and fathers were more likely to interrupt daughters than sons. Fathers participating in another study (Marianne Engle, 1980) used more directive statements (e.g., Let's build a truck) to their children than did mothers who asked for suggestions (e.g. What would you like to play with now?). Mothers of three-year-olds used sentences of greater complexity than did mothers of two-year-olds. The fathers' speech did not show this type of adaptation to the children's linguistic maturation (Engle, 1980).

Are fathers more likely to walk away, even out of the house, in response to family arguments (an action not as readily available to mothers or children?) Do mothers use more terms of endearment (perhaps to try to balance "unmotherly" outbursts of anger)? Do mothers, children, and fathers use crying and profanity in differing amounts, for differing purposes, and with differing results? Family members' speech strategies at home and in public have been little explored.

Reviewing *middle*-class Motherese strategies, Martha Coonfield Ward (1971) writes:

> In public or in the presence of witnesses the mother feels constrained not to smack or yell at her child. She must resort to suggestions, little lies, veiled threats, teasing, or whatever comprises her repertoire. In the privacy of her home she may not be forced to rely exclusively on such tactics. (p. 70)

In her study of interaction between the members of households in a small black working-class community near New Orleans, Ward seldom heard these verbal devices:

> For one reason, there are no public and private standards of socialization. For another, parents believe that children are so hardheaded that nothing subtle will penetrate. Only the most obvious and direct techniques, it is believed, will work. . . . To get a child to eat . . . dinner one does not say, "Don't your red beans and rice taste good today?" but "Eat your dinner!!" (p. 70)

Ward's research illustrates again the importance of considering race, social class, social structure and social values, while studying, categorizing, and explaining verbal strategies of family members. The nature of the relations between domestic and public spheres may differ significantly in different segments of society.

Studies of family interaction in various speech communitites should help define the linguistic opportunities of females and males and help explain how people learn to speak as female and male and with what effect.

GOALS AND RATIONALITY OF SPEECH INTERACTION

Studying verbal communication in the family has usually meant studying what researchers have called *power*. The amount of talk, the number of times individuals speak, who speaks to whom, who agrees with whom—these kinds of tabulations have been used as measurements of power. Yet these tabulations do not by themselves tell us the *functions* of speech acts. For example: One researcher of classroom interaction between students and teachers has proposed that asking questions is a method people use to control conversation (Elliot G. Mishler, 1975). He notes that teachers use questions to control the order of speakers and the topics of conversation. However, Fishman (1977, 1978), listening to tapes made in the apartments of three female/male couples, noted that women asked more questions—in order to obtain verbal responses from men, Fishman theorizes. Given that women (and men) may use talk to encourage interaction, merely comparing the number of times women and men ask questions—or the total amount of time they talk, or the number of times they initiate conversation—will not give us a satisfactory description or explanation of speech strategies. Another example: people sometimes use laughter to complement others' comments and thereby to encourage their further talk (Rose Laub Coser, 1960); people sometimes use laughter to put others down.

Hedges—statements that include a modifier to reduce the force and certainty of an otherwise "bald" declaration—are often posited as particularly associated with female speech, that is, as indicating a subordination and a willingness to please by remaining open to the opinions of others (Robin Lakoff, 1973). Females may use more hedges than males (although see Betty Lou Dubois and Isabel Crouch, 1975). Yet hedges are not always used to express subordination or uncertainty. Counting the number of hedges women and men use does not tell us much about social relationships. Consider the following possibilities: A woman responding to an invitation, which must also be approved by her spouse, says, "I suppose we might be able to go." A man assuming the right to approve or disapprove the social activities of a family responds to his wife's question about an outing by saying, "I suppose we might be able to go." In the first case the speaker thinks she is unable to answer with certainty. In the second case the speaker may not want to answer with certainty, but rather to make a tentative statement to produce uncertainty in others.

The verbal indices of power, then, cannot be straightforwardly determined outside of consideration of the addressee's power over the speaker, and the specific contexts. This argues for the importance of using an explicit theoretical framework for the study of the speech interaction of women and men. Studying family interaction within a discussion of societal arrangements of females and males will encourage a focus on *what* individuals are working to achieve, *what* resources they have to work with, and how their goals and their strategies perhaps reflect and reproduce an asymmetric gender order.

The strategy theory, then, encourages the study of interaction as a study of individuals' goals and rationality. Consideration of all speech as strategic perhaps places too much emphasis on individualistic, rational planning—neglecting social structure—and on people's attempts to control—neglecting other goals of behavior. For example, is it useful to look at all mother-to-child, and wife-to-husband offers to help in terms of personal goals? In stressing strategy are we not, for example, ignoring love?[8] Yet love can also affect our strategies. Our aims—pursued strategically—may be based not only on self-interest but also on altruistic other-interest. If the concept of strategies can be used to emphasize speech as *action,* the framework discussed here can be helpful in finding and explaining the relationship of family interaction to the larger social structure.

NOTES

1. The focus of literature on family and marriage *is* changing somewhat. For example, several economists are investigating the economics of family life (see Gary S. Becker, Elizabeth M. Landes, and Robert T. Michael, 1977, and George Farkas, 1976). Consideration of division of wealth in the family—including family goods, education, income—is important to explanations of family interaction. See Marianne A. Ferber and Bonnie G. Birnbaum (1977) for a critical review of studies of the economics of the household. A basic problem with most of the traditional literature on the family is a failure to consider the relations (historically and now) of the family members to the political economy. In a valuable critique of literature on the family, Nona Glazer-Malbin (1976) considers the social role of housewives and their work in our economic structure. Rayna Rapp (1978) points out that households and families vary by class in their access to wealth, wages, and welfare. She writes that if we are to understand what family means, we need to listen, seriously, to what people say about their experiences, and to consider the relationship between household and production resources. "The family," she argues, "is a topic which is ideologically charged" (p. 279). See also Rayna Rapp, Ellen Ross, and Renate Bridenthal, 1979.

2. Gillespie's analysis is clearly aligned with the view of social structure presented as the strategy theory. Women are discriminated against in the larger, more highly esteemed segment of society, the public domain. This discrimination affects the influence they have even within the domestic domain.

3. These results suggest the importance of distinguishing between distinctive strategies which only one or the other gender uses, and different rates of use of shared strategies.

4. According to a 1978 U.S. Commission on Civil Rights report, black males receive eighty-five percent the wages of white males with comparable qualifications; the percentages for white females and black females fall below that figure (reported in the *Saturday Review,* 25 November 1978, p. 7). See also Robert Staples (1978) for a discussion of the prevalent use of white standards for evaluating the black family.

5. Barry Silverstein and Ronald Krate (1975) also write about the verbal strategies of black women; in their work the writers stress some of what they see as the difference between the verbal strategies of whites and blacks rather than of females and males.

> It is not uncommon for ghetto girls to show similar traits to a degree that sets them apart from their female counterparts in most other American communities. Girls frequently compete successfully with boys in exchanges of insults and even in physical combat. (p. 105)

In their work Silverstein and Krate often write about the (singular, non-gender-specific) "speech of the children." Unfortunately, most of their examples come from exchanges involving boys only, and often their generalizations seem to concern primarily boys, with mention of girls sometimes tacked on, as in the following statements: "Often older boys (and girls) challenge a teacher who tries to control them" (p. 114).

6. Studying interaction between children and between child and parents would also indicate whether or not there is any or much gender-segregation in many families. In a study of interaction in families in Norway, Karen Larson (1978) found that girls and mothers were more likely to talk with other females in the family, and males were more likely to talk with other males.

7. Schulz's paper "Mother Tongue" was given at the Sprache und Geschlecht conference at the Universität Osnabrück, West Germany, 29-31 March 1979, one of several recent international conferences held to discuss language and gender topics. Others include the Language and Sex programs at the Ninth World Congress of Sociology, Uppsala, Sweden, 14-19 August 1978, and at the International Conference on Social Psychology and Language at the University of Bristol, England, 16-20 July 1979.

8. Nancy Chodorow (1979) does suggest ways that love can be discussed as part of asymmetrical power relationships between women and men. In discussing the inequality that comes from the public/domestic split she writes:

> Women's work in the home and the maternal role are devalued because they are outside of the sphere of monetary exchange and unmeasurable in monetary terms, and because love, though supposedly valued, is valued only within a devalued and powerless realm, a realm separate from and not equal to profits and achievement. (p. 89)

Domestic labor (and Chodorow reminds us that mothering others *is* work [p. 97]) does not have the same exchange value as public labor.

X

WOMEN (AND MEN) AS RATIONAL SPEAKERS

The strategy model posits that in our culture the goals of both women and men include independence, and influencing the actions of others. Women's role in social process will be different from men's because women and men are engaged in different activities and have unequal access to valued resources; thus they must work in different ways to achieve their goals.

Possible gender differences in verbal strategies are intriguingly suggested, if not often clearly elaborated, in studies of female/male interaction. As I have indicated, many references to "female strategies" occur in popular and even academic literature of sociology. Most often, reference to strategies is made in passing with only a few illustrations and sometimes with none. The scattered references may, however, be helpful in further work on the strategy theory. For example, the authors of a book on cocktail waitresses in one bar quote an informant who describes how she copes with what she sees as unequal male-female joking relationships (unequal because the male waiters and customers have more latitude in what they can say and do and still keep their job and friends):

> You just can't walk up and grab some guy. My way of getting back at them is to say something under my breath so that they hear one word of it and they know I said something really gross, but they can't hear most of it. They're shocked and dying to know what I said, but I won't tell them. There are very few ways that girls can get the boys back without making herself appear cheap. (James P. Spradley and Brenda J. Mann, 1975:97)

A more extensive study of how waitresses—who are pinched, sweet-talked, and propositioned much more frequently than waiters—deal with these responses while keeping their job and obtaining their tips would add to our information on the maintenance of status and power in public and private for women and men.[1] Women in many public places find that they are frequently stared at and their presence commented on in various ways. Women *can* be present in some public places without "inviting" stares and comments on their presence—such as in the department store, grocery store, and church. These places have materials and ideas thought necessary for the maintenance of the home.[2]

Some of the material reviewed indicates that whether or not most people give conscious thought to women's and men's differing relationships to public/domestic domains and the differing expectations of women's and men's speech, they are willing, if asked, to analyze their own verbal strategies. One research team studying the power strategies reported by university students asked them to write a paragraph on the general topic of "How I Get My Way." Less than a third of the men and almost half the women said they use a show of emotion to get their way; the men were more apt to report the use of anger, the women more apt to mention sadness, sulkiness, or tears (Paula B. Johnson and Jacqueline D. Goodchilds, 1976:69). Other studies involving university students found that women and men report using direct techniques when what they want from others is stereotypically correct for their gender but indirect techniques when they think what they want falls outside what is considered the norm for their gender (study by Naomi McCormick; reported in Johnson and Goodchilds, 1976).

In a study of power tactics, again in a laboratory experiment, Paula Johnson (reported in Johnson and Goodchilds, 1976) gave students a choice of written messages to send via a computer to other (unseen—and actually nonexistent) co-workers to encourage them, as a team, to work harder in a card-sorting task in competition with other teams. Female and male students, provided with an array of possible statements, chose the following most often and chose them equally: "Please sort faster, I think our group can be one of the best; let's all try to sort very fast," and "Please sort faster, we can make the most points and get done sooner if we sort very fast." However, four times as many women as men chose the message, "Help, please sort faster, I'm really depending on you," while three times as many men as women chose "Please sort faster, I know it's possible to go faster because I've worked on this sort of thing before and you can really go fast."

True, choosing a message to send via a computer to encourage unseen people to sort IBM cards quickly is not an everyday type of interaction. But the gender differences that were found in the messages chosen are intriguing. Johnson and Goodchilds (1976) suggest that realistic fears of being thought pushy, overbearing, or lesbian may keep women "from asserting themselves in ways that we expect and accept in men" (p. 70). (Barrie Thorne points out that men in this study were evidently more reluctant to express dependence—the other side of the coin.) If the strategy theory is employed the women's responses might be explained thus: women do not think they will win by trying to usurp directly the power or authority-attitude of males. One technique they may find useful is to try to gain power and value by seemingly acknowledging their inferior position and asking for help rather than commanding.

Working on the assumptions that women do employ different strategies to influence others and that women *do* have influence over others, Susan Kaplan (1976) has looked first at self-report data of dating heterosexual couples to assess perception of power and also at couples' behavior in a variety of decision-making tasks (set forth by the researcher). While ninety-five percent of the women and eighty-seven percent of the men said decisions *should* be egalitarian (i.e., the woman and the man "should have exactly the same amount of say"), only forty-nine percent of the women and forty-two percent of the men thought their current relationship equal; men were perceived as having more power. Observers, male and female, listened to tape-recorded discussions of couples engaged in the decision-making tasks, first to rate who they thought had the more power, and then to code the statements made by the couples when they were asked to discuss and resolve hypothetical dating relationship conflicts. The observers used Bales's IPA coding system (1950) and coded the verbal responses into four clusters which Kaplan labelled Placate and Propose (socio-emotional categories), and Request and Oppose (instrumental categories). The women who had been rated as powerful were found to be more likely than other women to use Request or Oppose statements, and to verbally attack their partners more. However, Kaplan reports the assertive style used by women as "still somewhat indirect" (p. 8). She writes:

> The women's use of questioning [asking for information and opinions] suggests that while instrumentality has become increasingly sex-role appropriate [for women], direct assertion by proposing ideas or stating opinions is still not a power strategy of choice for women when interacting with men. (p. 9)

Males who had been rated powerful used a high proportion of statements categorized as Propose.

The strategies studied are limited to those recognized in Bales's Interaction Process Analysis which assumes dichotomous socio-emotional and instrumental speech; statements are categorized according to whether they work (in the perception of the coder) toward task completion or toward easing tensions and maintaining a good social atmosphere. One *could* use many other types of categories (for example, support/competition; proof from personal experience/ proof from other sources) or measurements without dichotomous labels. Furthermore, as Kaplan points out, the ratings of power may reflect the observers' stereotypes of powerful women and men rather than the actual power of the partners. She does not give examples of what she labels assertive and indirect verbal styles. But her work does suggest that women and men at least in some situations may use different power strategies.

Quite possibly the indirect strategies popularly associated with females are involved primarily in initial interactions; that is, between and among strangers, but perhaps not to such a great degree in long-term relationships. In a 1963 study comparing the talk/decision-making in small groups of strangers to the talk/ decision-making of family members, Robert K. Leik concluded:

> The traditional male role (instrumental, non-emotional behavior) as well as the traditional female role (emotional, non-task behavior) appear when interaction takes place among strangers. These emphases tend to disappear when subjects interact with their own families. Particularly is this true for instrumentality, because of a dual role for mothers [who issue many commands to children yet who are given primary responsibility for providing soothing, loving support for the children]. (p. 144)

This study, it should be noted, was limited to the study of people talking on a researcher-determined topic in a laboratory. The two observers coded only two aspects of interaction—those thought to be "emotional" and those considered "task" behavior.

"Emotion" and "task" orientation are neatly dichotomous on coding sheets and in research reports but perhaps not so neatly dichotomous in actual interaction. In most cases the *researcher* not the speakers has determined the salience and the operational definition of these terms. High consensus between or among raters can be reached with training and practice. But consensus likely will not be high across a number of teams of coders (Jesse Delia, conversation). And the observed speakers might put still different interpretations on their own interaction. The Leik study comparing the interaction among strangers and among family members was based on Robert Bales's assumptions about "appropriate sex roles" which should, he writes, be based on "traditional social order" (Robert F. Bales, 1970:212).

The "sex role differentiation hypothesis"—that men specialize in instrumental or task behaviors and women specialize in expressive or social activities—has been influential in communication studies of the past twenty-five years. Experimenters have used the hypothesis, often assumed to be fact, in setting up categories of observation and in explaining research results. (It is interesting that these categories most often used in studies of group interaction are categories of behavior that are thought to be gender specific. Work in small group research, of course, reflects the gender divisions of the larger society.) Usually the coding models treat the expressive, female-linked traits and the instrumental, male-linked traits as bipolar opposites. Yet, in a review of studies dealing with "sex differences" in small groups, B. F. Meeker and P. A. Weitzel-O'Neill (1977) write that *status* not task/social differentiation is the crucial concept; "status affects performance expectations and expectations for legitimacy of competitive or dominating behavior" (p. 101).

Often the procedures and the underlying assumptions in the "socio-emotion/task" studies are not as thoroughly reported as are the conclusions. One of the difficulties of trying to summarize these various materials, which seem to me to have a relevance to the strategy theory, is that the studies discussed here have not been explicitly governed by that theory. The questions posed, procedures used, and conclusions drawn are not discussed in terms of the assumptions of the strategy theory.

Yet a process of reuse and reinterpretation of the information from studies and personal experience is going on constantly. We can see an example of this in a study area that has relevance for the testing of the strategy framework. A study widely referenced in "sex role" literature that appears to provide support for the strategy theory is Mirra Komarovsky's 1946 report in which she concluded that women often play inferior to men in dating situations. Over the years this finding has become a "fact" which has been used as the underpinning for additional theorizing on female/male relationships. Recently a research team (Dwight Dean et al., 1975) has questioned the methodology and interpretation of the 1946 Komarovsky study and the one replication of that study (Paul Wallin, 1950) that they found. This research team replicated those earlier studies. Once again, university students were asked to complete questionnaires containing such questions as "How often [on dates] have you pretended to be intellectually inferior?" The answers resulted in raw data similar to that obtained in the two earlier studies. However, while the earlier investigators collapsed categories ("very often," "often," "several times," and "once or twice") into one, Dean et al.

reasoned that (a) lumping "once or twice" responses with "very often" responses means the final conclusions give little indication of the extent to which women play inferior, and (b) the women's answers should be put into a context of the number of opportunities they had to "play inferior," in other words, the number of dates should be considered. Furthermore, they thought it important to also ask men to complete questionnaires on *their* reported propensity to "play inferior." The men reported "playing inferior" about as frequently as did the women. The report concluded that the evidence "is insufficient to sustain the widespread and uncritical acceptance of the belief that women pretend inferiority on dates" (p. 213).

Of course, the questionnaires were structured by the investigators and were completed by individuals who were consciously reporting on their own behavior within the context of the questions provided. The completed questionnaires should not be confused with transcripts of couples' speech. Perhaps these women (and only university women and men students were involved in the study) *are* actually more likely to use what the researchers would call "playing inferior" strategies. Perhaps one sex is more likely to report "playing inferior." (Eleanor Emmons Maccoby and Carol Nagy Jacklin [1974] have reported that females are more willing than males to reveal "weaknesses" [p. 151].) Perhaps women and men do not agree on what constitutes "playing inferior." Additionally, acting inferior is certainly not the only type of verbal strategy that can be played in dating situations. However, the results of the study provide a caution against accepting too readily the proposal that women have a gender-particular repertoire of responses and methods to deal with others, especially men. Because stereotypes about what we expect from males and females run so strong and thus affect our generalizations of what we have seen and heard, Maccoby and Jacklin (1974) in their reviews of studies of social behavior of females and males place more reliance on observational data obtained from frequency counts of "relatively unambiguous categories" of behavior rather than on one-time overall ratings of observers. If we are concerned, for example, with the number of times girls and boys initiate talk with their teachers we can obtain discrete counts relatively easily. However, relatively unambiguous categories for speech strategies, for, say, the verbal or nonverbal behavior used to initiate talk, are not as easy to come by.

Very few investigators report the exact words, the talk, from which study conclusions are drawn. The exchanges have been interpreted and coded, and in the interest presumably of time, space, and expense, category scores have been presented rather than transcripts. (Even transcripts do not usually give us information on nonverbal and paralinguistic cues.) From my own searches for the actual speech upon which much of the marital power work of the 1960s and 1970s is based, I know that often no audio or video tapes now exist (in some cases tapes never were made), so reassessment of the strategies used by the women and men whose speech was studied is now impossible. The current prevalence of tape recorders, the continuing interest in symbolic interaction (with researchers observing and participating more and thus showing more consciousness of the origin of analytical categories rather than acting as omnipotent director, tester, and measurer), and the increasing willingness of journal reviewers and editors, especially in Great Britain, to accept passages of transcript as scholarly evidence will likely mean the actual speech of the observed will be more readily available. While many researchers doing work on gender differences in interaction have used Bales's categories, I would think that work undertaken specifically from the strategy theory framework would most usefully use categories related to the particular verbal strategies and motivations considered important by the participants as well as by observers.

SMALL GROUP INTERACTION

In the study of all types of interaction we need to be conscious that individual verbal strategies are likely to interact with gender and situational expectations. This is a perspective that is seldom taken in small group interaction study (Mercilee Jenkins, in press). In a review of small group research as that research affects the study of women in small groups, Mercilee Jenkins and I (Jenkins and Kramer, 1978) set forth some of the problems we found with most small group research; first, the focus is usually on problem-solving and on topics more relevant to the public sphere than to the private sphere (topics, that is, more aligned with interests and activities of males); second, most studies are conducted in the laboratory, and focus on competition, hierarchies, and leadership (with little attention to cooperation); third, generalizations about small group interaction of both males and females are often drawn from studies of all-male groups (the reverse, drawing conclusions about *mankind* from studies of all-female groups, does not occur); fourth, the social status of the individuals in the group is often ignored. We concluded from our review that it is likely that women and men have developed strategies for behavior based on their different experiences and on the existence of different social evaluations and expectations for men and women. Patterns of communication should, we argue, be studied and evaluated through a framework that recognizes the factors that determine the relationships between women and men and between their activities in private and public domains.

A few studies give some indications of what we might find if we were to ask some new questions about women's and men's interaction in small groups. Elizabeth Aries (1976) studied two all-male groups, two all-female groups, and two mixed groups, all of which met in five hour-and-a-half sessions. She could thus observe group formation rather than the aggregate behavior of assembled individuals meeting once. In the same-gender groups, men established hierarchies which remained relatively stable, while the leadership in the all-female groups rotated. In the all-male groups men told more stories with themes of aggression and superiority, and revealed less about themselves, than did women in same-gender groups, who were more likely to establish a sense of intimacy through self-revelation. In the mixed-gender groups women in general spoke less and interacted less with each other than with men. The differing behavior of men and women in the same- and mixed-gender groups needs to be explained in terms of their standing in the larger society. Using the strategy model we might be led to new insights into group dynamics of men's and of women's and of mixed-gender groups in formal and informal settings.

Some of the statements made by the *Woman, Culture, and Society* authors suggest that the strategy model will be of particular aid in studying small group interaction. Discussing activities in other cultures, both Louise Lamphere (1974) and Michelle Zimbalist Rosaldo (1974) mention the value of gossiping among women—as the exchange of valuable information, some of which can be used to influence men's public activities. Additionally, Lamphere writes that through interaction in neighborhood groups women can exercise influence over men's activities "through subtle manipulation of opinion and by creating rumors that will damage reputations or 'lose face' for the menfolk" (p. 105). These observations do not seem foreign to our culture.

The women in groups formed as part of the Women's Liberation movement—consciousness-raising groups, professional support groups, feminist spirituality groups, for example—are in some cases attempting to wield additional power in areas that have been men's domain and in others working toward a sisterhood that is consciously, deliberately, different from brotherhood. See discussions of these contemporary groups in *Chrysalis: A Magazine of Women's Culture* (1978, No. 6). Women's friendship networks of the eighteenth and nineteenth centuries are described in Nancy Cott's (1977) *The Bonds of Womanhood* and in Carroll Smith-Rosenberg's (1975) essay on female friendship. Smith-Rosenberg writes that the women whose letters and diaries she studied valued each other; "Women, who had little status or power in the larger world of male concerns, possessed status and power in the lives and worlds of other women" (p. 14). See also Mary Ryan (1979).

In all cases women are seeking to control and enrich their lives. Often women who are perceived as having or wanting power to influence men's lives are called bitches or witches; but considering men and women as people seeking to gain influence over their own and others' actions will give us a new conceptual approach to the study of women's and men's speech in small group interaction.

ASSERTIVENESS TRAINING

Currently in the United States, assertiveness training programs and writings, based evidently on different premises from those of the strategy theory, are receiving a great deal of attention. I mention them here because I think comparing these different approaches may indicate some of the popular beliefs about women's speech, as we work through and on the strategy theory, and because I think comparing these approaches may help in an evaluation of assertiveness training by looking at the assumptions of such programs.

While most advocates of assertiveness training programs propose that such training is useful to all individuals who need help in expressing their individuality, the training is often held to be of particular benefit to women because, first of all, women are thought less likely than men to be prepared to act on their own behalf; women, it is claimed, have been encouraged to be more concerned about social approval than about their own rights and wishes. Second, because more women are trying to move into a predominantly male professional milieu and are facing challenges and behaviors that are unfamiliar to them. Third, because the types of verbal behavior commonly associated with women are thought damaging to their mental health; one writer gives the following definition to point up the importance of learning to speak in an assertive manner: Nonassertive or acquiescent speaking is "emotionally dishonest, indirect, self-denying, inhibited." Assertive speaking is "(appropriately) emotionally honest, direct, self-enhancing, expressive" (Patricia Jakubowski-Spector, 1973:77). And, fourth, because many of the strategies traditionally thought to be used frequently by women are ineffective. Quite obviously, we can learn much about stereotypes and expectations about female and male verbal behavior by discussing various verbal devices women might use to accurately and effectively convey to others their feelings and goals. Assertiveness training programs, which can be considered in part programs to help people expand their repertoires of strategies, can provide valuable advice and support to those who desire to experiment with different speaking styles in order to be more effective speakers.

Several criticisms or qualifications, however, deserve attention. First, the assertiveness training literature seems to be telling women once again that we need to modify our behavior; once again we are told to adjust to the speech norms of others. For years etiquette books have been advising women that they need to work on their speech, to make it conform to social expectations or restrictions on how a woman does or should speak. While now the advice is to make the voice firm and certain rather than soft and hesitant, still the suggestions for change are directed, once again, at women (Connie C. Eble, 1976; Kramer, 1975a). While in the past women have been encouraged to be different from men in their speech, women are now seemingly encouraged to be more like men. In each case suggestions for women's responses are made in relationship to those of men, rather than in terms of a reassessment of the speech behavior of both women and men.

Many writers deal with possible criticism of this type by writing that assertive speaking is beneficial to both men and women but to women in particular because in the past they have not, as Barbara Bate (1976) points out, had equal preparation for meeting the challenges now increasingly faced in work outside the home (pp. 55-56). Also, others point out that being assertive does not necessarily mean being "masculine." Two coordinators of training groups write, "In our assertion groups we have stressed that high quality assertive responses are in no way antagonistic to warmth or sensitivity" (Kathleen Adams and Linda Wukasch-Williamson, 1976:2). Masculinity and femininity and the accompanying traditional concepts do not have to be considered as bipolar elements.

However, several problems remain. Before decisions are made about the importance of assertion training for either women or men we need information on and discussion of what are considered typical characteristics of the speech of women and men, and information on the types and strengths of restrictions placed on the type of talk "allowed" women in various situations. For example, white middle-class speakers in the Southwest of the United States rated stereotyped female terms such as "oh dear" as more "gentle" and less "aggressive" than such stereotyped male terms as "shit" (Carole Edelsky, 1976b). A study I completed with the cooperation of 466 white high school and university students found that women rated their own individual speech as close to ideal speech characteristics as did the men. While the study results are based on a questionnaire and not on men's and women's evaluation of their own speech in particular situations, and while "ideal" speech may be considered proper but not effective in actual interaction, the results indicate that assertiveness training programs need to consider what both women and men perceive as valuable, positive qualities of female, as well as male, speech (Kramer, 1978).

Furthermore, the speech stereotypically associated with men can be heard to have some social disadvantages. A student, describing to members of my language and gender class his interaction with roommates, said, "Even if we have problems, we don't usually talk about them, except indirectly. We have an all-purpose word—not a polite word—which we use a lot. That word and a sock on the arm—that's how we talk about problems." Feeling oneself limited to verbal and nonverbal displays of bravado certainly seems to me to be an unfortunate restriction of self-expression, a restriction that women should not be advised to unthinkingly emulate. A number of writers have shown concern with the way male inexpressiveness may be detrimental to men's mental health and to good husband-wife relationships. For example, Sidney M. Jourard (1964) and a colleague asked several hundred women and men to indicate on questionnaire forms what types of personal information they gave to whom. Men did not report as much self-disclosure as did women. Jourard writes that men, trained to assume the instrumental role, tend to relate to other people on an impersonal level while women, trained otherwise, "sense and respond to the feelings of the *other* person even in a supposedly official transaction" (p. 49).

"Inexpressive" usually seems to refer to more than keeping self-knowledge to oneself. The authors of an article on "The inexpressive male: A tragedy of American society" suggest two basic styles: the "cowboy—John Wayne" style of inarticulateness and the "playboy" style of saying just what is necessary to exploit women sexually (Jack O. Balswick and Charles W. Peek, 1976). The authors explain that these styles are expressed by males because societal norms encourage males to learn to be inexpressive as a part of being tough, courageous, and competitive, and suggest that men who have learned to be inexpressive can and should unlearn their inexpressiveness. These analyses at least recognize that male speech can be considered as a species in itself, not merely the base of "real" speech against which the speech of women is evaluated.[3] Assertiveness training readings and programs might well consider the many implications of encouraging women to practice, say, making more impositions on others and omitting "extra" polite terms.

An additional criticism of assertiveness training literature is that authors seldom discuss how employment of assertive techniques does or does not change the social structure. The literature on assertiveness training has not created much interest in Great Britain, where analysis of social structures is a central concern of feminists' discussions. (In the spring of 1977 and again in the summer of 1978 I searched in London bookstores and each time found only one assertiveness training book, and that one was imported from the United States.) When I introduced mention of assertiveness training in several study groups in London, the ensuing discussions centered on the limitations of the political orientation of such training. How is self-improvement related to the wider society? What types of strategies did women start with?[4] Were the same programs of equal benefit to women of all social classes? On this point Nancy Henley (1977) has written, "While the assertive training movement is vaguely understood by many to be advancing women's cause, we may ask which women it is helping" (p. 201). She suggests that the time, transportation, and fees involved mean that training is not available for the poorest women—who in any event might only lose jobs if they become "uppity." These questions point to the benefits that would accrue from further evaluation of the assertiveness training proposals and programs. The assumptions of such programs do not appear to be the same as those set forth by the strategy theory. But that theory might be used as a base from which, initially, to work to conceptualize the processes involved in assertiveness training.

In sum, often enough the references to verbal strategies are very general, useful primarily as an indicator of how widespread the belief is that women do exercise power—by subterfuge. Women are thought much more likely to use circumlocution in their speech. Men's speech is considered blunt, straightforward, direct. Men are thought to just say what needs to be said—no extra words. Even, or perhaps especially, when women are heard as "just talking" (not, that is, as manipulating), they are heard (stereotypically, at least) to be using "extra" words (Kramer, 1977).

Referring to men's speech as direct, blunt, straightforward, implies that there is nothing strategic in men's speech. It is heard as representing logic, reason. What they say is just what should be said. Women's speech has frills, and quirks; when it is not silly it is often devious. The implicit and explicit connection between men's speech and rationality is made continually.

The strategy model provides a less reductive examination of people's talk. While recording conversation among a group of four people (including myself) eating in a restaurant I taped the following exchange between one member of the group and the person serving the table:

Patron: I'm sorry, but this isn't mine.
Server: What did you order?
Patron: The turkey plate.
Server: Must be someone else's.
Patron: Sorry.
Server: I'll get yours in a minute.
Patron: That's fine. Thank you.

I showed the transcript to a dozen people and asked if they would be willing to guess the gender of the speakers. Most guessed (accurately) that the patron was a woman and the server a male (although some people were unwilling to guess the gender of the server). The patron was thought to be female because she was "overly polite," more apologetic than a man would be or "than she had to be."

Let us assume for a minute that women are, in many settings and to many people, more polite than men.[5] Why should women choose to express themselves this way? Penelope Brown (1977) suggests that rather than dismissing women's speech as curiously weak, trivial, and overpolite, we should rather consider the social pressures and constraints on women's behavior.

Politeness, Brown writes, is behaving in a way that attempts to take into account the feelings of the people addressed. "What a fantastic dress that is, Cynthia" shows interest and approval of the addressee (unless the intonation is that which we call sarcastic). One way of making a polite request is to apologize for the imposition and make it easy for the person addressed to refuse to comply with the request. "I hate to bother you, but would you have time to check in on our cat while we're away?" That is, when we are polite we show concern for the addressee's face (the desire to have the approval of others and the desire not to be imposed on). Brown points out that people are more likely to be polite when they speak to superiors or when they speak to socially distant persons or when they are involved in potentially face-threatening acts or have a high assessment of what counts as impositions.

While many men spend much of their working days interacting with superiors (e.g., in employment hierarchies) or dealing with socially distant people (in clerking jobs), women in our culture are, as women, a subordinate class and are likely to be more cautious when they are in public places to remain socially and physically distant from males who are not relatives or friends. Their reputation is determined in part by whether or not they make efforts to maintain distance from unrelated males. Also, the seriousness of impositions is perhaps weighed differently by women and by men. I asked the woman who apologized to the waiter why *she* had said "sorry" when it was *his* mistake. She said she hated to ask him to take the plate of food back to the kitchen. I asked her if she ever issued direct, bald, commands to people (such as "Take this back, and tell the chef to try again"). She said, "Only at home. Mostly to the kids." Perhaps women and men do not evaluate impositions in the same way, especially when requests are made in public domains.

If we start from the strategy model, the more useful question is not "Why are women overpolite?" but, rather, "What is the interaction between social structure and language use?" When and where do women use more polite expressions than do men? Unlike the correlational studies which line up, say, speakers' phonological variations according to age and gender classes, the strategy framework places speech within a social structure and considers speakers' social relationships, social status, and motivations.[6]

Jack W. Sattel, entitling his article "The Inexpressive Male: Tragedy or Sexual Politics?" (1976), asks whether the male is socialized to inexpressiveness or whether he finds it a handy, socially acceptable tactic. He argues that male inexpressiveness is a technique used by men to consolidate and maintain positions of power and privilege. Sattel sees inexpressiveness not merely as a cultural variable but as a determinant and consequence of the differing power positions of the sexes (p. 475), a method used to control threats to the male position. He uses empirical work, dialogue from fiction, and his experiences in consciousness-raising groups to provide examples of how inexpressiveness can be used to assume and maintain superior power positions.

In this view, men are more likely than women to be inexpressive not because the society teaches men to be inexpressive, but because society teaches them that they have the right to wield power over women. For example, a man's refusal to let others know about his joys and sorrows can be seen as a refusal to let others know the limits of his abilities and power.

I suggest that women's speech to men is thought to be more strategic and manipulative than is men's speech to women primarily because women's attempts to control are regarded as socially illegitimate. The strategy framework encourages us to look at women's and men's verbal interaction as indications of and responses to a differential distribution of power.

NOTES

1. In his collection of the words of workers—farmers, miners, cleaners, clerks, sports players, teachers, nurses, writers, police officers, and many others—Studs Terkel (1972) records many different ways women and men "maintain a sense of self" while keeping sometimes unsatisfying and humiliating jobs. ,

2. We are acquiring greater knowledge of these public and private boundaries and where women and men can speak "naturally" because of recent challenges to the boundaries. Women in religious organizations are requesting, sometimes demanding, public speaking roles. Several times small groups of women have violated the private/public boundaries by standing together on street corners staring at and commenting on males passing by. This activity has been considered unusual enough for mention to be made of it in the literature of the Women's Liberation movement as a technique to raise the consciousness of both men and women. However, women's standard, and safer, response to men's comments on women's public appearance is to pretend not to hear or see the speakers, and to avoid areas where men congregate. Men have a much wider spatial domain than women (Nancy Henley, 1977). Studies using the strategy framework can help us locate the boundaries and the methods of boundary maintenance.

3. Other authors discuss some of the fears of men that lead to "inexpressiveness": for example, the viewing of all other males as competitors, and the fear of homosexuals or homosexuality (Robert A. Lewis, 1978). Still others have looked at the directors and programmers of military and Boy Scout organizations as powerful agents which construct "masculinity" (Jeffrey P. Hantover, 1978).

4. In their analysis of speech style in a courtroom setting, Bonnie Erickson, Bruce C. Johnson, E. Allan Lind, and William O'Barr (1978) argue that so-called "women's language" (frequent use—in comparison with stereotypical men's speech—of intensifiers such as "very," "so"; hedges; grammar-book-correct speech; hand gestures; polite expressions; wide and frequent pitch shifts) is not gender specific but status and setting specific. "Women's speech" was not used by either men or women in high-status positions in the court. (This research is also discussed by William M. O'Barr and Bowman K. Atkins, 1980.) Of course, men have more high-status positions than do women. See Rosabeth Moss Kanter's *Men and Women of the Corporation* (1977) for a discussion of the relationship of job position and behavior.

5. Testing for the number and kind of hedges (examples: "kinda," "sorta," "I guess") and polite words (examples: "please," "excuse me," "thanks") used by people who make

inquiries of a female or a male attendant at a municipal center information booth, Faye Crosby and Linda Nyquist (1977) found women using more "female register" although the results were not statistically significant. Another factor that may be involved in such a situation is the perceived weightiness of the imposition. Women may be more reluctant to ask for the attendant's time and attention and thus may try to make brief requests for information.

6. The strategy framework needs and deserves much more exploration than is possible in these chapters. While this approach contains a valuable recognition of and appreciation for women's rationality and for the complexities of gender arrangements in our culture, the framework also contains the risk of a tautology for its advocates. If we say that all women's and men's speech is rational and strategic, we are more likely to hear only rationality and strategies in interactions. Colleagues and I have noticed that if we begin an examination of tapes of adult conversation by assuming that speakers' intentions are guiding their speech and thus that it is important that we try to decipher intentions, we are very capable of assigning motives to the speakers. The more time we spend discussing a tape, the more elaborate the motivations of the speakers seem to become. Yet it is not clear to me how many moves ahead speakers actually can and do plan or how carefully plotted their speech is.

Epilogue

Several conceptions of *language* are implicit in these chapters. In some cases language is taken primarily as a system, a medium of communication for speakers. In other cases it is dealt with primarily as an activity, as speech. It is often useful to make some distinctions between the language as a structure, a resource for speakers; and language as interaction. Yet as these explorations should illustrate, no neat boundary lines can be drawn between language as a code and language as a practice. The material in this book in general presents language structure as a social form, a product of social interaction, which affects and is affected by the rest of the social life of its speakers. Language use, or speech, is presented as interaction in which the speakers often have unequal influence and speaking rights.

This perspective on language is different from that taken by many people who write and talk about language. As I have read and reread many popular and academic essays on language while working on this book, I have made a listing of the (usually unexplicated) assumptions that seem to serve as a base for many statements about the relationship of language and gender, especially those published in periodicals and books designed for a "general" audience. The statements I quote here are all from a short essay by a British columnist (Philip Howard, 1977). Additional examples can be found in the preceding chapters and in the sources cited in the essays by Wendy Martyna (1978a, 1978b, 1980), Maija S. Blaubergs (1978a, 1978b, 1980), Barbara Bate (1978), and Norma J. Shepelak (1977).

1. Language structure is autonomous, quite separate from the social conditions and the social hierarchy of speakers. ("Social practice rather than linguistic regulation will gradually and happily remove the adventitious masculine connotations from such vocation words as stockbroker, pilot, miner, and Prime Minister" [p. 94]. "We need to end the real injustice in jobs, and homes, and mortgages, and other aspects of life, and the language can look after itself" [p. 95].)

2. Language changes slowly over time, but in the past it has changed in correct, natural ways. Language change should not be, perhaps cannot be, forced.

("For advertisements for jobs and products we can agree to give up or smudge some feminine designations. . . . But we must firmly resist other misguided attempts to emasculate or spay the language in the name of sexual equality" [p. 94].)

3. Language is considered a wonderful, even mystical gift from the heavens which can serve all needs of reasonable people. ("The English language, with its magnificently Protean flexibility, is quite capable of meeting [the current] challenge without the whimsical convolutions around the theme of Madam Chairperson invented by mockers and even, it is said, by the zanier supporters of Women's Lib" [p. 93].)

4. Language is a precious structure which can be damaged by lunatics and thus must be protected by language specialists. ("To reduce the number and scope of available discriminations, however worthy the purpose, is silly because it harms the language. . . . Such nonsense as chairpersons . . . is not just loony, but also mischievous . . . it corrupts the language" [pp. 94-95].)

5. Language structure has sufficient categories for the world. No more labels need to be added—at least not by feminists or other traitors of the culture. (See example under No. 4.)

6. Social practices and language usage are quite separate, operating with different value systems. ("[The new law making it illegal for advertisers to specify gender of person-wanted advertisements] is socially desirable, but linguistically deplorable" [p. 94].) (Howard's essay on language is titled: "One area where sexism is welcome.")

These are powerful assumptions because they are popular assumptions. I am not arguing that language is synonymous with social life; we can and should make distinctions. We can do this by setting forth some of the popular assumptions about the relationships and distinctions between language and the rest of the social structure; and by discussing and evaluating those assumptions in terms of theoretical approaches that deal with the ways people acquire, use, and evaluate language.

Most of the researchers whose work is described and quoted in the preceding chapters desire or at least do not fear changes in relationships between women and men. In their critical look at language they are pointing out concept-omissions in the language, they are studying the process of naming, they are indicating the ways that sexist language can affect the perception of self and others and can affect interaction among males and females, they are suggesting guidelines for eliminating sexist language, they are renaming themselves, and they are analyzing past and contemporary linguistic, sociolinguistic, social psychological, and sociological theory. They consider the language structure not as primarily an abstract system of lexicon and grammar, but as a social structure that has, in the past, been produced and directed more by men than by women.

The concern here has been with the relationship of women, men, and language. But as Blanche Wiesen Cook (1978) points out, a study of the relationship of women and men eventually leads to much more—to a study of, for example, the connections between racism, poverty, sexism, and imposed institutional restrictions (p. vii). The columnist who concludes his essay on sexism in language with the suggestion that perhaps the next step in this "fuss" will be to rename the movement Wopersons' Lib (Howard, 1977:95) announces that he has very little knowledge, or wishes to show little knowledge, of the work in language and gender research, and of the implications of this research for other linguistic and social issues.

Speech is often, although not always, an important element of interaction; but speech when it occurs is always socially situated behavior, a part of social reality, not merely a reflection of it (Philip M. Smith and Howard Giles, 1978). As the work presented here illustrates, speech in our culture cannot be adequately studied apart from some attention to the social structure—which includes the division of labor and of speaking rights by gender, and a language structure that does not represent equally the concerns of women and men.

To say this is not, of course, to explain the specifics of how social interaction is to be studied. We are only beginning to learn how to do conversational analysis—that is, learning what cues we as speakers use—word choice, tone, speech norms, setting, perceived intentions, gestures, and the like—to make sense of our interaction and to be effective interactants. Penelope Brown and Stephen Levinson (1978) have written a detailed explanation of one speech function—politeness—demonstrating some of the complexities of human planning represented by the words, tone, and gestures chosen. Their illustrations persuasively attest that conversations cannot be drawn up apart from knowledge of social relationships. The common assumption that conversations are, in general, a cooperative effort among equals is misleading.

The problems for those of us who want to understand social power are complex. However, increasingly we are finding that language study can be a useful ingress to an analysis of power—of who influences others and compels obedience. The studies reviewed in the preceding chapters support the conclusions reached by Rolv Mikkel Blakar (1977), who was working with the Norwegian language:

> The simplest way to get an idea of the social power and influence exerted by a language system is to analyse an area where the constellation of power is relatively clear. An example of this is the sex role division in our male-dominated society. Through a fairly comprehensive analysis of Norwegian, it was demonstrated how language in different ways (a) *reflects* and (b) *conserves* the existing sex role pattern, even to the extent that language can be said to (c) *counteract change*. Further it was shown (d) how boys and girls, both directly and indirectly, learn their traditional sex roles as they learn and understand their mother tongue. (p. 12)

Additionally, through language study we are learning how speech in everyday interaction reflects and conserves the existing social structure.

Power increasingly is a topic of women's discussions and writings. Yet many fear the topic. Women have not been rewarded for trying to obtain power or to use power for their own interests. Many women, resentful at being the objects upon which the power structure is built, are yet worried that working for more power for women will just alter the names of the people who have power but will not alter the hierarchies themselves. The often unstated assumption is that there is a finite amount of power; if someone or some group finds a way to power, someone else or some other group loses power. Women talk about (and try to practice in many of their groups) power diffusion. Leadership is rotated, and information sharing is encouraged as alternatives to traditional power structures are sought. (Florence Howe [1975] and Lee Jenkins and I in an [1978] essay discuss some of these fears and some group attempts to change interaction procedures.) Individually many women are working, through formal assertiveness training programs or self-initiated programs, to change habitual verbal and nonverbal behavior that indicates weakness and submissiveness, behavior such as averting one's gaze when stared at, not protesting when interrupted, allowing others to touch or cuddle, smiling a lot, and using many qualifying statements and acknowledgments that one might be wrong.

Increased attention to our own interests, preferences, and personal power is, of course, important. However, as Nancy Henley (1978) reminds us, personal power is not so very personal. "Weaknesses" such as sensitivity to the needs of others, acknowledgment that one may be wrong, crying, smiling, and open discussion of feelings may be considered strengths. These behaviors become "weaknesses" when the powerful people take advantage of the vulnerability of those who are more open (Henley, p. 36). Women's language has never really been in a class by itself. It has been a part of the structure of knowledge and beliefs designed by men to express, explain, and sanction their power.

Discussion of language and power, and of the reactions of the powerful to women's claims to custody of naming and speaking rights can be, I believe, greatly facilitated by discussions of and development of theoretical frameworks that deal with the relationships of women and men and the theories and rituals that support those relationships. What is vital in this process is that both men and women are involved in the discussions of perceptions and definitions of themselves and their place in their world and in the production of symbols and values.

Each of the frameworks for analysis presented here discusses the effects on language use of the unequal distribution of power that results from a gender hierarchy. Each provides an explicit perspective from which to look at the dynamics of social interaction among women and men, and to explain some of the gender-based differences in speech and in the evaluation of speakers.

The four frameworks are of value in that they encourage the examination of women's and men's speech from several perspectives. Yet all have to do with relations between men and women, and all take account of dominance as part of the relations. Although I discuss in each section studies that seemed particularly relevant to the questions and assumptions highlighted by each theory, I know that the same material could be analyzed through more than one theoretical framework. I am not suggesting that the theories are equally valuable. Because it is an attempt to specity the dynamics of speech as socially situated behavior influenced by social institutions, the strategy approach used as the basis for the last three chapters seems to me, at this time, to be the most stimulating and useful. And I think that discussion of the variables of the speech styles framework will be particularly helpful in exploring the influence of social institutions. However, each of these frameworks and others can help us inspect different aspects of women's and men's interaction and involvement in institutional and symbolic systems.

I have learned a great deal in working with each framework. In each case I used the framework as a guide to questions about the language of women and men and to possible explanations about what people are hearing women and men say, and how that speech is evaluated. I worked from an assumption that we are all, in an important and practical sense, social theorists in our everyday life, sorting through our experiences in every social encounter and revising our theories. I need to say again that my analyses of these frameworks are exploratory. Further work with these and other frameworks, additional language and gender research, continuing changes in the roles taken by women and men, and our understanding of those changes will alter somewhat the questions we ask. Continued discussion of various theoretical approaches should help us work toward coherent conceptual schemes relating language code and use to men's and women's differing economic, political, and social activities and status.

References

Abrahams, Roger. 1972. Joking: The training of the man of words in talking broad. In Thomas Kochman (ed.). *Rappin' and stylin' out.* Urbana, Ill.: Univ. of Illinois Press.

———. 1973. The advantages of black English. In Johanna S. DeStefano (ed.), *Language, society, and education: A profile of black English.* Worthington, Ohio: Charles A. Jones Publishing Company.

———. 1975. Negotiating respect: Patterns of presentation among black women. In Claire R. Farrer (ed.), *Women and folklore.* Austin: Univ. of Texas Press.

Adams, Kathleen, and Linda Wukasch-Williamson. 1976. Assertiveness training, androgyny, and professional women. Paper read at American Psychological Association, Washington, D.C.

Addington, D. W. 1968. The relationship of selected vocal characteristics to personality perception. *Speech Monographs,* 35, 492-503.

Adlam, Diana, and Couze Venn. 1977. Introduction to Irigaray. *Ideology & Consciousness,* No. 1 (May), pp. 57-61.

Aldous, Joan, and N. Dahl. 1974. *International bibliography of research in marriage and the family.* Volume II, 1965-1972. Minneapolis: Univ. of Minnesota Press.

Aleguire, David. 1978. Interruptions and dominance. Paper read at Ninth World Congress of Sociology, Uppsala, Sweden.

Andelin, Helen B. 1975. *Fascinating womanhood.* New York: Bantam.

Ardener, Edwin. 1973. Some outstanding problems in the analysis of events. Paper read at Association of Social Anthropologists' Decennial Conference.

———. 1975. The "problem" revisited. In Shirley Ardener (ed.), *Perceiving women.* London: Malaby Press.

Ardener, Shirley (ed.). 1975. *Perceiving women.* London: Malaby Press.

———. 1978. *Defining females: The nature of women in society.* New York: John Wiley & Sons.

Aries, Elizabeth. 1976. Interaction patterns and themes of male, female, and mixed groups. *Small Group Behavior,* 7 (1), 7-18.

Bailey, F. Lee, and Henry B. Rothblatt. 1971. *Successful techniques for criminal trials.* Rochester, N.Y.: Bancroft-Whitney Publishing Company.

Bakeman, Roger, and Barbara Bianchi. 1976. Social interactions among preschool children: Sex differences and environmental influences. Paper read at American Psychological Association, Washington, D.C.

Baker, Oleda. 1975. *Be a woman!* New York: Ballantine.

Bales, Robert F. 1950. *Interaction process analysis.* Cambridge, Mass.: Addison-Wesley.

———. 1970. *Personality and interpersonal behavior.* New York: Holt, Rinehart and Winston.

Ballou, Maturin M. 1971. *Notable thoughts about women: A literary mosaic.* Ann Arbor, Mich.: Gryphon Books.

Balswick, Jack O., and Charles W. Peek. 1976. The inexpressive male: A tragedy of American society. In Deborah S. David and Robert Brannon (eds.), *The forty-nine percent majority.* Reading, Mass.: Addison-Wesley.

Barzun, Jacques. 1974. A few words on a few words. *The Columbia Forum,* (Summer), pp. 17-19.

Bate, Barbara. 1975. Generic man, invisible woman: Language, thought, and social change. *University of Michigan Papers in Women's Studies,* 2 (1), 83-95.

———. 1976. Assertive speaking: An approach to communication education for the future. *Communication Education,* 25 (January), 53-59.

———. 1978. Sex bias in language: An issue worth talking about. *Thresholds in Education,* 4 (1), 27-31.

Battle-Sister, Ann. 1971. Conjectures on the female culture question. *Journal of Marriage and the Family,* 33, 411-420.

Baym, Nina. 1978. *Woman's fiction: A guide to novels by and about women in America, 1820-1870.* Ithaca, N.Y.: Cornell Univ. Press.

Beardsley, Elizabeth Lane. 1976. Referential genderization. In Carol C. Gould and Marx W. Wartofsky (eds.), *Women and philosophy: Toward a theory of liberation.* New York: C. P. Putnam's Sons.

———. 1977. Traits and genderization. In Mary Vetterling-Braggin, Frederick A. Elliston, and Jane English (eds.), *Feminism and philosophy.* Totowa, N.J.; Littlefield, Adams.

Beatts, Anne. 1975. Can a woman get a laugh and a man too? *Mademoiselle,* 81 (11), 140, 182, 184, 186.

de Beauvoir, Simone. 1964. *The second sex.* Translated and edited by H. M. Parshley. New York: Bantam.

Becker, Gary S., Elisabeth M. Landes, and Robert T. Mitchell. 1977. An economic analysis of marital instability. *Journal of Political Economy,* 85, 1141-1187.

Bem, Sandra L., and Daryl J. Bem. 1973. Does sex-biased job advertising "aid and abet" sex discrimination? *Journal of Applied Social Psychology,* 3 (1), 6-18.

Bernard, Jessie. 1973a. My four revolutions: An autobiographical history of the ASA. In Joan Huber (ed.), *Changing women in a changing society.* Chicago: Univ. of Chicago Press.

———. 1973b. Sex differences: An overview. *Module 26.* N.p.: MSS Modular Publications.

Blakar, Rolv Mikkel. 1977. Language as a means of social power. In J. L. Mey (ed.), *Pragmalinguistics: Theory and practice.* Lisse: Peter de Ridder.

Blaubergs, Maija S. 1975. On "The nurse was a doctor." In R. Ordoubadian and Walburga von Raffler Engel (eds.), *Views on language.* Murfreesboro, Tenn.: Inter-University Publishing.

———. 1978a. Changing the sexist language: The theory behind the practice. *Psychology of Women Quarterly,* 2, 244-261.

———. 1978b. Sociolinguistic change towards nonsexist language: An overview and analysis of misunderstandings and misapplications. Paper read at Ninth World Congress of Sociology, Uppsala, Sweden.

———. 1980. An analysis of classic arguments against changing sexist language. *Women's Studies International Quarterly,* 3 (2/3), 135-147. These issues also appear as: Cheris Kramarae (ed.). 1980. *The voices and words of women and men.* Oxford: Pergamon Press.

Blood, Robert O., Jr., and Donald M. Wolfe. 1960. *Husbands and wives.* New York: Free Press.

Bochner, Arthur P. 1976. Conceptual frontiers in the study of communication in families: An introduction to the literature. *Human Communication Research,* 2, 381-397.

Bodine, Ann. 1975. Androcentrism in prescriptive grammar: Singular "they," sex-indefinite "he," and "he or she." *Language in Society,* 4, 129-146.

Booth, Alan, and Susan Welch. 1978. Spousal consensus and its correlates: A reassessment. *Journal of Marriage and the Family,* 40, 23-32.

Bornstein, Diane. 1978. As meek as a maid: An historical perspective on language for women in courtesy books from the middle ages to Seventeen Magazine. In Douglas Butturff and Edmund L. Epstein (eds.), *Women's language and style.* Published with the assistance of the Department of English, Univ. of Akron.

Bosmajian, Haig. 1977. Sexism in the language of legislatures and courts. In Alleen Pace Nilsen, Haig Bosmajian, H. Lee Gershuny, and Julia P. Stanley (eds.), *Sexism and language.* Urbana, Ill.: National Council of Teachers of English.

Braude, Jacob M. 1958. *Braude's handbook of humor for all occasions.* Englewood Cliffs, N.J.: Prentice-Hall.

Bristol [England] Women's Liberation Group, The. N.d. The Journal of the Bristol Women's Liberation Group.

Brown, George W., and Michael Rutter. 1966. The measurement of family activities and relationships: A methodological study. *Human Relations,* 19, 241-263.

Brown, Penelope. 1976. Women and politeness: A new perspective on language and society. *Reviews in Anthropology,* 3, 240-249.

———. 1980. How and why are women more polite: Some evidence from a Mayan community.

In Sally McConnell-Ginet, Nelly Furman, and Ruth Borker (eds.), *Women and language in literature and society.* New York: Praeger, 111-136.

———, and Stephen Levinson. 1978. Universals in language usage: Politeness phenomena. In Esther N. Goody (ed.), *Questions and politeness: Strategies in social interaction.* Cambridge, England: Cambridge Univ. Press.

Buffery, Anthony W. H., and Jeffrey A. Gray. 1972. Sex differences in the development of spatial and linguistic skills. In Christopher Ounsted and David C. Taylor (eds.), *Gender differences: The ontogeny and significance.* Edinburgh: Churchill Livingstone.

Burke, Carolyn Greenstein. 1978. Report from Paris: Women's writing and the women's movement. *Signs: Journal of Women in Culture and Society,* 3, 843-855.

Byatt, A. S. 1977. A. S. Byatt reviews George Steiner's latest artifact. [London] *Times Educational Supplement,* April 8, p. 18.

Callan, Hilary. 1978. Harems and overlords: Biosocial models and the female. In Shirley Ardener (ed.), *Defining females: The nature of women in society.* New York: John Wiley & Sons.

Campbell, Karlyn Kohrs. 1973. The rhetoric of women's liberation: An oxymoron. *Quarterly Journal of Speech,* 59, 74-86.

Campbell, Patricia B. 1976. Adolescent intellectual decline. *Adolescence,* 11, 629-635.

Cantwell, Mary, and Amy Gross. 1975. How to be funny: The all-time, surefire, great guide. *Mademoiselle,* 81 (11), 136-137, 210.

Carlson, Rae. 1972. Understanding women: Implications for personality theory and research. *Journal of Social Issues,* 28 (2), 17-32.

Catt, Carrie Chapman. 1902. Quoted (without source) in Alison M. Jaggar and Paula Rothenberg Struhl (eds.). 1978. *Feminist frameworks: Alternative theoretical accounts of the relations between women and men.* New York: McGraw-Hill, p. xiv.

Chapman, Antony J., and Nicholas J. Gadfield. 1976. Is sexual humor sexist? *Journal of Communication,* 26 (3), 141-153.

Cheshire, Jenny. 1978. Present tense verbs in Reading, England. In Peter Trudgill (ed.), *Sociolinguistic patterns in British English.* London: Edward Arnold.

Chesler, Phyllis. 1972. *Women and madness.* New York: Avon.

———, and Emily Jane Goodman. 1976. *Women, money & power.* New York: William Morrow.

Chodorow, Nancy. 1979. Mothering, male dominance and capitalism. In Zillah R. Eisenstein (ed.), *Capitalist patriarchy and the case for socialist feminism.* New York: Monthly Review Press.

Cixous, Hélène. 1976. The laugh of the Medusa. *Signs: Journal of Women in Culture and Society,* 1, 875-893. Translated by Keith Cohen and Paula Cohen.

Collier, Jane Fishburne. 1974. Women in politics. In Michelle Zimbalist Rosaldo and Louise Lamphere (eds.), *Woman, culture, and society.* Stanford, Calif.: Stanford Univ. Press.

Condon, John. 1975. *Semantics and communication.* 2nd edition. New York: Macmillan.

Condry, John, and Sandra Condry. 1976. Sex differences: A study of the eye of the beholder. *Child Development,* 47, 812-819.

Conklin, Nancy Faires. 1974. Toward a feminist analysis of linguistic behavior. *University of Michigan Papers in Women's Studies,* 1 (1), 51-73.

Conrad, Cinthia Lee Gannett. 1978. Sex and the single brain. Paper read at Ninth World Congress of Sociology, Uppsala, Sweden.

Continuation of the story of the collective that has no name, A. 1970. *Ain't I a Woman,* 1(8), 9.

Cook, Blanche Wiesen (ed.). 1978. *Crystal Eastman on women and revolution.* Oxford: Oxford Univ. Press.

Cooper, Lee. 1974. "Publish" or perish: Negro Jehovah's Witness adaptation in the ghetto. In Irving I. Zaretsky and Mark P. Leone (eds.), *Religious movements in contemporary America.* Princeton, N.J.: Princeton Univ. Press.

Coser, Rose Laub. 1960. "Laughter among colleagues": A study of the social functions of humor among the staff of a mental hospital. *Psychiatry*, 23, 81-95.

Cott, Nancy F. 1977. *The bonds of womanhood: "Woman's sphere" in New England, 1780-1835.* New Haven: Yale Univ. Press.

Crosby, Faye, and Linda Nyquist. 1977. The female register: An empirical study of Lakoff's hypotheses. *Language in Society*, 6, 313-322.

Daly, Mary. 1973. *Beyond God the father.* Boston: Beacon Press.

———. 1978. *Gyn/Ecology*: The metaethics of radical feminism. Boston: Beacon Press.

Dean, Dwight, Edward A. Powers, Rita Braito, and Brent Bruton. 1975. Cultural contradictions and sex roles revisited: A replication and a reassessment. *Sociological Quarterly,* 16, 207-215.

Delamont, Sara. 1976. *Interaction in the classroom*. London: Methuen.

DeStefano, Johanna S., Mary W. Kuhner, and Harold B. Pepinsky. 1978. An investigation of referents of selected sex-indefinite terms in English. Paper given at the Ninth World Congress of Sociology, Uppsala, Sweden.

Dewhurst, C. Kurt, Betty MacDowell, and Marsha MacDowell. 1977. Beyond expectations: Folk art by American women. Unpublished manuscript. The Museum: Michigan State Univ.

Dill, Bonnie Thornton. 1979. The dialectics of black womanhood. *Signs: Journal of Women in Culture and Society*, 4, 543-555.

Dillard, J.L. 1972. *Black English: Its history and usage in the United States.* New York: Random House.

———. 1975. *All-American English*. New York: Random House.

———. 1976. *American talk: Where our words came from*. New York: Random House.

Dobler, Lavinia, and Muriel Fuller (eds.). 1970. *The Dobler world directory of youth periodicals.* 3rd edition. New York: Citation Press.

Doglin, Janet. 1974. Latter-Day sense and substance. In Irving I. Zaretsky and Mark P. Leone (eds.), *Religious movements in contemporary America.* Princeton, N.J.: Princeton Univ. Press.

Donovan, Jane. 1976. Poet as woman: Poetry as becoming. Unpublished manuscript. Univ. of Illinois.

Dubois, Betty Lou, and Isabel Crouch. 1975. The question of tag questions in women's speech: They don't really use more of them, do they? *Language in Society* 4, 289-294.

———. 1976. *Proceedings of the conference on the sociology of the languages of American women.* Papers in Southwest English, 4. San Antonio, Texas: Trinity Univ.

———. 1978. Introduction to special issue (American minority women in sociolinguistic perspective). *International Journal of the Sociology of Languages,* 17, 5-15.

Duke, Daniel Linden. 1978. Why don't girls misbehave more than boys in school? *Journal of Youth and Adolescence*, 4, 141-157.

Eagly, Alice H. 1978. Sex differences in influenceability. *Psychological Bulletin,* 85, 86-116.

Eakins, Barbara Westbook, and R. Gene Eakins. 1978. *Sex differences in human communication.* Boston: Houghton Mifflin.

Eble, Connie C. 1976. Etiquette books as linguistic authority. In Peter Reich (ed.), *LACUS Forum* II 1975. Columbia, S.C.: Hornbeam Press.

Edelsky, Carole. 1976a. The acquisition of communicative competence: Recognition of linguistic correlates of sex roles. *Merrill-Palmer Quarterly of Behavior and Development,* 22, 47-59.

———. 1976b. Subjective reactions to sex-linked language. *Journal of Social Psychology,* 99, 97-104.

Edwards, John R. 1979. Social class differences and the identification of sex in children's speech. *Journal of Child Language,* 6, 121-127.

Ehrmann, Jacques (ed.). 1970. *Structuralism.* New York: Doubleday Anchor.

Eisenstein, Zillah R. (ed.). 1979. *Capitalist patriarchy and the case for socialist feminism.* New York: Monthly Review Press.

Elliott, John. 1974. Sex role constraints on freedom of discussion: A neglected reality of the classroom. *New Era*, 55, 147-155.

Ellmann, Mary. 1968. *Thinking about women*. New York: Harcourt Brace Jovanovich.

Emswiler, Sharon Neufer, and Thomas Neufer Emswiler. 1974. *Women and worship: A guide to non-sexist hymns, prayers, and liturgies*. New York: Harper & Row.

Enck, John J., Elizabeth T. Forter, and Alvin Whitley (eds.). 1960. *The comic in theory and practice*. New York: Appleton-Century-Crofts.

Engle, Marianne. 1980. Sex differences in parent-child conversations. *Women's Studies International Quarterly*, 3 (2/3), 259-266. These issues also appear as: Cheris Kramarae (ed.). 1980. *The voices and words of women and men*. Oxford: Pergamon Press.

Erickson, Bonnie, Bruce C. Johnson, E. Allan Lind, and William O'Barr. 1978. Speech style and impression formation in a court setting: The effects of "powerful" and "powerless" speech. *Journal of Experimental and Social Psychology*, 14, 266-279.

Ervin-Tripp, Susan. 1976. "What do women sociolinguists want?": Prospects for a research field. In Betty Lou Dubois and Isabel Crouch (eds.), *Proceedings of the conference on the sociology of the languages of American women*. San Antonio, Texas: Trinity Univ.

Esar, Evan (ed.). 1949. *The dictionary of humorous quotations*. Garden City, N.Y.: Doubleday.

Farkas, George. 1976. Education, wage rates, and the division of labor between husband and wife. *Journal of Marriage and the Family*, 38, 473-483.

[Farrar, Eliza W. R.]. 1836. *The young lady's friend*. Boston: American Stationers' Company.

Fast, Julius. 1971. *The incompatibility of men and women: And how to overcome it*. New York: M. Evans and Company.

Felman, Shoshana. 1975. Women and madness: The critical phallacy. *Diacritics*, 5 (4), 2-10.

Feminist English dictionary: An intelligent woman's guide to dirty words. 1973. Chicago: Loop Center YWCA.

Ferber, Marianne A., and Bonnie G. Birnbaum. 1977. The "new home economics": Retrospects and prospects. *Journal of Consumer Research*, 4, 19-28.

Fine, Gary Alan. 1976. Obscene joking across cultures. *Journal of Communication*, 26 (3), 134-140.

Firestone, Shulamith. 1970. *The dialectic of sex: The case for feminist revolution*. New York: William Morrow.

Fishman, Pamela M. 1977. Interactional shitwork. *Heresies: A Feminist Publication on Art & Politics*, No. 2 (May), 99-101.

–––. 1978. Interaction: The work women do. *Social Problems*, 25, 397-406.

Fletcher, Ronald. 1973. *The family and marriage in Britain*. 3rd edition. Harmondsworth, Middlesex: Penguin.

Flexner, Stuart Berg. 1975. Preface. In Harold Wentworth and Stuart Berg Flexner (eds.), *Dictionary of American Slang*. 2nd supplemental edition. New York: Thomas Y. Crowell.

Foster, Brian. 1976. *The changing English language*. London: Macmillan.

Frank, Francine Wattman. 1978. Women's language in America: Myth and reality. In Douglas Butturff and Edmund L. Epstein (eds.), *Women's language and style*. Published with the assistance of the Dept. of English, Univ. of Akron.

Fransella, Fay, and Kay Frost. 1977. *On being a woman: A review of research on how women see themselves*. London: Tavistock Publications.

Freeman, Jo. 1975. The politics of women's liberation: A case study of an emerging social movement and its relation to the policy process. New York: David McKay.

Freire, Paulo. 1970 *Pedagogy of the oppressed*. Translated by Myra Bergman Ramos. New York: Herder and Herder.

Friedan, Betty. 1963. *The feminine mystique*. New York: Dell.

Gall, Meredith D., Amos K. Hobby, and Kenneth H. Craik. 1969. Non-linguistic factors in oral language productivity. *Perceptual and Motor Skills*, 29, 871-874.

Gallatin, Judith E. 1975. *Adolescence and individuality: A conceptual approach to adolescent psychology*. New York: Harper & Row.

Gallop, Jane. 1975. The ghost of Lacan, the trace of language. *Diacritics*, 5 (4), 18-24.

———. 1976. The ladies' man. *Diacritics*, 6 (4), 28-34.

Garry, Leon (ed.). 1973. *The standard periodical directory*. 4th edition. New York: Oxbridge Publishing.

Gerbner, George, and Nancy Signorielli. 1979. *Women and minorities in television drama 1969-1978*. Philadelphia: Univ. of Pennsylvania. The Annenberg School of Communications.

Gershuny, H. Lee. 1977. Sexism in the language of literature. In Alleen Pace Nilsen, Haig Bosmajian, H. Lee Gershuny, and Julia P. Stanley (eds.), *Sexism and language*. Urbana, Ill.: National Council of Teachers of English.

———. 1978. The doublespeak of sexism. Paper read at Modern Language Association convention, New York.

Giles, Howard. 1977. Social psychology and applied linguistics: Towards an integrative approach. *ITL: Review of Applied Linguistics*, No. 35, pp. 27-42.

———, Richard Y. Bourhis, and Donald M. Taylor. 1977. Towards a theory of language in ethnic group relations. In Howard Giles (ed.), *Language, ethnicity and intergroup relations*. European monographs in social psychology, 13. London: Academic Press.

———, and Peter F. Powesland. 1975. *Speech style and social evaluation*. European monographs in social psychology, 7. London: Academic Press.

Gillespie, Dair L. 1971. Who has the power? The marital struggle. *Journal of Marriage and the Family*, 33, 445-458.

Gilman, Charlotte Perkins. 1911. *The man-made world; or our androcentric culture*. London: T. Fisher Unwin.

Glasgow University Media Group. 1976. *Bad News*, volume 1. London: Routledge & Kegan Paul.

Glazer-Malbin, Nona. 1976. Housework: Review essay. *Signs: Journal of Women in Culture and Society*, 1, 905-922.

Gleason, Jean Berko. 1975. Fathers and other strangers: Men's speech to young children. In Daniel P. Dato (ed.), *Developmental psycholinguistics: Theory and applications*. Washington, D.C.: Georgetown Univ. Press.

Glick, Bruce R., and Steven Jay Gross. 1975. Marital interaction and marital conflict: a critical evaluation of current research strategies. *Journal of Marriage and the Family*, 37, 505-512.

Goffman, Erving. 1976. Gender advertisements. *Studies in the Anthropology of Visual Communication*, 3, 65-154.

———. 1977. The arrangement between the sexes. *Theory & Society*, 4, 301-331.

Goldstein, Jeffrey H. 1976. Theoretical notes on humor. *Journal of Communication*, 26 (3), 104-112.

Goodwin, Marjorie Harness. 1978. Conversational practices in a peer group of urban black children. Unpublished dissertation. Dept. of Anthropology, Univ. of Pennsylvania.

———. 1980. Directive-response speech sequences in girls' and boys' task activities. In Sally McConnell-Ginet, Nelly Furman, and Ruth Borker (eds.), *Women and language in literature and society*. New York: Praeger, 157-173.

Graham, Alma. 1975. The making of a nonsexist dictionary. In Barrie Thorne and Nancy Henley (eds.), *Language and sex: Difference and dominance*. Rowley, Mass.: Newbury House.

Green, Laura. 1973. Dictionaries think just like male chauvinist pigs. *Chicago Sun-Times*, May 22, section 2, p. 3.

Greif, Esther Blank. 1980. Sex differences in parent-child conversations. *Women's Studies International Quarterly*, 3 (2/3), 253-258. These issues also appear as: Cheris Kramarae (ed.). 1980. *The voices and words of women and men*. Oxford: Pergamon Press.

Griffin, Susan. 1978. *Women and nature: The roaring inside her*. New York: Harper & Row.

Griffiths, Dot, and Esther Saraga. 1977. " . . . fundamentally suited to different social roles": Sex differences in a sexist society. Paper read at Woman and Science Conference, University of Sussex.

Grim, Patrick. 1977. Sexism and semantics. In Mary Vetterling-Braggin, Frederick A. Elliston, and Jane English (eds.), *Feminism and philosophy*. Totowa, N.J.: Littlefield, Adams.

Grimstad, Kirsten, and Susan Rennie (eds.). 1973. *The new woman's survival catalog*. New York: Coward, McCann and Geoghegan/Berkley Publishing.

Gross, Elizabeth, 1976. Lacan, the symbolic, the imaginary and the real. *Working Papers in Sex, Science & Culture*, 1 (2), 12-32.

Grotjahn, Martin. 1957. *Beyond laughter*. New York: McGraw-Hill.

Gurewitch, Morton. 1975. *Comedy: The irrational vision*. Ithaca, N.Y.: Cornell Univ. Press.

Hale, Beatrice Forbes-Robertson. 1914. *What women want: An interpretation of the feminist movement*. New York: Frederick A. Stokes.

Hall, Judith. 1977. Female intuition measured at last? *New Society*, June 9, pp. 502-503.

Hantover, Jeffrey P. 1978. The Boy Scouts and the validation of masculinity. *Journal of Social Issues*, 34 (1), 184-195.

Harding, Susan. 1975. Women and words in a Spanish village. In Rayna R. Reiter (ed.), *Toward an anthropology of women*. New York: Monthly Review Press.

Hardwick, Elizabeth. 1975. In Women novelists: A distinct group? (a panel discussion). *Women's Studies: An Interdisciplinary Journal*, 3, 5-28.

Harrison, Linda. 1975. Cro-Magnon woman—in eclipse. *The Science Teacher*, 42 (4), 8-11.

———, and Richard N. Passero. 1975. Sexism in the language of elementary school textbooks. *Science and Children*, 12 (4), 22-25.

Hartman, Maryann. 1976. A descriptive study of the language of men and women born in Maine around 1900 as it reflects the Lakoff hypotheses in "Language and Women's Place." In Betty Lou Dubois and Isabel Crouch (eds.), *Proceedings of the conference on the sociology of the languages of American women*. San Antonio, Texas: Trinity Univ.

Heath, Stephen. 1978. Difference. *Screen*, 19 (3), 51-112.

Heer, David M. 1963. The measurement and bases of family power: An overview. *Marriage and Family Living*, 25, 133-139.

Helgeson, Candace. 1976. The prisoners of texts: Male chauvinism in college handbooks and rhetorics. *College English*, 38, 396-406.

Henley, Nancy. 1977. *Body politics: Power, sex, and nonverbal communication*. Englewood Cliffs, N.J.: Prentice-Hall.

———. 1978. Changing the body power structure. *Women*, 6 (1), 34-38.

———, and Barrie Thorne. 1975. *She said / he said: An annotated bibliography of language and sex including nonverbal communication*. Old Westbury, N.Y.: Feminist Press.

———, Barrie Thorne, and Cheris Kramarae (eds.). In preparation. *Language and sex II* (working title). Rowley, Mass.: Newbury House.

Hennig, Margaret, and Anne Jardim. 1978. *The managerial woman*. New York Pocket Books.

Henry, Alice. 1979. Comment on "On the term 'sex roles,' " by Lopata and Thorne. *Signs: Journal of Women in Culture and Society*, 4 (4), 812-813.

Herman, Simon N. 1961. Explorations in the social psychology of language choice. *Human Relations*, 14, 149-164.

Herschberger, Ruth. 1970. *Adam's Rib*. New York: Harper & Row (HAR/ROW BOOKS).

Hiatt, Mary. 1977. *The way women write*. New York: Teachers College Press.

Highet, Gilbert. 1962. *The anatomy of satire*. Princeton, N.J.: Princeton Univ. Press.

Hoagland, Sarah L. 1980. Androcentric rhetoric in sociobiology. *Women's Studies International Quarterly*, 3 (2/3), 285-293. These issues also appear as: Cheris Kramarae (ed.). 1980. *The voices and words of women and men*. Oxford: Pergamon Press.

Hochschild, Arlie Russell. 1973. A review of sex role research. In Joan Huber (ed.), *Changing women in a changing society*. Chicago: Univ. of Chicago Press.

———. 1975. Inside the clockwork of male careers. In Florence Howe (ed.), *Women and the power to change*. New York: McGraw-Hill.

Hoke, Helen (ed.). 1957. *The family book of humor*. New York: Hanover House.

Hole, Judith, and Ellen Levine. 1972. *Rebirth of feminism*. New York: Quadrangle Books.

Homans, George C. 1961. *Social behavior: The elementary forms*. New York: Harcourt Brace.

Howard, Philip. 1977. *New words for old*. New York: Oxford Univ. Press.

Howe, Florence. 1975. Women and the power to change. In Florence Howe (ed.), *Women and the power to change*. New York: McGraw-Hill.

Howe, Louise Kapp. 1978. *Pink collar workers: Inside the world of women's work*. New York: Avon.

Huber, Elaine C. n.d. *The Woman's Bible* vs. the patriarchy: Elizabeth Cady Stanton's radical perspective. *Movement Pamphlet: Journal of the Student Christian Movement of Britain and Ireland*, No. 24.

Husserl-Kapit, Susan. 1975. An interview with Marguerite Duras. *Signs: Journal of Women in Culture and Society*, 1, 423-434.

Hymes, Dell. 1971. Sociolinguistics and the ethnography of speaking. In Edwin Ardener (ed.), *Social anthropology and language*. [ASA monographs 10] London: Tavistock.

———. 1972. Introduction. In Courtney B. Cazden, Vera P. John, and Dell Hymes (eds.), *Functions of language in the classroom*. New York: Teachers College Press.

———. 1973. On the origins and foundations of inequality among speakers. *Daedalus*, 102 (3), 59-85.

———. 1974. *Foundations in sociolinguistics: An ethnographic approach*. Philadelphia: Univ. of Pennsylvania Press.

Irigaray, Luce. 1974. *Speculum de l'autre femme*. Paris: Editions de Minuit.

———. 1977. Women's exile [an interview]. *Ideology & Consciousness*, No. 1 (May), pp. 62-76.

Jakobson, Roman. 1956. Two aspects of language and two types of aphasic disturbances. In *Fundamentals of Language*, by Roman Jakobson and Morris Halle. The Hague: Mouton.

Jakubowski-Spector, Patricia. 1973. Facilitating the growth of women through assertive training. *The Counseling Psychologist*, 4 (1), 75-86.

Janeway, Elizabeth. 1975. *Between myth and morning: Women awakening*. New York: William Morrow.

Jardine, Alice. 1979. Interview with Simone de Beauvoir. *Signs: Journal of Women in Culture and Society*, 5 (2), 224-236.

Jenkins, Lee, and Cheris Kramer. 1978. Small group process: Learning from women. *Women's Studies International Quarterly*, 1, 67-84.

Jenkins, Mercilee M. 1980. Toward a model of human leadership. In Virginia Eman and Cynthia L. Berryman (eds.), *Communication, language and sex*. Rowley, Mass.: Newbury House.

Jespersen, Otto. 1922. *Language: Its nature, development and origin*. London: George Allen & Unwin.

Joan, Polly, and Andrea Chesman. 1978. *Guide to women's publishing*. Paradise, Calif. (P.O. Box 100): Dustbooks.

Johnson, Paula B., and Jacqueline D. Goodchilds. 1976. How women get their way. *Psychology Today*, 10 (5), 69-70.

Johnston, Jill. 1973. *Lesbian nation: The feminist solution*. New York: Simon and Schuster.

Jones, Deborah. 1980. Gossip: Notes on women's oral culture. *Women's Studies International Quarterly*, 3 (2/3), 193-198. These issues also appear as: Cheris Kramarae (ed.). 1980. *The voices and words of women and men*. Oxford: Pergamon Press.

Jong, Erica. 1973. The artist as housewife: The housewife as artist. In Francine Klagsbrun (ed.), *The first Ms. reader*. New York: Warner Paperback Library.

———. 1975. In Women novelists: A distinct group? (a panel discussion). *Women's Studies: An Interdisciplinary Journal*, 3, 5-28.

Jourard, Sidney M. 1964. *The transparent self: Self disclosure and well-being*. Princeton, N.J.: D. Van Nostrand.

Kalčik, Susan. 1975. . . . like Ann's gynecologist or the time I was almost raped: Personal narratives in women's rap groups. In Claire R. Farrar (ed.), *Women and folklore*. Austin: Univ. of Texas Press.

Kanter, Rosabeth Moss. 1977. *Men and women of the corporation*. New York: Basic Books.

Kaplan, Cora. 1975. *Salt and bitter and good: Three centuries of English and American poets*. London: Paddington Press.

———. 1976. Language and gender. *Papers on patriarchy*. Lewes, Sussex: Women's Publishing Collective.

Kaplan, Susan. 1976. The assertion of power: Ideals, perceptions, and styles. Paper read at American Psychological Association, Washington, D.C.

Keenan, Elinor. 1974. Norm-makers, norm-breakers: Uses of speech by men and women in a Malagasy community. In R. Bauman and J. Sherzer (eds.), *Explorations in the ethnography of speaking*. Cambridge: Cambridge Univ. Press.

Kelly, George. 1955. *The psychology of personal constructs*. 2 volumes. New York: Norton.

Kernan, Alvin B. 1965. *The plot of satire*. New Haven, Conn.: Yale Univ. Press.

Kessler, Suzanne, and Wendy McKenna. 1978. *Gender: An ethnomethodological approach*. New York: John Wiley & Sons.

Kett, Joseph F. 1973. Adolescence and youth in nineteenth-century America. In Theodore K. Rabb and Robert I. Rotberg (eds.), *The family in history: Interdisciplinary essays*. New York: Harper & Row.

———. 1977. *Rites of passage: Adolescence in America 1790 to the present*. New York: Basic Books.

Key, Mary Ritchie. 1975. Male/female language. Metuchen, N.J.: The Scarecrow Press.

Kilpatrick, James J. 1976. And some are more equal than others. *American Sociologist*, 11, 85-93.

King, Josephine, and Mary Stott (eds.). 1977. *Is this your life? Images of women in the media*. London: Virago.

Kingston, Albert, and Terry Lovelace. 1978. Sexism and reading: A critical review of the literature. *Reading Research Quarterly*, 13, 133-161.

Klement, Alice. 1974. Sex life of words spelled out. Newspaper clipping in the Women's Collection, Northwestern Univ. Library, Evanston, Ill.

Kolodny, Annette. 1975a. *The lay of the land: Metaphor as experience and history in American life and letters*. Chapel Hill, N.C.: Univ. of North Carolina Press.

———. 1975b. Some notes on defining a "feminist literary criticism." *Critical Inquiry*, 2 (1), 75-92.

Komarovsky, Mirra. 1946. Cultural contradiction and sex roles. *American Journal of Sociology*, 52, 182-189.

———. 1967. *Blue-collar marriage*. New York: Vintage Books.

Korsmeyer, Carolyn. 1977. The hidden joke: Generic uses of masculine terminology. In Mary Vetterling-Braggin, Frederick A. Elliston, and Jane English (eds.), *Feminism and philosophy*. Totowa, N.J.: Littlefield, Adams.

Kramarae, Cheris. 1978. Resistance to the public female voice. Paper read at Ninth World Congress of Sociology, Uppsala, Sweden.

——— (ed.). 1980. *The voices and words of women and men*. Oxford: Pergamon Press.

Kramer, Cheris. 1974a. Folklinguistics. *Psychology Today*, 8 (1), 82-85.

———. 1974b. Stereotypes of women's speech: The word from cartoons. *Journal of Popular Culture*, 8, 622-638.

———. 1975a. Excessive loquacity: Women's speech as presented in American etiquette books. Paper read at Speech Communication Association, Austin, Texas.

———. 1975b. Sex-linked differences in address systems. *Anthropological Linguistics*, 17, 198-210.

———. 1975c. Women's speech: Separate but unequal? In Barrie Thorne and Nancy Henley (eds.), *Language and sex: Difference and dominance.* Rowley, Mass.: Newbury House.

———. 1977. Perceptions of female and male speech. *Language and Speech,* 20, 151-161.

———. 1978. Women's and men's ratings of their own and ideal speech. *Communication Quarterly,* 26 (2), 2-11.

———, Barrie Thorne, and Nancy Henley. 1978. Review essay: Perspectives on language and communication. *Signs: Journal of Women in Culture and Society,* 3, 638-651.

Labov, William. 1966. *The social stratification of English in New York City.* Washington, D.C.: Center for Applied Linguistics.

———. 1972. *Sociolinguistic patterns.* Philadelphia: Univ. of Pennsylvania Press.

Lacan, Jacques. 1970. The insistence of the letter in the unconscious. Translated by Jan Miel. In Jacques Ehrmann (ed.), *Structuralism.* New York: Doubleday Anchor.

———. 1977. *Écrits: A selection.* Translated by Alan Sheridan. New York: W. W. Norton.

Ladner, Joyce A. 1971. *Tomorrow's tomorrow: The black woman.* Garden City, N.Y.: Doubleday.

La France, Marianne, and Clara Mayo. 1979. A review of nonverbal behaviors of women and men. *Western Journal of Speech Communication,* 43, 96-107.

Lakoff, Robin. 1973. Language and woman's place. *Language in Society,* 2, 45-80.

———. 1974. Why women are ladies. In Charles Fillmore, George Lakoff, and Robin Lakoff (eds.), *Berkeley Studies in Syntax and Semantics,* Volume 1. Berkeley, Univ. of California.

———. 1975. *Language and woman's place.* New York: Harper & Row.

Lamm, Bob. 1977. Learning from women. In Jon Snodgrass (ed.), *For men against sexism.* New York: Monthly Review Press.

Lamphere, Louise. 1974. Strategies, cooperation, and conflict among women in domestic groups. In Michelle Zimbalist Rosaldo and Louise Lamphere (eds.), *Woman, culture, and society.* Stanford, Calif.: Stanford Univ. Press.

Lane, Ann J. (ed.). 1977. *Mary Ritter Beard: A sourcebook.* New York: Schocken.

Larson, Karen. 1978. Role-playing and the real thing: Socialization and standard speech in Norway. Paper read at Ninth World Congress of Sociology, Uppsala, Sweden.

Leach, Edmund. 1976. *Culture & communication: The logic by which symbols are connected.* Cambridge, Eng.: Cambridge Univ. Press.

Leacock, Eleanor. 1975. Class, commodity, and the status of women. In Ruby Rohrlich-Leavitt (ed.), *Women cross-culturally: Change and challenge.* The Hague: Mouton.

———. 1977. Review of Rayna R. Reiter (ed.), *Toward an anthropology of women. Signs: Journal of Women in Culture and Society,* 3, 495-497.

Leik, Robert K. 1963. Instrumentality and emotionality in family interaction. *Sociometry,* 26, 131-145.

Lesage, Julia. 1975. The human subject—you, he, or me? (Or the case of the missing penis). *Screen,* 16 (2), 77-83.

Lever, Janet. 1976. Sex differences in the games children play. *Social Problems,* 23, 478-487.

Levin, Harry. 1972. Introduction. In Harry Levin (ed.), *Veins of humor.* Harvard English Studies, 3. Cambridge, Mass.: Harvard Univ. Press.

Levine, Jacob. 1969. Approaches to humor appreciation. In Jacob Levine (ed.), *Motivation in humor.* New York: Atherton Press.

Levine, Lewis, and Harry J. Crockett, Jr. 1966. Speech variation in a Piedmont community: Postvocalic *r.* In Stanley Lieberson (ed.), *Explorations in sociolinguistics.* The Hague: Mouton.

Lewis, Robert A. 1978. Emotional intimacy among men. *Journal of Social Issues,* 34 (1), 108-121.

Lipinski, Ann Marie. 1979. The selling of women takes a scholarly twist in publishing. *Chicago Tribune,* Lifestyle section, pp. 1, 4.

Lipman-Blumen. Jean. 1976. Toward a homosocial theory of sex roles: An explanation of the sex segregation of social institutions. *Signs: Journal of Women in Culture and Society*, 3, 718-721.

McArthur, Leslie Zebrowitz, and Susan V. Eisen. 1976. Achievements of male and female storybook characters as determinants of achievement behavior by boys and girls. *Journal of Personality and Social Psychology*, 33, 467-473.

Macaulay, Ronald K. S. 1978. The myth of female superiority in language. *Journal of Child Language*, 5, 353-363.

McBride, Sarah Elizabeth, and Karen J. Garvin. 1976. The rhetoric of women in religion: A premature celebration. Paper read at Speech Communication Association, San Francisco.

MacCabe, Colin. 1975. Presentation of "The imaginary signifier." *Screen*, 16 (2), 7-13.

Maccoby, Eleanor Emmons, and Carol Nagy Jacklin. 1974. *The psychology of sex differences*. Stanford, Calif.: Stanford Univ. Press.

McConnell-Ginet, Sally. 1978a. Address forms in sexual politics. In Douglas Butturff and Edmund L. Epstein (eds.), *Women's language and style*. Published with the assistance of the Dept. of English, Univ. of Akron.

———. 1978b. Intonation in a man's world. *Signs: Journal of Women in Culture and Society*, 3, 541-559.

———. 1979. Review of Mary Hiatt's *The way women write*. *Language in Society*, 8 (3), 466-469.

———, Nelly Furman, and Ruth Borker (eds.). 1980. *Women and language in literature and society*. New York: Praeger.

McDaniel, Judith. 1978. In The transformation of silence into language and action (a panel discussion). *Sinister Wisdom*, 6 (Summer), 15-17. [P.O. Box 30541, Lincoln, NE 68503.]

McDowell, Margaret B. 1971. The new rhetoric of woman power. *Midwest Quarterly*, 12, 187-198.

McGhee, Paul E. 1976. Sex differences in children's humor. *Journal of Communication*, 26 (3), 176-189.

MacKay, Donald G. 1979. Singular *they* and the principles of prescriptive grammar. Unpublished manuscript. Psychology Department, Univ. of California at Los Angeles.

———, and David C. Fulkerson. 1979. On the comprehension and production of pronouns. *Journal of Verbal Learning and Verbal Behavior* 18, 661-673.

———, and Toshi Konishi. 1980. Personification and the pronoun problem. *Women's Studies International Quarterly*, 3 (2/3), 149-163. These issues also appear as: Cheris Kramarae (ed.). 1980. *The voices and words of women and men*. Oxford: Pergamon Press.

McMillan, Julie R., A. Kay Clifton, Diane McGrath, and Wanda S. Gale. 1977. Women's language: Uncertainty or interpersonal sensitivity and emotionality? *Sex Roles*, 3, 545-559.

McRobbie, Angela, and Jenny Garber. 1975. Girls and subcultures. *Working Papers in Cultural Studies* [Univ. of Birmingham], 7-8, 209-229.

Martyna, Wendy. 1978a. Using and understanding the generic masculine: A social-psychological approach to language and the sexes. Unpublished dissertation. Stanford Univ.

———. 1978b. What does "he" mean?: Use of the generic masculine. *Journal of Communication*, 28 (1), 131-138.

———. 1980. Beyond the "he/man" approach. *Signs: Journal of Women in Culture and Society*, 5, 482-493.

Marx, Patricia. 1966. Interview with Anne Sexton. *Hudson Review*, 18 (4), 546-570.

Mathieu, Nicole-Claude. 1973. Man-culture and woman-nature? Translated by D. M. Leonard Barker. *Women's Studies International Quarterly*, 1, 55-65.

Media Report to Women. 3306 Ross Place, N.W., Washington, D.C. 20008.

Meeker, B. F., and P. A. Weitzel-O'Neill. 1977. Sex roles and interpersonal behavior in task-oriented groups. *American Sociological Review*, 42 (February), 91-105.

Mellor, Caltha, and Judy Miller. 1970. What we think is happening. . . . *Women: A Journal of Liberation*, 1 (2), 78-79.

Mencken, H. L. 1977. *The American language: An inquiry into the development of English in the United States.* 4th edition. Annotations and new material by Raven I. McDavid, Jr. New York: Alfred A. Knopf.

Micossi, Anita Lynn. 1970. Conversion to women's lib. *Trans-action,* 8 (1-2), 82-90.

Miles, Rosalind. 1974. *The fiction of sex: Themes and functions of sex difference in the modern novel.* New York: Barnes & Noble.

Miller, Casey, and Kate Swift. 1976. *Words and women: New language in new times.* Garden City, N.Y.: Doubleday Anchor.

Miller, Jean Baker. 1976. *Toward a new psychology of women.* Boston: Beacon Press.

Mishler, Elliot G. 1975. Studies in dialogue and discourse: II. Types of discourse initiated by and sustained through questioning. *Journal of Psycholinguistic Research,* 4, 99-121.

Mitchell, Juliet.1975. *Psychoanalysis and feminism.* Harmondsworth, Middlesex: Penguin.

Moffat, Mary Jane. 1975. Foreword. In Mary Jane Moffat and Charlotte Painter (eds.), *Revelations: Diaries of women.* New York: Vintage.

———, and Charlotte Painter (eds.). 1975. *Revelations: Diaries of women.* New York: Vintage.

Montemayor, Raymond. 1974. Children's performance in a game and their attraction to it as a function of sex-typed habits. *Child Development,* 45, 152-156.

Morgan, Robin. 1978. *Going too far: The personal chronicle of a feminist.* New York: Vintage.

Morton, Nelle. 1972. The rising woman consciousness in a male language structure. *Andover-Newton Quarterly,* 12 (4), 177-190.

Moulton, Janice. 1977. The myth of the neutral "man." In Mary Vetterling-Braggin, Frederick A. Elliston, and Jane English (eds.), *Feminism and philosophy.* Totowa, N.J.: Littlefield, Adams.

The Moynihan Report. 1965. *The Negro family: The case for national action.* Washington, D.C.: Government Printing Office.

Murray, Jessica. 1972. Male perspective in language. *Women: A Journal of Liberation,* 3 (2), 46-50.

Newman, Philip R., and Barbara M. Newman. 1976. Early adolescence and its conflict: Group identity versus alienation: Adolescence in the context of the life-span. *Adolescence,* 11, 261-274.

Newton, Esther. 1972. *Mother camp: Female inpersonators in America.* Englewood Cliffs, N.J.: Prentice-Hall.

Nichols, Patricia C. 1976. Black women in the rural South: Conservative and innovative. In Betty Lou Dubois and Isabel Crouch (eds.), *Proceedings of the conference on the sociology of the languages of American women.* San Antonio, Texas: Trinity Univ.

———. 1978. Dynamic variation theory as a model for the study of language and sex. Paper read at the Ninth World Congress of Sociology, Uppsala, Sweden.

Nilsen, Alleen Pace. 1977. Sexism in the language of marriage. In Alleen Pace Nilsen, Haig Bosmajian, H. Lee Gershuny, and Julia P. Stanley (eds.), *Sexism and language.* Urbana, Ill.: National Council of Teachers of English.

Oakley, Ann. 1974. *The sociology of housework.* London: Martin Robertson.

O'Barr, William M., and Bowman K. Atkins. 1980. 'Women's language' or 'powerless language'? In Sally McConnell-Ginet, Nelly Furman, and Ruth Borker (eds.), *Women and language in literature and society.* New York: Praeger, 93-110.

Obatala, J. K. 1979. The unlikely story of blacks who were loyal to Dixie. *Smithsonian,* 9 (12), 94-101.

O'Connell, Walter E. 1969. The social aspects of wit and humor. *Journal of Social Psychology,* 79, 183-187.

Ohmann, Carol. 1971. Emily Brontë in the hands of male critics. *College English,* 32, 906-913.

Olsen, Tillie. 1979. *Silences.* New York: Delta/Seymour.

Omwake, Louise. 1937. A study of sense of humor: Its relation to sex, age and personal characteristics. *Journal of Applied Psychology,* 21, 688-704.

One, Varda. 1970. Manglish. *Everywoman,* October 23.

Ong, Walter J. 1977. *Interfaces of the word: Studies in the evolution of consciousness and culture.* Ithaca, N.Y.: Cornell Univ. Press.

Parker, Rozsika. 1977. Portrait of the artist as housewife. *Spare Rib,* 60 (July), 5-8.

Parsons, Elsie Clews. 1913a. *The old-fashioned woman: Primitive fancies about the sex.* New York: G. P. Putnam's Sons.

———. [published under pseudonym John Main]. 1913b. *Religious chastity: An ethnological study.* New York: Macaulay.

Parsons, Talcott, and Robert F. Bales. 1955. *Family: socialization and interaction process.* Glencoe, Ill.: Free Press.

Pateman, Trevor. 1980. *Language, truth and politics.* Revised edition. Nottingham: Jean Stroud and Trevor Pateman (at the Russell Press).

Pei, Mario. 1967. *The story of the English language.* Revised edition. Philadelphia: J. B. Lippincott Co.

Plaza, Monique. 1978. "Phallomorphic power" and the psychology of "woman." Translated by Miriam David and Jill Hodges. *Ideology & Consciousness,* No. 4 (Autumn), pp. 5-36.

Prochnow, Herbert V., and Herbert V. Prochnow, Jr. 1962. *A dictionary of wit, wisdom, and satire.* New York: Harper.

Quaggiotto, Pamela. 1979. Review of Shirley Ardener (ed.), *Perceiving women. Women's Studies International Quarterly,* 2, 133-134.

Quinn, Jane Bryant. 1979. A woman's place. *Newsweek*, February 26, p. 73.

Rainwater, Lee. 1970. *Behind the ghetto walls: Black families in a federal slum.* Chicago: Aldine Publishing.

Rapp, Rayna. 1978. Family and class in contemporary America: Notes toward an understanding of ideology. *Science & Society*, 42, 278-300.

———. 1979. Review essay: Anthropology. *Signs: Journal of Women in Culture and Society*, 4, 497-513.

———, Ellen Ross, and Renate Bridenthal. 1979. Examining family history. *Feminist Studies,* 5 (1), 174-200.

Rausch, Harold L., William A. Barry, Richard K. Hertel, and Mary Ann Swain. 1974. *Communication, conflict and marriage.* San Francisco: Jossey-Bass.

Reiter, Rayna R. (ed.). 1975. *Toward an anthropology of women.* New York: Monthly Review Press.

Adrienne Rich's Poetry. 1975. Barbara Charlesworth Gelpi and Albert Gelpi (eds.). New York: W. W. Norton.

Rich, Adrienne. 1978. In The transformation of silence into language and action (a panel discussion). *Sinister Wisdom*, 6 (Summer), 17-25. [P.O. Box 30541, Lincoln, NE 68503.]

Rogers, Anne, and Aleen Holly. 1971. On feeling superior to other women. *Women: A Journal of Liberation,* 2 (3), 53-55.

Rohrlich-Leavitt, Ruby (ed.). 1975. *Women cross-culturally: Change and challenge.* The Hague: Mouton.

Rosaldo, Michelle Zimbalist. 1974. Woman, culture, and society: A theoretical overview. In Michelle Zimbalist Rosaldo and Louise Lamphere (eds.), *Woman, culture, and society.* Stanford, Calif.: Stanford Univ. Press.

———. 1978. Thoughts on domestic/public. Working paper prepared for Rockefeller Foundation conference on Women, Family, and Work. New York City.

——— 1980. The use and abuse of anthropology: Reflections on feminism and cross-cultural understanding. *Signs: Journal of Women in Culture and Society,* 5, 389-417.

———, and Louise Lamphere (eds.). 1974. *Woman, culture, and society.* Stanford, Calif.: Stanford Univ. Press.

Rossi, Alice S. 1965. Naming children in middle-class families. *American Sociological Review*, 30, 499-513.

Roszak, Betty, and Theodore Roszak (eds.). 1969. *Masculine/feminine: Readings in sexual mythology and the liberation of women*. New York: Harper Colophon.

Roussel, Jean. 1968. Introduction to Jacques Lacan. *New Left Review*, No. 51 (September-October), pp. 63-70.

Rowbotham, Sheila. 1973. *Woman's consciousness, man's world*. Harmondsworth, Middlesex: Penguin.

Rubin, Lillian Breslow. 1976. *Worlds of pain: Life in the working-class family*. New York: Basic Books.

Ruether, Rosemary. n.d. Male clericalism and the dread of women. In *For the banished children of Eve: An introduction to feminist theology*. N.p.: Student Christian Movement of Britain and Ireland.

Ryan, Mary P. 1979. The power of women's networks: A case study of female moral reform in antebellum America. *Feminist Studies* 5 (1), 66-85.

Sachs, Jacqueline. 1975. Cues to the identification of sex in children's speech. In Barrie Thorne and Nancy Henley (eds.), *Language and sex: Difference and dominance*. Rowley, Mass.: Newbury House.

Sacks, Harvey, Emmanuel Schegloff, and Gail Jefferson. 1974. A simplest systematics for the organization of turn-taking for conversation. *Language*, 50, 696-735.

Safilios-Rothschild, Constantina. 1969. Family sociology or wives' family sociology? A cross-cultural examination of decision-making. *Journal of Marriage and the Family*, 31, 290-301.

———. 1974. *Women and social policy*. Englewood Cliffs, N.J.: Prentice-Hall.

Sattel, Jack W. 1976. The inexpressive male: Tragedy or sexual politics? *Social Problems*, 23, 469-477.

Schneider, Joseph W., and Sally L. Hacker. 1973. Sex role imagery and use of the generic "man" in introductory texts: A case in the sociology of sociology. *American Sociologist*, 8, 12-18.

Schulz, Muriel. 1975. The semantic derogation of woman. In Barrie Thorne and Nancy Henley (eds.), *Language and sex: Difference and dominance*. Rowley, Mass.: Newbury House.

———. 1978. As others see us: What English says about women. Paper read at Modern Language Association, New York City.

———. 1979. Mother tongue. Paper read at Sprache und Geschlecht Conference, Universität Osnabrück, West Germany.

Scott, Kathryn. 1980. Perceptions of communication competence: What's good for the goose is not good for the gander. *Women's Studies International Quarterly*, 3 (2/3), 199-208. These issues also appear as: Cheris Kramarae (ed.). 1980. *The voices and words of women and men*. Oxford: Pergamon Press.

Shepelak, Norma J. 1977. Does "he" mean "she" too?: The case of the generic anomaly. Paper read at Fourth National Conference on Feminist Psychology, St. Louis.

———, D. Ogden, and D. Tobin-Bennett. 1976. Students' perceptions of careers as a function of gender cues. Unpublished paper. Indiana Univ.

Sheppard, Alice. 1976. Humor and sex-role stereotypes. Paper read at Pioneers for Century III, Conference on the Power of Women and Men, Cincinnati.

Shields, Stephanie A. 1975. Functionalism, Darwinism, and the psychology of women: A study in social myth. *American Psychologist*, 30, 739-754.

Shimberg, Edmund. 1971. Letter printed in *APA Monitor*, 2 (10), 2, 9.

Shuy, Roger W., Walter A. Wolfram, and William K. Riley. 1967. *Linguistic correlates of social stratification in Detroit speech*. Final Report, Project 6-1347. Washington, D.C.: U.S. Office of Education.

Silveira, Jeanette. 1978. *Women on the fringes: Generic masculine words and their relation to thinking*. Seattle, Wash.: Privately printed.

———. 1980. Generic masculine words and thinking. *Women's Studies International Quarterly*,

3 (2/3), 165-178. These issues also appear as: Cheris Kramarae (ed.). 1980. *The voices and words of women and men.* Oxford: Pergamon Press.

Silverstein, Barry, and Ronald Krate. 1975. *Children of the dark ghetto.* New York: Praeger.

Skolnick, Arlene. 1973. *The intimate environment: Exploring marriage and the family.* Boston: Little, Brown.

Smith, Dorothy E. 1974. Women's perspective as a radical critique of sociology. *Sociological Inquiry,* 44, 7-13.

———. 1978. A peculiar eclipsing: Women's exclusion from men's culture. *Women's Studies International Quarterly,* 1, 281-295.

Smith, Philip M., and Howard Giles. 1978. Sociolinguistics: A social psychological perspective. Paper read at Ninth World Congress of Sociology, Uppsala, Sweden.

Smith-Rosenberg, Carroll. 1975. The female world of love and ritual: Relations between women in nineteenth-century America. *Signs: Journal of Women in Culture and Society,* 1, 1-29.

Snow, Catherine E. 1976. The language of the mother-child relationship. In Sinclair Rogers (ed.), *They don't speak our language: Essays on the language world of children and adolescents.* London: Edward Arnold.

Soskin, William F., and Vera P. John. 1963. The study of spontaneous talk. In Roger G. Barker (ed.), *The stream of behavior.* New York: Appleton-Century-Crofts.

Spender, Dale. 1977. The namer and the named. Unpublished manuscript. Univ. of London Institute of Education.

———. 1979. "Free Speech" in the classroom. *Osnabrücker Beiträge zur Sprach Theorie* [*Sprache und Geschlecht*], 9 (February), 52-59.

Spradley, James P., and Brenda J. Mann. 1975. *The cocktail waitress: Woman's work in a man's world.* New York: John Wiley & Sons.

Stack, Carol B. 1974. *All our kin: Strategies for survival in a black community.* New York: Harper & Row.

Stahlecker, James E. 1978. Parental and literature stereotype modeling: An investigation of their influence on second grade children. Paper read at Communication, Language and Sex Conference, Bowling Green Univ., Ohio.

Stanley, Julia P. 1972. The semantic features of the machismo ethic in English. Paper read at South Atlantic Modern Language Association, Jacksonville, Florida.

———. 1974. What's in a label: The politics of naming. Paper read at South Central Modern Language Association, Houston, Texas.

———. 1975a. Passive motivation. *Foundations of Language,* 13, 25-39.

———. 1975b. Prescribed passivity: The language of sexism. In Reza Ordoubadian and Walburga von Raffler Engel (eds.), *Views on language.* Murfreesboro, Tenn.: Inter-University Pub.

———. 1976. The stylistics of belief. In Daniel J. Dieterich (ed.), *Teaching about double speak.* Urbana, Ill.: National Council of Teachers of English.

———. 1977a. Gender-marking in American English: Usage and reference. In Alleen Pace Nilsen, Haig Bosmajian, H. Lee Gershuny, and Julia P. Stanley (eds.), *Sexism and language.* Urbana, Ill.: National Council of Teachers of English.

———. 1977b. Paradigmatic women: The prostitute. In David L. Shores and Carole P. Hines (eds.), *Papers in language variation.* University, Alabama: Univ. of Alabama Press.

———. 1978. Sexist grammar. *College English,* 39, 800-811.

———, and Susan J. Wolfe. 1976. Sexist slang and the gay community: Are you one, too? *Michigan Occasional Paper,* No. XIV, summer, 1979.

———, and Susan J. Wolfe (Robbins). 1978. Toward a feminist aesthetic. *Chrysalis: A Magazine of Women's Culture,* No. 6 (Winter), pp. 57-71.

———, and Susan W. Robbins. 1978a. Going through the changes: The pronoun *she* in Middle English. *Papers in Linguistics,* 11 (1-2), 71-88.

———, and Susan W. Robbins. 1978b. Sex marked predicates in English. *Papers in Linguistics* 11 (3-4), 487-516.

Stannard, Una. 1977. *Mrs. Man.* San Francisco: Germainbooks.

Stanton, Elizabeth Cady. 1898. *The woman's Bible,* 2 volumes. New York: European Publishing Company.

Staples, Robert. 1978. Masculinity and race: The dual dilemma of black men. *Journal of Social Issues,* 34 (1), 169-183.

Steadman, J. M., Jr. 1938. Affected and effeminate words. *American Speech,* 13, 13-18.

Steinem, Gloria. 1972. Introduction. *Wonderwoman* [book of reprinted comics of the strip by Charles Moulton]. New York: Holt, Rinehart and Winston.

Stillman, Deanne, and Anne Beatts (eds.). 1976. *Titters: The first collection of humor by women.* New York: Collier Books.

Stimpson, Catharine B. 1979. Editing *Signs. Bulletin of the Midwest Modern Language Association,* 12 (1), 37-42.

Stone, Lucy. 1894. The progress of fifty years. In Mary Kavanaugh Oldham Eagle (ed.), *The congress of women.* Chicago: Monarch Book Company.

Stone, Merlin. 1977. *The paradise papers: The suppression of women's rites.* London: Virago.

Strainchamps, Ethel. 1971. Ethel Strainchamps wrote this. *New York Times,* October 4, Section C, p. 39.

Svebak, Sven. 1975. Styles in humor and social self-images. *Scandinavian Journal of Psychology,* 16, 79-84.

Swacker, Marjorie. 1976. Women's verbal behavior at learned and professional conferences. In Betty Lou Dubois and Isabel Crouch (eds.), *Proceedings of the conference on the sociology of the languages of American women.* San Antonio, Texas: Trinity Univ.

Tajfel, Henri. 1974. Social identity and intergroup behavior. *Social Science Information,* 13 (2), 65-93.

Terkel, Studs. 1972. *Working: People talk about what they do all day and how they feel about what they do.* New York: Pantheon Books.

Thompson, Spencer K. 1975. Gender labels and early sex role development. *Child Development,* 46, 339-347.

Thompson, Wayne N. 1967. *Quantitative research in public address and communication.* New York: Random House.

Thorne, Barrie, and Nancy Henley (eds.). 1975. *Language and sex: Difference and dominance.* Rowley, Mass.: Newbury House.

Tiger, Lionel. 1970. *Men in groups.* New York: Vintage.

Todasco, Ruth. 1973. Women and the English language. In *Feminist English dictionary: An intelligent woman's guide to dirty words.* Chicago: Loop Center YWCA.

Treichler, Paula. In press. Verbal subversions in Dorothy Parker: "trapped like a trap in a trap." *Language and Style.*

Trenfield, Karen. 1978. Feminist sf: Reality or fantasy? A review of recent sf by women. *Hecate: A Woman's Interdisciplinary Journal,* 4 (1), 99-108.

Trible, Phyllis. 1978. *God and the rhetoric of sexuality.* Philadelphia: Fortress Press.

Trudgill, Peter. 1975. Sex, covert prestige, and linguistic change in the urban British English of Norwich. In Barrie Thorne and Nancy Henley (eds.), *Language and sex: Difference and dominance.* Rowley, Mass.: Newbury House.

Turkle, Sherry. 1978. *Psychoanalytic politics: Freud's French revolution.* New York: Basic Books.

Turner, Rosa Shand. 1977. The increasingly visible female and the need for generic terms. *Christian Century,* May 16, pp. 248-252.

Unger, Rhoda Kesler. 1979. Toward a redefinition of sex and gender. *American Psychologist,* 34 (11), 1085-1094.

U.S. Commission on Civil Rights. 1979. *Window dressing on the set: An update.* Washington, D.C.: U.S. Government Printing Office.

Uroff, Margaret Dickey. 1979. *Sylvia Plath and Ted Hughes.* Urbana, Ill.: Univ. of Illinois Press.

Valian, Virginia. 1977. Linguistics and feminism. In Mary Vetterling-Braggin, Frederick A. Elliston, and Jane English (eds.), *Feminism and philosophy*. Totowa, N.J.: Littlefield, Adams.

Wallin, Paul. 1950. Cultural contradictions and sex roles: A repeat study. *American Sociological Review*, 15, 288-293.

Ward, Martha Coonfield. 1971. *Them children: A study in language learning*. New York: Holt, Rinehart and Winston.

Weisstein, Naomi, and Heather Booth. 1978. Will the women's movement survive? [British] *Catcall*, June, pp. 16-27.

Weitz, Shirley. 1976. Sex differences in nonverbal communication. *Sex Roles*, 2, 175-184.

Wells, Richard. 1892. *Manners, culture and dress of the best American society*. Omaha: Clark Publishing Company.

Wentworth, Harold, and Stuart Berg Flexner (eds.). 1975. *Dictionary of American slang*. 2nd supplemental edition. New York: Thomas Y. Crowell.

West, Candace, and Don H. Zimmerman. 1977. Women's place in everyday talk: Reflections on parent-child interaction. *Social Problems*, 24, 521-529.

Whitehead, Ann. 1976. Sexual antagonism in Herefordshire. In Diana Leonard Barker and Sheila Allen (eds.), *Dependence and exploitation in work and marriage*. London: Longman.

Wilden, Anthony. 1968. Lacan and the discourse of the other. In Anthony Wilden (trans.), *The language of the self: The function of language in psychoanalysis by Jacques Lacan*. Baltimore, Maryland: The Johns Hopkins Press.

---. 1972. *System and structure: Essays in communication and exchange*. London: Tavistock.

Williams, Drid. 1975. The brides of Christ. In Shirley Ardener (ed.), *Perceiving Women*. London: Malaby Press.

Williams, Jennifer A., and Howard Giles. 1978. The changing status of women in society: An intergroup perspective. In Henri Tajfel (ed.), *Differentiation between social groups: Studies in the social psychology of intergroup relations*. European monographs in social psychology, 14. London: Academic Press.

Williams, Raymond. 1976. *Keywords: A vocabulary of culture and society*. New York: Oxford Univ. Press.

Willy, Margaret. 1964. *Three women diarists: Celia Fiennes, Dorothy Wordsworth, Katherine Mansfield*. London: Longmans, Green.

Wisby, Gary. 1979. Name of this game is the game of her name. *Chicago Sun-Times*, March 4, p. 52.

Wittig, Monique. 1975. *The lesbian body*. Translated by David Le Vay. New York: William Morrow.

Wolfe (Robbins), Susan J. 1978. Stylistic experimentation in Millett, Johnston, and Wittig. Paper read at Modern Language Association, New York City.

Wolfram, Walter A. 1969. *A sociolinguistic description of Detroit Negro speech*. Washington, D.C.: Center for Applied Linguistics.

Woll, B., L. Ferrier, and Gordon Wells. 1975. Children and their parents—Who starts the talking—Why and when? Paper read at Conference on Language and the Social Context, Stirling, Scotland.

Wollheim, Richard. 1979. The cabinet of Dr. Lacan. *The New York Review of Books*, January 25, pp. 36-45.

A woman's new world dictionary. 1973. In the Women's Collection, Northwestern University Library, Evanston, Illinois.

Woods, Peter. 1976. Having a laugh: An antidote to schooling. In Martyn Hammersley and Peter Woods (eds.), *The process of schooling: A sociological reader*. London: Routledge & Kegan Paul.

Woolf, Virginia. 1972. *A room of one's own*. In *Collected Essays*, Volume 2, ed. Leonard Woolf. London: Chatto and Windus.

Wrather, Nancy, and Mary Sanches. 1978. The acceptability of racist and sexist humor. Paper read at Speech Communication Association convention, Minneapolis.

Wright, Milton. 1936. *The art of conversation: And how to apply its technique*. New York: McGraw-Hill.

Young, Michael, and Peter Willmott. 1975. *The symmetrical family*. Harmondsworth, Middlesex: Penguin.

Zaretsky, Eli. 1976. *Capitalism, the family, and personal life*. New York: Harper Colophon.

Zigler, Edward, Jacob Levine, and Laurence Gould. 1969. Cognitive challenge as a factor in children's humor appreciation. In Jacob Levine (ed.), *Motivation in humor*. New York: Atherton Press, 139-148.

Zimmerman, Don H., and Candace West. 1975. Sex roles, interruptions and silences in conversation. In Barrie Thorne and Nancy Henley (eds.), *Language and sex: Difference and dominance*. Rowley, Mass.: Newbury House.

———. 1978. Male-female differences in patterns of interruption and responses to interruption in two-party conversations. Paper read at Ninth World Congress of Sociology, Uppsala, Sweden.

Index

Montemayor, Raymond, 48
Morgan, Robin, 23, 24, 40
Morton, Nelle, 22, 25
Motherese, 137, 138
Mothers
    coiners of words, 37
    decision-making power, 128
    offering suggestions, 138
    working outside home, 128, 129
Moulton, Janice, 48
Moynihan Report, 133
Ms., 46
Murray, Jessica, 41
Murray, Melissa, 53
"Muted" speakers, 1-62
Myths about gender, v, vi. *See also*
        Proverbs *and* Stereotypes.

Naming, viii, ix, 8. *See also* Labels.
    after marriage, viii, ix, 110, 116, 117
    as revolutionary activity, 26-28, 40-43,
        49, 114
    for status, 40
    the world, 40
New Left, 22-24, 40
Newman, Barbara M., 89
Newman, Philip R., 89
News, men's activities, 9
Newspapers, 28, 29
    feminist underground, 14, 21, 29
Newton, Esther, 87
Nichols, Patricia C., 5, 6, 97, 98, 104, 124
Nilsen, Alleen Pace, 42, 110
Nonverbal communication, ix, 17, 18
    adaptive shifts, 104
    control of space, 153
    gestural slang, 43
    messages of teen journals, 87
    overlooked, 19
    politics of touch, 24
Norms for women's and men's speech, 121.
        See also Masculine, Stereotypes,
        Expectations.
Nyquist, Linda, 154

Oakley, Ann, 133
O'Barr, William M., 153
Obatala, J. K., 117
Obscenities, 23
    nonverbal, 43
O'Connell, Walter E., 56
Ogden, D., 48

Ohmann, Carol, 31, 32
Olsen, Tillie, 21
Omwake, Louise, 54
One, Varda, 110
Ong, Walter J., 50, 51
Opposition to change, 109-117
Orators, ix, 29, 34
Other, woman as, vi, 8, 34, 68, 119

Painter, Charlotte, 13
Parent/child talk, 121, 137
Parker, Dorothy, 32
Parker, Rozsika, 17
Parsons, Elsie Clews, 43, 95, 107
Parsons, Talcott, 131
Passero, Richard N., 48
Passive voice, 26, 28
Passive, women portrayed as, 85
Pateman, Trevor, 80, 81
Paternal voice, 2, 26, 65
Patriarchal attitudes, 26, 27, 28
    expressed through language, 71
Pauses, 132
Peek, Charles W., 150
Pei, Mario, 33, 45, 46
Pepinsky, Harold B., 49
Person, as generic, 117
Persuasibility, 112
Persuasion techniques, 143
Phonological variants, 5, 6, 93, 98
    shifts, 104, 106
Photographs, 86, 87
Pitch, 96
    children, 104
    stereotypical female, 153
Plath, Sylvia, 31
Plaza, Monique, 68
Poetry, 19-20, 26-28, 70, 72, 78, 80
Political activism, 22-25
    variables affecting language, 91
Political language, 22-24
Politeness
    definition, 152
    expectations, 76, 105
    tests of, 153
Politics
    participation in, ix, 22, 23
    of research, iv-vii
Posture, xiv
Power, 32, 37, 38, 157, 158. *See also*
        Language as reflection of social
        structure.